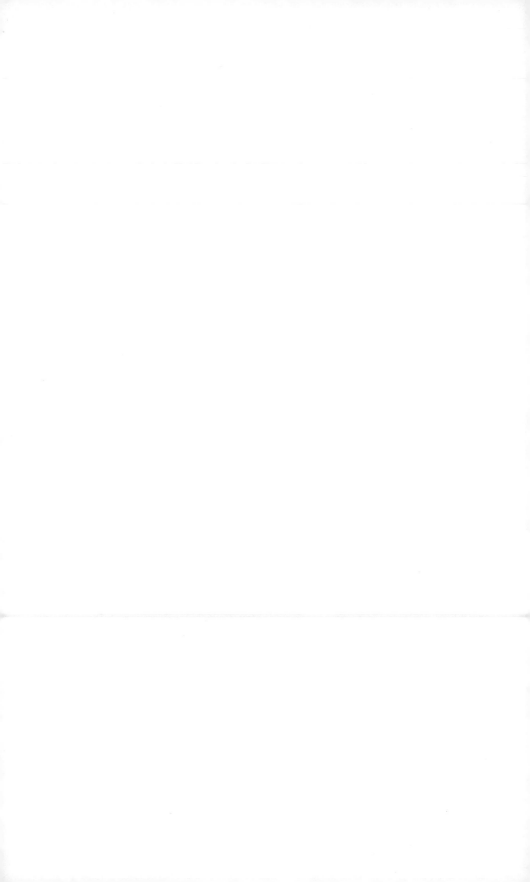

DISABILITY, CULTURE, AND DEVELOPMENT

DISABILITY, CULTURE, AND DEVELOPMENT

A Case Study of Japanese Children at School

Misa Kayama

Wendy Haight

OXFORD
UNIVERSITY PRESS

Oxford University Press is a department of the University of Oxford.
It furthers the University's objective of excellence in research, scholarship,
and education by publishing worldwide.

Oxford   New York
Auckland   Cape Town   Dar es Salaam   Hong Kong   Karachi
Kuala Lumpur   Madrid   Melbourne   Mexico City   Nairobi
New Delhi   Shanghai   Taipei   Toronto

With offices in

Argentina   Austria   Brazil   Chile   Czech Republic   France   Greece
Guatemala   Hungary   Italy   Japan   Poland   Portugal   Singapore
South Korea   Switzerland   Thailand   Turkey   Ukraine   Vietnam

Oxford is a registered trademark of Oxford University Press
in the UK and certain other countries.

Published in the United States of America by
Oxford University Press
198 Madison Avenue, New York, NY 10016

© Oxford University Press 2014

Library of Congress Cataloging-in-Publication Data
Kayama, Misa.
Disability, culture, and development : a case study of Japanese children at school / Misa
Kayama, Wendy Haight.
  pages cm
ISBN 978-0-19-997082-7 (hardback)
1. Developmentally disabled children—Education (Elementary)—Japan—Case studies.
2. Education, Elementary—Japan—Case studies.   3. Parent–teacher relationships—Japan—
Case studies.   I. Haight, Wendy L., 1958–   II. Title.
LC4037.J3K39 2013
371.90952—dc23
2013016833

9 8 7 6 5 4 3 2 1
Printed in the United States of America
on acid-free paper

The book is dedicated to:

My family and friends in Japan (Misa)

My family in California and Minnesota (Wendy)

CONTENTS

PREFACE

In this book, we consider a key moment in the history of how disabilities are envisioned in Japan: the transition between two different understandings of what it means when children have difficulties learning in school. In 2007, children who were formerly viewed as "difficult" or "slow" were recognized as having "disabilities" and in need of special intervention. We describe how educators, parents, and children created change and adapted to change, weaving new policy-generated perspectives of disabilities into traditional, Japanese cultural beliefs and practices. Through this glimpse into the everyday experiences of these Japanese families and professionals, readers may recognize some of the culturally widespread challenges they faced but also discern the distinctly Japanese cultural hue of adults' and children's responses. Japanese adults and children creatively addressed the "dilemma of difference" arising when children are singled out on the basis of deficits to receive necessary educational support that is different from that of their peers, and thus potentially stigmatizing. This early twenty-first century Japanese case provides us with an instance of how disabilities are socially, culturally, and historically constructed and invites us to reflect on our own taken-for-granted cultural assumptions about the nature and remediation of "invisible" disabilities.

This project has roots that extend back at least 15 years. Then, Misa Kayama was a doctoral student in Chemistry at the Institute for Molecular Science in Japan preparing to begin her dissertation research. Before completing her experiments, she suffered a skiing accident that left her paralyzed from the waist down. The Chemistry lab was not accessible to her crutches or wheelchair, so her advisor kindly offered to conduct the experiments for her. Under these circumstances, however, Misa saw little future for herself as a chemist with a disability in Japan. Rather, during her period of recovery and rehabilitation, Misa was introduced to a new field, Social Work, which interested her very much. She decided to pursue graduate studies in social work in the United States, where she specialized in school social work. During her MSW studies she first learned about special education for children with disabilities affecting cognition, social relations, attention, and executive functioning.

During her graduate education in the United States, Misa was encouraged to think of her own cultural knowledge as a resource from which to reflect on U.S. ways of addressing disability and to use the resulting insights to reflect back on Japanese ways. In other words, her experiences as an international graduate student in the United States provided her with an opportunity to simultaneously learn about her own culture and her new culture. As a student in Japan, from preschool through university, Misa interacted with peers who, in retrospect, may have had mild cognitive and behavioral disabilities. At that point in history, however, special education services were not available for these students. Rather, they received informal support, as needed, from classroom teachers and other students. Yet classroom teachers and peers did not always have the knowledge or resources to provide effective support. Several of Misa's peers who did not fit in with peer groups became socially isolated.

Misa's first experience with specialized interventions for children with mild cognitive and behavioral disabilities occurred in the United States. The formal system of special education in the United States promised to provide all children with disabilities with an appropriate education. Misa was fascinated. Yet from her "Japanese eyes," the U.S. system of special education appeared somewhat rigid, even coercive of some children and their parents. Children were frequently pulled out from their classrooms by adults for interventions and assessments of their needs. Misa was initially confused during her internship at a public middle and elementary school when she was told to go to classrooms and pull out several children. Misa had not established any relationships with these children, and she worried about how they and their peers would react to this support outside of their classrooms. In addition, parents attended meetings where educators and administrators discussed their children's difficulties including while filling out paperwork. Although educators generally attempted to minimize the emotional impact of such meetings on parents and help them to participate in decision making, some parents and educators were dissatisfied with the meetings. Eventually, Misa became used to the U.S. way of interacting and working with children with disabilities but wondered how children with mild cognitive and behavioral disabilities and their families were treated in Japan. She began communicating with Japanese educators and learned that a new formal system of special education for such children was being implemented in Japan.

When Misa entered the PhD program in Social Work at the University of Illinois, Urbana-Champaign, she decided to conduct research on disability in cultural context. This decision was motivated both by her experiences as an

MSW student and also by her own experiences in a wheelchair in the United States and Japan. The differences she observed in people's reactions to her wheelchair, as well as the greater availability of accommodations in the United States than in Japan raised important questions about how cultural contexts affect the experiences of individuals with disabilities. Ten years ago in Japan, many buildings and other public places were not accessible to Misa. Once her wheelchair was accepted by others, however, a lack of accessibility became *their* concern as well as hers. She experienced the comfort of kindness and belonging. In the United States, however, Misa has enjoyed the freedom of accessibility, and also from other peoples' "eyes" as individuals with disabilities more typically inhabit public places.

Fifteen years ago, Wendy Haight was a social work professor at University of Illinois, Urbana-Champaign and mother of young children, one of whom was diagnosed with dyslexia. Over the years, she and her family have appreciated the many resources available in the United States to identify and address children's learning differences but also have experienced many frustrations navigating the complex U.S. education system to secure resources for their child to learn, participate, and engage in school. They sought resources to build on their child's many strengths and support his self-concept as smart and a competent learner. They especially wanted to avoid potentially stigmatizing practices that could undermine their child's motivation, interactions with peers, and teacher expectations. At the middle school and high school levels, these goals were only met by opting out of an overcrowded, underfunded public school system. Yet it was only through the impressive technological and human resources available at public U.S. universities that this child gained full access to learning as a young adult. Today, he is poised to graduate with a master's degree in social work (MSW) and launch into an exciting and meaningful professional career. These insider experiences with U.S. educational policy, beliefs, and practices for individuals with learning disabilities from the elementary through graduate school levels have provided Wendy with an important context for viewing Japanese beliefs and practices and for reflecting back on U.S. practices.

Wendy' scholarship examines adults' socialization beliefs and practices and children's experiences within culturally diverse and marginalized families. She began collaborating with Japanese colleagues in 2005 examining socialization beliefs, practices, and policies pertaining to children vulnerable because of their history of maltreatment. The overarching commitment across her career has been to build a more culture-inclusive understanding of diverse children's well-being and development. This has required engaging deeply with a variety of perspectives and scrutinizing "mainstream" North

American assumptions that undergird so much research in developmental psychology, education, and child welfare. For example, her ethnographic work within an African-American community examined Sunday School as an important socialization context for African-American children and considered what U.S. public school policy makers and educators might learn from this context to better support the school learning of African-American children (Haight, 2002. *See also* Hudley, Haight & Miller, 2003/2009).

The current project is Wendy's latest effort to engage multiple sociocultural perspectives but also is an ongoing engagement with Japanese perspectives. She and Sachiko Bamba (Bamba & Haight, 2007, 2009a, 2009b, 2011) conducted an ethnographic study of children with histories of maltreatment. Japanese educators and child welfare professionals typically located the origins of maltreatment not within parents' individual pathology (although such cases certainly were recognized), but within social relationships. Professionals viewed child abuse and neglect, in part, as a problematic response to a rapidly urbanizing society in which the traditional social and community support optimal for childrearing have broken down and parents are relatively isolated from extended family and community. Maltreatment was viewed as partly emerging from parents' lack of *Ibasho*, a place where one feels comfort, belonging, and acceptance. The absence of *Ibasho* leads to emotional instability and irritability that can result in child maltreatment. Similarly, supporting children's recovery from child maltreatment did not primarily involve individual therapy (although such services were available) but helping children to find their *Ibasho* where they felt comfort, security, acceptance, and belonging to a group. This focus on children's *Ibasho* is also observed at Greenleaf Elementary School, the site of our current study. Misa became interested in examining the cultural meaning of Japanese practices, as she talked with Wendy and Sachiko about *Ibasho*, a concept typically taken-for-granted by Japanese people.

Over the past 6 years, Misa's and Wendy's close international collaboration has become a major strength of this joint research. Misa can understand education in Japan both from a Japanese perspective and from the perspective of a person with a disability. Her insider understanding of Japanese culture provided a necessary context for identifying relevant research questions, and interpreting participants' responses. Her study and experiences as a person with a disability in the United States also gave her an outsider perspective from which to reflect back on her own culture. Wendy's outsider status illuminated for systematic study Japanese constructs that often are taken for granted by cultural insiders, such as the role of education for *kokoro* (heart, mind) in shaping how formal, special education services are designed and implemented. Her insider status as the parent of a child with learning differences also sensitized her to similarities in parent and child responses to "disability" across two very distinct cultures.

Each culture encompasses diverse perspectives and each person occupies multiple roles that afford multiple cultural vantage points. Our personal experiences with disability deepen our access to particular corners of cultural knowledge, compared with those who have not had such experiences. In other words, we all have access within our own experiences to multiple roles and perspectives. It is the constant dialogue within ourselves as well as with others that is a major strength of a comparative outlook. Our multiple cultural lenses are a key strength in offering a clearer line of sight on the Japanese case that is not occluded by that which is taken for granted by any single cultural perspective.

We wrote this book for U.S. and Japanese colleagues and students. It is accessible to advanced undergraduate students but should also be of interest to graduate students, teachers, and scholars in education, social work, developmental cultural psychology, and East Asian and disability studies. Our overall aim is to encourage contemplation of what we in the United States can learn from a culture (Japan) in which children's school learning difficulties are localized primarily within social interactions, especially for supporting children's concepts of a competent, social self and for discouraging stigmatization. At the same time, we are interested in what Japanese educators might learn from the U.S. experience of administering a structured system of special education for the widespread, consistent support of all children with learning difficulties.

ACKNOWLEDGEMENTS

Over the years, many people have supported and encouraged us on this project. We would like to acknowledge a few of them. First of all, we would like to thank the children, parents, and educators at Greenleaf Elementary School (a pseudonym), especially, the principal who allowed us to conduct this project at her school, the three children followed longitudinally and their parents who kindly shared their experiences, the special education coordinator who gave Misa day-to-day guidance in how to work with Japanese children with disabilities at school, and the special education director who gave us continuous support and comments on our findings. We also would like to thank our colleagues who provided support and helpful comments on this project, including the reviewers. Thanks to Dr. Peggy Miller for stimulating conversations and her thoughtful reviews of early drafts. Dr. Ross Parke provided helpful comments especially on the implications of our findings. Dr. Brenda Lindsey's comments helped us to interpret practices in both countries. Dr. Jan Carter-Black provided insights into cultural analyses. Finally, we would like to acknowledge the continuous support we received from the University of Illinois at Urbana-Champaign School of Social Work, especially from Dean Wynne Korr. The University of Minnesota, Twin Cities, School of Social Work was our academic home during the writing of this book where we received generous support from the Gamble-Skogmo endowment.

Copyright permission/acknowledgement

Chapter 1

In this book, we have expanded and elaborated a report originally published as Kayama, M. & Haight, W. (2012). Cultural sensitivity in the delivery of disability services to children: A case study of Japanese education and socialization. *Children and Youth Services Review, 34,* 266-275. We have obtained permission to reproduce texts from this report (*see also* chapters 3–8).

Chapter 5

In this book, we have expanded and elaborated a report originally published as Kayama, M. & Haight, W. (in press). Disability and stigma: How Japanese educators help parents accept their children's differences. *Social Work*. We have obtained permission to reproduce texts from this report (*see also* chapters 1 and 8).

Chapter 7

In this book, we have expanded and elaborated a report originally published as Kayama, M. & Haight, W. (in press). The experiences of Japanese elementary-school children living with "developmental disabilities": Navigating peer relationships. *Qualitative Social Work*. (Available online: http://qsw.sage pub.com/content/early/2012/03/06/1473325012439321.full.pdf.) We have obtained permission to reproduce texts from this report (*see also* chapter 8).

A GUIDE TO JAPANESE TERMS

Throughout the book, we have retained some Japanese words and terms used by our participants and in Japanese literature. These terms were used in Japanese cultural contexts and were difficult to translate into English. For example, several concepts, such as *Ibasho* (see the definition below), do not have corresponding English terms. We have provided here definitions of some of the Japanese terms.

Henken

A Japanese term referring to discriminative, negatively biased views in society, prejudice, and stigma. In this book, it is used to describe the cultural attitudes directed toward individuals with disabilities, especially children with mild, relatively invisible cognitive and behavioral disabilities.

Ibasho

A place to belong. *Ibasho* connotes a physical and psychological place where one feels cozy, at home, fully accepted, and able to express oneself fully. It is considered to be basic to mental health and well-being throughout the lifespan.

Jibun

A Japanese word for self. *Jibun* literally means "one's share" of something beyond oneself. Japanese people view *jibun* as emerging within a social context, changing form from time to time as relationships between the self and other people change.

Manabi

A Japanese word to refer to learning. Especially for younger children, *manabi* refers not only to learning academic skills but also the social skills and moral attitudes necessary to function successfully as a Japanese adult.

Kokoro

An individual's inner world: heart, mind, soul, spirit, attitude, value system, personality, character, humanity, and so forth. Education for *kokoro* is a fundamental purpose of elementary education in Japan.

Mimamori

Adults support children's development largely through the practice of *mimamori*: They watch over children with affection and empathy as protective figures while allowing them the autonomy to freely explore activities, interact with others, and learn from these experiences.

Omoiyari

Empathy and sympathy. For Japanese people, empathy involves sensing, anticipating, and responding to other people's needs, and is critical to establishing trusting relationships. The responsibility of the individual is more to sense what others are feeling and thinking than to express his or her own emotions and thoughts. This sensitivity and ability to attend to other people's feelings and thoughts is referred to as *omoiyari*.

Sensei

Honorific used to respectfully acknowledge another's status and expert knowledge. Used for teachers, professors, medical doctors, legal, art, and other professionals. For example, children called Misa "Kayama *sensei*" or just "*Sensei*" when she was at Greenleaf Elementary School as a teaching assistant during her field work.

DISABILITY, CULTURE, AND DEVELOPMENT

1 RAISING CHILDREN WITH DISABILITIES AND THEIR PEERS AT A JAPANESE PUBLIC ELEMENTARY SCHOOL

Third-grade hallway: Children's first calligraphy of the year (*kakizome*), "Friends." A class photo from the annual choir concert. Children's self-introductions

Nagai *sensei*[1] shared her experiences with Naoto, 1 of 3 first graders in her class *of* 35 who required special attention because of social or learning difficulties. Naoto had a diagnosis of ADHD and frequently became upset and fought with other children. Nagai sensei discussed the need to "raise" all children to recognize, understand, and empathize with the struggles of others... "I explained to [Naoto's classmates] that everyone has a different amount that they are able to bear/tolerate (*gaman*). Everyone has a cup [of tolerance], but it's different one by one. Someone has a large cup, but there is someone who has a small cup. We can't change the size of our cups easily. So, there is a person who wants to *gaman* but can't... When [Naoto] became upset, other children said, 'His cup has overflowed.'" As a result of such interactions, another teacher explained, "When there is a child with a disability in a classroom, the classroom becomes kind to other people...." (based on Misa's fieldnote and interviews)

Physical and mental conditions that impact children's functioning create challenges affecting children, families, schools, and other social systems around the world. Yet how such conditions impact children's development varies considerably and can be understood as a transaction with culturally shared beliefs, practices, and social policies. In the first decade of the twenty-first century, special education in Japanese public elementary schools underwent a major reform. Before the reform, children such as Naoto who have mild[2] cognitive and behavioral disabilities were fully included in their general education classrooms (e.g., Stevenson & Stigler, 1992) but were taught by teachers who had neither specialized training nor support services (Kataoka, van Kraayenoord, & Elkins, 2004). The implementation of new special education services, called "special needs education[3]," provided invaluable support for Naoto and many other children with learning disabilities, Attention Deficit Hyperactivity Disorders (ADHD), high-functioning autism, Asperger's syndrome[4], and other relatively mild disabilities. The new services also created significant challenges for children, their parents, and educators to shape and respond to a formal system of individualized special education in a Japanese context where children are educated largely within peer groups. By treating individual children differently from members of their peer groups, special needs education can place them at risk of stigmatization, an especially devastating experience in Japan. As one teacher explained, "This is a society where you are called 'stranger' if you are a little bit different from others."

In many cultures, including the United States, disability is a sensitive issue because of lingering stigma. As we will see in this book, Japanese educators, parents, and children addressed the challenges posed by special needs education with sensitivity, flexibility, and creativity. Adults were aware of children's diagnostic labels but focused steadfastly on the whole child including competencies that could be a source of self-esteem and status within peer groups. Educators also respected parents' sensitivity to "other people's eyes" and spent time building trusting, collaborative, and non-coercive relationships with them and their children. As illustrated by Naoto's teacher in the opening excerpt, educators incorporated support for children who are struggling in their everyday activities at school as naturally as possible. They used metaphor and ritual to help children understand and respond to their own and their classmates' differences and created contexts that supported children's communication. For their parts, children with disabilities actively responded to the implementation of special needs education, for example, through pretend play. At the same time, Japanese educators encountered significant system-level obstacles. Some Japanese educators were frustrated by inadequate resources and procedures for consistently identifying and providing services to all children with mild cognitive and behavioral disabilities, and insufficient professional training and preparation for teaching them.

In this book, we focus on children like Naoto with mild disabilities of language, cognition, attention, behavior, and executive functioning whose struggles can be especially challenging to interpret. In many respects, they appear to be typically developing children. Unlike challenges faced by children with more severe or visible disabilities (e.g., involving vision, hearing, mobility, and global cognitive deficits), those experienced by children with less apparent disabilities can be difficult for the children and others to understand. They may view themselves as "stupid" or "bad." Peers who do not understand their classmates' difficulties may avoid or reject them (Ochs, Kremer-Sadlik, Solomon & Sirota, 2001). Adults may misattribute their difficulties to laziness, disobedience, or disrespect (e.g., McNulty, 2003; Portway & Johnson, 2005). Such misinterpretations can increase children's risk of academic failure, delay their access to the support necessary for their development, including special education services, and, in some cases, may leave them vulnerable to maltreatment. Indeed, Helton and Cross (2011) found that among a U.S. national probability sample of families investigated for maltreatment, children with minor language deficits were at greater risk for physical abuse by parents than those with severe language impairments.

Clearly, universal, biologically based conditions that result in relatively mild cognitive, language, and attention difficulties also have profound social consequences. These consequences, however, may vary widely. Cultures differ in which physical and mental conditions are considered "disabilities," how such conditions are grouped or categorized, societal responses deemed appropriate, how individuals with disabilities are valued, and the extent to which stigmatization affects individuals' everyday experiences (e.g., Kock et al., 2012; Varenne & McDermott, 1998). Japanese educators use the term "developmental disabilities" to refer to relatively mild cognitive and behavioral disabilities.[5] As we will describe below, understanding the meanings of "developmental disabilities" requires examination of Japanese social, historical, and cultural contexts. Relatively little sociocultural research written in English, however, has focused on non-Western children with disabilities (e.g., Peters, 1993). This limited focus restricts our understanding of the extent to which and how cultures vary in their beliefs and responses to disability, as well as the impact of any differences on the developing child (see also Fadiman, 1997; Jegatheesan, Fowler, & Miller, 2010; Jegatheesan, Miller, & Fowler, 2010; Ochs et al., 2001; Ochs & Solomon, 2010). By stepping outside of those sociocultural contexts that we take for granted to consider culturally diverse responses to disability, new dimensions of these complex experiences emerge.

Our goal is to create a "conversation" between alternative cultural under-standings of mild cognitive and behavioral disabilities.[6] This conversation includes how adults, through educational policies and practices, can consis-tently provide children with support that is both different from their peers and necessary to their success in school while minimizing their risk of stigmatiza-tion. Our research is situated in an emerging tradition of international, collab-orative research on children intended to engage multiple cultural perspectives each on its own terms (e.g., Bamba & Haight, 2011; Miller, Fung, Lin, Chen, & Boldt, 2012; Rogoff, 2011; Rogoff, Mistry, Göncü, & Mosier, 1993; Shweder, 2009; Tobin, Hsueh, & Kasrasawa, 2009; Tobin, Wu, & Davison, 1989). This tradition contrasts with research and professional practice that would elevate one way of doing things (typically North American and European) as "best practice" over other ways. The Japanese case allows us to explore what we (in the West) might learn from a culture in which children's school learning difficulties are localized primarily within relationships between individuals rather than individual pathology. It also allows us to consider what we (in Japan) might learn from a Western culture in which structured procedures help to ensure the timely receipt of services by all children with disabilities from educators with professional-level training in special education. Such cross-cultural "conversations" allow us all (in the West and in Japan) to con-sider the implications of cultural variation for improving our support for children with disabilities and their families. It is our belief that significant advances in practice and policy for the United States, Japan and other cultures will occur when multiple cultural perspectives are engaged in a deep, bal-anced, and respectful way.

Theoretical Models of Disability

An examination of Japanese models of "developmental disabilities" increases the range of cultural cases available for theoretical analyses of the role of cul-tural context in shaping the development of children with disabilities. There are many models of disability, including the medical model (e.g., see Llewellyn & Hogan, 2000; Mackelprang & Salsgiver, 2009), prominent in some U.S. edu-cational contexts (Peters, 1993). Those employing the medical model view the challenges experienced by individuals with disabilities as caused primarily by physiological impairments resulting from damage or a disease process. Expert practitioners treat the condition so that the individual can adapt to the environment. Identifying children's specific disabilities provides guide-lines to establishing service eligibility and delivery for *all* children who meet requirements. In 1975, PL.94-142 (currently, the Individuals with Disabilities

Education Act, or IDEA) provided specific guidelines to U.S. educators for special education. In 2008, 11.2% of U.S. children between the ages of 6 and 17 years received special education services (Data Accountability Center, 2012), which is about four times higher than in Japan. Many of them received services for relatively mild, "high-incidence disabilities" including learning disabilities (43%), emotional-behavioral disorders (20%), and speech-language disorders (7%).

At the same time, classification of children by disability may not always illuminate the educational and social needs of individual children (Peters, 1993). In addition, an unintended result of educators' focus on deficits and differences from typically developing children may be exposing children with disabilities and their families to stigmatization. Further, by focusing on children's challenges, educators may lose sight of the "whole child," including their strengths and competences (e.g., Ho, 2004; McDermott & Varenne, 1995).

In contrast to the medical model, our perspective on disability integrates a biological and sociocultural developmental perspective (e.g., Varenne & McDermott, 1998). We recognize biologically based variations in human neurological functioning as well as cultural differences in how people understood and respond to these variations—for example, how support for children with disabilities is provided. Consistent with the orientation of our Japanese participants, however, our focus is on the transactions of children with disabilities within specific culturally structured developmental contexts, including everyday interpersonal interactions at school and at home. For example, Kasahara and Turnbull (2005) found that Japanese parents of children with a broad range of disabilities emphasized educators' culturally valued expressions of empathy. Mothers expected educators' commitment and empathy and expected to work collaboratively with them for their children. They expressed a willingness to engage with teachers who showed enjoyment in working with their children and whose work was rooted in love and respect for children. Mothers also described the negative impact on their families and children of professionals who did not have these qualities.

Developmental contexts such as school and family are culturally structured to support the acquisition and display of valued competencies and attitudes (e.g., Corsaro & Rosier, 1992). Public elementary schools in the United States and Japan, for example, include classrooms comprised of same-aged children with a teacher, whose focus includes children's progressive mastery of basic literacy skills and social-emotional development. For children with certain biologically based variations in cognition, attention regulation, or executive functioning, some characteristics of school contexts may actually impede learning. Children with ADHD, for example, may have difficulty focusing and staying on task when learning is structured around sustained reading and writing at desks and tables.

Individuals' beliefs and responses to disabilities, however, are not determined by culture nor are they static. Through everyday social interactions within developmental contexts, children not only come to share beliefs and practices with others, they also actively contribute to recreating and reshaping them (e.g., Gaskins, Miller, & Corsaro, 1992; Shweder et al., 2006). As children with disabilities and their families participate in various activities at home, at school, and in the community, they encounter others' beliefs and expectations for them. They may respond to these beliefs and expectations in a variety of ways, including ignoring, denying, accepting, and actively embracing (e.g., Cohen & Napolitano, 2007; Lutz & Bowers, 2005). For example, Lalvani (2008) explored the experiences of U.S. mothers of children with Down Syndrome. Over time, as they and their children interacted with an increasingly broad array of individuals, who responded in diverse ways to their children's disability, their perspectives of Down Syndrome shifted away from an emphasis on medical to social issues. In another example, some Japanese parents of children with disabilities actually resisted stigma. These parents rejected responses from others, such as, "I'm sorry for you" and "You must be unhappy and hopeless" (Kasahara & Turnbull, 2005, p. 256). They preferred the new emerging concept of a consumer's right to receive necessary services.

Individuals' understanding and responses to disability also may vary developmentally (*see also* McNulty, 2003). For example, a 7-year-old child's understanding of his struggles to read, write, or control his behavior may change throughout his childhood, adolescence, and adulthood. Similarly, appropriate and effective support will vary with the individual's development. For example, educators' thoughtful use of play and ritual may facilitate the young elementary school-aged child's understanding and response to disability, whereas providing medical and scientific findings may be most appropriate for the adolescent or adult.

As others interact with children with disabilities and their families, their understanding and expectations likewise may develop. Family members, educators, social workers, adults with disabilities, and others can provide a bridge between children with disabilities and society by advocating for appropriate services and accommodations, thereby impacting cultural beliefs, values, social structures, and available educational resources. Japanese parent advocates, for example, have helped to bring about an historical turning point in Japanese education: the implementation of special education services within general elementary schools for their children with learning disabilities (Abe, 1998; *see also* Chapter 3). Changes in the attitudes of those around them, as well as broader social changes, may then impact children's own perceptions of self and participation in developmentally and culturally significant activities (Takahashi, 2003).

Within complex, contemporary societies, diverse views of disability may co-exist. Attention to such diversity is important to providing appropriate support to children and their families. For example, Jegatheesan, Miller, and Fowler (2010) examined parental beliefs about their children's autism in South Asian Muslim immigrants in the United States. One of the primary goals for these parents was the full inclusion of their children in daily activities at home and in the community, including religious rituals. Parents' beliefs about how to support their children's development conflicted with those of educators, who emphasized a structured and controlled environment to facilitate their children's individual learning. As a result of these conflicts, many parents were dissatisfied with schools and services for their children and conducted repeated, unsuccessful searches for service providers who understood their views of disability and with whom they could engage to support their children. Similarly, Fadiman (1997) described the struggles of Hmong refugee parents and their child with epilepsy. Their struggles illustrate a tragic collision between the family's traditional, largely spiritual understanding of epilepsy and the American medical construction of illness.

Through the research described in this book, we begin to elaborate an integrated biological and sociocultural developmental model of disability. A relatively unique feature is our cultural analysis of policy. We consider how new Japanese national policies intersected with local cultural contexts in the everyday lives of developing children, their parents, and educators. We will see, for example, how Japanese educators responded with exquisite sensitivity to the anxiety of some parents and children about the risk of stigmatization posed by national special education reforms. In other words, through our study of Japan, we came to appreciate the study of everyday lives of children as reflecting the interface of public policy and local culture as well as the richness of this interface for understanding the development of children.

Disability and Stigma

The importance for professionals of developing empathetic and trusting relationships with families and children may be especially important when the child's difference results from a disability. Throughout recorded history, many people with disabilities have been marginalized as morally objectionable or pathological and in need of assistance (Mackelprang & Salsgiver, 2009). In Europe, education for individuals with disabilities originated as charity projects, which evolved in the eighteenth century into schools for children who were "deaf and blind." Charity projects provided individuals with disabilities opportunities to receive an education. They also were intended to relieve poverty, which inadvertently reinforced the lower status of individuals with disabilities (Nakamura & Arakawa, 2003). In many cultures, disability remains a sensitive issue, in part because of continued stigma (e.g., Goffman, 1963; Kock et al., 2012).

Stigma may be defined as the co-occurrence of labeling, stereotyping, separation, status loss, and discrimination (Link & Phelan, 2001). According to Goffman (1963), individuals with socially defined "undesired differentness" experience varying degrees of stigma. Further, their difference from "normal" may affect not only others' attitudes and behaviors toward them (social stigma) but also their own concepts of self (e.g., internalized stigma) (Crystal, Watanabe, & Chen, 1999; Goffman, 1963). Social and psychological barriers created by stigma are experienced by some people with disabilities as presenting the greatest challenges to their full participation in society (Mackelprang & Salsgiver, 2009).

For many children, special education services are invaluable bridges providing access to school learning. On the other hand, receiving special education services can mark children as different from their peers and become a source of stigma (Minow, 1990). Indeed, children receiving special education around the world express challenges that are not directly related to difficulties emerging from their neurologically based disorders or educational interventions *per se*. These challenges include feelings of isolation from peers, difference from others, lack of belonging, teasing by peers, and perception that they are "less than" their peers (e.g., Davis & Watson, 2001; Kelly, 2005; Mackelprang & Salsgiver, 2009; McMaugh, 2011; McNulty, 2003; Meadan & Halle, 2004; Nugent, 2008; Portway & Johnson, 2005; Zambo, 2004). Some children may even develop secondary disabilities not directly caused by their "primary" disabilities but developed in interaction with their environments. These secondary disabilities including emotional and behavioral disorders may then require additional intervention (e.g., Saito, 2009).

Stigma can affect not only individuals with disabilities but their families as well. Goffman (1963) defines courtesy stigma as occurring when both the stigmatized person and his or her intimates are treated as one negatively valued social unit. Courtesy stigma can be experienced by parents of children with disabilities, particularly mothers who may be viewed as "bad mothers" for raising "less-than-perfect" children. Internalizing and responding to courtesy stigma can add another layer of stressful demands to raising a child with a disability (Koro-Ljungberg & Bussing, 2009). For example, Jegatheesan (2009) examined the perspectives of first-generation Asian-American mothers of children with disabilities. Some mothers shared others' negative beliefs about having a child who was not "normal" and feared bringing shame to their families. They discussed the strains of being part of a community where there is an emphasis on children being smart and talented. These mothers felt that community members looked down on their children and felt pity for them as parents.

McDermott and others (Hood, McDermott & Cole, 1980; McDermott, Goldman & Varenne, 2006; McDermott, & Varenne, 1995; Mehan, 1998; Varenne, & McDermott, 1998) have observed that cultural frameworks help to define developmental goals, address common human challenges, and support the development of various abilities. On the other hand, the ways in which cultural frameworks are used to address particular human problems and interpret individual variation also may make visible and consequential particular differences in individuals. Consider, for example, the experiences of children with dyslexia and their parents in contemporary U.S. schools. We conduct education largely through the manipulation of written symbols, expect children to display their knowledge through written symbols, and highly value early literacy (e.g., Artiles, Thorius, Bal, Neal, Waitoller, & Hernandez-Saca, 2011; McDermott et al., 2006). Intelligent and otherwise capable children with neurological differences making discrimination of written symbols difficult are singled out in school as "learning disabled" and in need of intervention. As a consequence of a focus on what the child cannot do in a competitive school context, children may become frustrated (e.g., Assouline & Whiteman, 2011), and their self-esteem and relationships with peers may be threatened (Mackelprang & Salsgiver, 2009; McNulty, 2003; Meadan & Halle, 2004; Portway & Johnson, 2005; Zambo, 2004). In addition, their parents may be suspect among other parents and educators as providing insufficient support and stimulation to their children at home (e.g., Koro-Ljungberg & Bussing, 2009). Yet in many other contexts such as home, clubs, and sports, these children function well and the label of "disability" has as little meaning (McDermott & Varenne, 1995; Varenne & McDermott, 1998) as it would have had at an earlier time in U.S. history before widespread public schooling.

Developmental Disabilities: A New Category in Japan

In this book, we describe how Japanese adults integrated traditional socialization and educational goals, beliefs, and practices within a new, formal, and potentially stigmatizing special education system and how this transition was experienced by children with "developmental disabilities," their parents, teachers, and peers at "Greenleaf Elementary School.⁷" Understanding the challenges faced by Japanese educators, parents, and children in transitioning to the new special education system highlights the issue of stigma and disability for analysis and raises questions regarding developmentally appropriate and culturally sensitive ways of framing "disabilities" for children, their parents, and peers.

Japanese educators use the term "developmental disabilities" to refer to various neurologically based conditions considered to cause relatively mild difficulties in children's school functioning. These conditions include learning disabilities such as dyslexia, ADHD, and certain autism spectrum disorders including high-functioning autism and Asperger's syndrome (Ministry of Health, Labour and Welfare, 2004a; *see* Chapter 3 for Japanese definitions of developmental disabilities). Educators formed this category, in part to avoid the stigma attached to particular medical diagnoses. In addition, they were dissatisfied with the utility of medical diagnoses for guiding educational interventions. They believed that children with developmental disabilities share many similar struggles and thus could benefit from similar educational programs and approaches (Tsuge, 2004). Despite different diagnoses, children with developmental disabilities appear "normal" and healthy but struggle to interact with others; learn to read, write, or calculate; or control their emotions and behaviors. They also share a risk for the development of secondary disabilities, such as emotional and behavioral disorders, that arise in response to how others treat them (Saito, 2009). Further, their struggles may overlap because medical diagnoses are not clear or mutually exclusive categories. For example, many children with learning disabilities also exhibit some behaviors in common with children diagnosed with ADHD and high-functioning autism (Tsuge, 2004; Sato, 2009). Finally, all of these children and their families may be vulnerable to stigmatization.

Until recently, Japanese children with developmental disabilities were considered to be among any number of children who were "difficult" or "slow learners" and were socialized within general education classrooms without special services. Rather, classroom teachers and peers provided individual support as needed. Children with more severe cognitive, mobility, and sensory disabilities were provided with services in special education schools or classrooms separated from their typically developing peers (e.g., Abe, 1998; Mogi, 1992). At the time of the present study (2009–2010), the Japanese education system was in transition, as public schools implemented formal special education services for children with developmental disabilities who were being educated within general education classrooms (Ministry of Education[8], 2007a). The recent implementation of formal special education services for these children provided a unique context for adults and children to reflect on otherwise unexamined beliefs about "disability" and appropriate responses to such children.

By the late 1970s, Japanese government leaders and scholars had become increasingly aware of children with learning difficulties in general education classrooms (National Institute of Special Needs Education, 1978). It was not until the 1990s, however, that their special needs received wider public attention as a result of internal and external pressure on the Japanese government. In 1990, a support group was established for Japanese parents of children with learning disabilities (National Association of Parents of Children with Learning Disabilities, 2013). Some parents of children with developmental disabilities were dissatisfied with the level of support provided to their children who were struggling in general education classrooms. Around this same time, the Japanese government was pressured by a movement across the world to protect children's rights. This movement included the Convention on the Rights of the Child that identified appropriate education as a basic human right (United Nations, 1989) and the Salamanca Statement that called on governments to provide inclusive education (UNESCO, 1994).

By the late 1990s, the special education system in Japan entered a period of reform (e.g., Abe, 1998). There was concern about the potential dangers of stigmatizing children through labeling them as having disabilities (*see* Abe, 1998). Kadomoto (1990), for example, indicated that the new formal support system for children with learning disabilities and other "mild" disabilities had to be designed with careful consideration of appropriate evidence-based, non-stigmatizing practices.

After a series of studies of children with learning difficulties and their needs spanning over a decade, schools in Japan implemented a new system of formal special education during the 2007–2008 academic year (Ministry of Education, 2007a). Under the new law, educators are required to provide individualized support for children with developmental disabilities. It requires schools to assign an educator to serve as a special education coordinator to work collaboratively with parents and other educators and plan and implement support for each child who is struggling in general education classrooms regardless of whether the child has a documented disability. This support is highly individualized, flexible, and somewhat dependent on school resources. It could range from extra support from a classroom teacher or a part-time teacher in the general education classroom to several hours a week of individual or small-group instruction outside of the classroom. If children require a more intensive level of support, then their formal eligibility for special education services is assessed by an outside team of professionals including a psychologist assigned by the local board of education. If they are eligible, children may attend a resource room or a special education classroom as needed while retaining their "seats" in their age-appropriate, general education classrooms.

Japanese Concepts of Self in Relationships and Place

Understanding the challenges of formulating and implementing culturally sensitive, formal systems of support for Japanese children with disabilities requires an understanding of broader, inter-related concepts of self in relationships and place. In Japan, a society that is often described as placing a high value relative to Western societies on interdependence, the self is understood as primarily relational and contextual (e.g., Markus & Kitayama, 1991; *see also* Lebra, 1976). The Japanese word for self, *"jibun,"* literally means "one's share" of something beyond oneself (*see* Lebra, 1976). As the Japanese consciousness of self, *jibun* is discovered from time to time between oneself and another (Kimura, 1972). Japanese people view *jibun* as emerging within a social context, changing form as relationships between the self and world change (Hagiwara, 2001). Accordingly, what people say and how they behave may be adjusted to be appropriate and acceptable to the social groups to which they belong (Markus & Kitayama, 1991).

In some contexts, individuals may face social interactions that conflict with their *kokoro,* their inner world and heart. When individuals have to act against their *kokoro* because of external social relationship demands and pressures, they may lose *jibun* and struggle to recover it (e.g., Lebra, 1976; Shimizu, 2001a). Accordingly, individuals must balance their own *kokoro* (individual-self) and *jibun* (interpersonal-self) within their social relationships with friends, parents, educators, colleagues, and so forth. (e.g., Hosaka, 2005). Some children, however, lose this balance. For example, children with disabilities may not be able to produce or display socially appropriate and acceptable behaviors, causing a conflict between their *kokoro* and *jibun.* They may develop a fear of school and interacting with their peers, for example, because of the lack of understanding of their struggles and frequent problems caused by their disabilities. As a result, they may drop out of peer groups, which may compound their problems. For example, Japanese children who do not belong to any group may become isolated from other children and lonely (Kennedy & Yaginuma, 1991). Eventually this isolation can result in extended absenteeism from school (Hosaka, 2005). From this perspective, children's struggles are located within their relationships with others, especially their peer groups. For children with disabilities and their parents, differences from typically developing children that may lead to stigmatization can become a major concern, probably more than biological descriptions of disabilities based on medical diagnoses.

A sense of place and belonging are important elements in connecting with others in meaningful social relationships. *Ibasho* is a physical and psychological place where one feels safe, at ease, accepted, and able to freely and fully express oneself. According to Japanese folk psychology, *Ibasho* forms a basis from which to face challenges and to which one can return for comfort and strength. *Ibasho* creation is necessary for the psychological well-being of all people, throughout the lifespan (Bamba & Haight 2007, 2009a, 2009b 2011). Children find their *Ibasho* through empathetic and mutually accepting relationships, the opportunity to contribute to others' well-being, and the performance of clear roles within the group. Finding their *Ibasho* is critical to children with disabilities who may experience many challenges, including stigma and interpersonal struggles.

Japanese Socialization Beliefs and Practices

In part to support the development of interpersonal relationships, Japanese socialization from early childhood emphasizes sensitivity and caring for other's feelings (e.g., Azuma, 1994; Shimizu, 2001b; Tobin et al., 2009). For Japanese people, empathy involves sensing, anticipating, and responding to other people's needs (Lebra, 1976) and is critical to establishing trusting relationships (Kayama, 2010). The responsibility of the individual is more to sense what others are feeling and thinking than to express his or her own emotions and thoughts. This sensitivity and ability to attend to other people's feelings and thoughts is referred to as *omoiyari* (Bamba & Haight, 2011). Japanese teachers, for example, emphasize the importance of children's skills in listening over speaking (Tobin et al., 1989). They generally are highly sensitive (relative to U.S. teachers) to children's behavioral cues indicating, for example, interpersonal struggles (Haynes et al., 2000). Japanese children also generally express higher levels of concern and empathy for peers with disabilities relative to U.S children (Crystal et al., 1999). At home, where parents prioritize children's abilities to control their feelings without disturbing other people, Japanese children are exposed to multiple opportunities in their everyday lives to guess and sense what other people feel and think (Azuma, 1994).

A basic Japanese socialization belief is that children are naturally good and sensible and will voluntarily acquire socially acceptable attitudes and behaviors through their close interpersonal relationships (Walsh, 2004). Hence, adults typically focus on socialization practices that are primarily indirect, non-coercive, and respectful of the child's autonomy. These practices frequently create physical and social ecologies that support children's emerging sense of place, self, and relationships. Adults support children's development largely through the practice of *mimamori*: They watch over children with affection and empathy as protective figures while allowing them the autonomy to freely explore activities, interact with others, and learn from these experiences (e.g., Bamba & Haight, 2011). Their guidance may involve creating opportunities and contexts for children to contribute to peer groups—for example, by serving food, planning and engaging in enjoyable activities, and developing positive relationships with others. For example, the city in which our research site is located implemented an "*Ibasho* creation project for children with disabilities." The primary purpose of this project was to provide a supportive, physical place in the community for children with disabilities after school hours, so that they can stay mentally and physically healthy, feel free, and improve communication and interpersonal skills. In addition, this *Ibasho* creation project provides children's parents with some respite.[9] Once children recognize the space as their *Ibasho*, they can initiate relationships with adults in the community who provide them with support and *mimamori*.

When children are struggling, Japanese educators and caregivers tend to focus on the child's relationship to the group. For example, Hirotada Ototake (1998), a Japanese educator born in 1976 without arms and legs, received a public education through high school in general education classrooms. At that time in Japan, it was uncommon for children with severe physical disabilities to attend general public schools, but his parents worked with educators to provide him with the opportunity to study with other children his own age. His power wheelchair was attractive to elementary school-aged children, and his peers were eager to help him complete tasks and participate in activities. This concerned his classroom teacher, who believed that Ototake should learn to be as independent of others' help as possible. Ototake, who did not like to be treated differently from others, appreciated the teacher's "equal" treatment of him. Eventually, his peers followed the lead of their teacher. As they became used to his disability, other children considered him as just "one of their classmates." Rather than "helping" him, they spontaneously created rules so that he was able to participate in activities. For example, if he scored a goal while playing soccer, then children gave his team 3 points[10]. Ototake and his classmates learned how to solve problems together, without focusing on the negative aspects of his disability.

The preference of Japanese adults for focusing on the social contexts of children's difficulties also was observed with a child struggling with a less visible challenge (Bamba & Haight, 2011). When Ayako, a young adolescent girl with a history of physical and sexual abuse, was suspended from school because of behavioral problems, her caregivers at the children's institution where she lived focused on creating a caring and supportive social ecology in which she could find a role and feel accepted (find her *Ibasho*) and in providing her with *mimamori*. They considered her developmental potential and watched over her with compassion and "long eyes" turned towards her future. During her school suspension, they allowed her to help take care of babies and toddlers, an activity meaningful and enjoyable to her and from which she found acceptance and success. In other words, these Japanese professionals located Ayoko's struggles within the context of, and intervened at the level of, interpersonal relationships.

Japanese Elementary School Education

Through elementary school, Japanese education is broadly viewed as "raising children" in partnership with parents. Parents expect educators to assume broad roles in their children's development, not only teaching academic skills but also providing opportunities for children to learn basic life skills, manners, discipline, and morality. Indeed, Japanese educational practices through elementary school focus on teaching not only academic content during formal instruction but attitudes and values from everyday interactions with educators, other children, parents, and people in the community. Japanese educators emphasize the spiritual function of education, including the development of personality and mind as well as emotional and social well-being. Okamoto (2006) explains this emphasis through the Japanese notion of "*kokoro*":

> "*Kokoro*" is a concept with a wide range of connotations including heart, mind, soul, spirit, attitude, value system and humanity. As witnessed by the frequent use of slogans extolling the virtues of "education for *kokoro*," it can be said that the fundamental purpose of education in Japan is surprisingly defined in nothing but spiritual, loftier terms such as "*kokoro*" or character development. (p. 9)

In addition, phrases such as "children who are physically and mentally healthy" are frequently used in Japanese education, including the National Curriculum Standards and mission statements of each school.[11] The Fundamental Law of Education (Ministry of Internal Affairs and Communication, 2006) clearly identifies the primary purpose of education as broadly supporting children's development, including the development of character and personality:

> Education has to be provided in order to promote full character/personality development and raise children who are healthy both physically and mentally and who have abilities to contribute to the formation of a peaceful and democratic nation and society. (Article 1, paragraph 1)

Cultivating *omoiyari* in children is one of the most important goals of Japanese elementary education (Ministry of Education, 2008). In middle childhood, the peer group is a central socialization and educational context (Chen, French, & Schneider, 2006), including for acquiring *omoiyari*. Children's relationships with their peers and educators are clearly recognized in the National Curriculum Standard for elementary schools (Ministry of Education, 2008) as a primary means of teaching academic skills as well as the social skills and moral attitudes necessary to function successfully as a Japanese adult. At school, teachers promote children's cooperation and ability to work with peers with diverse abilities and interests—for example, by utilizing small groups to which children are assigned regardless of their levels of skill and understanding (e.g., Benjamin, 1997; Lewis, 1995; Tsuneyoshi, 2001; White, 1987). Small groups are used in both academic and non-academic activities such as completing group projects (e.g., Lewis, 1995; Cave, 2007), eating lunch, and cleaning classrooms (e.g., Cave, 2007; Lewis, 1995; Mansfield, 2000; Tsuneyoshi, 1994, 2001). Through these activities, children learn by working collaboratively and contributing to their groups (Tsuneyoshi, 1994). Further, by working with others, children with special needs are inspired and motivated to learn (e.g., White, 1987).

Collaboration within peer groups is viewed as central to children's education for *kokoro* and holistic development into a competent member of Japanese society. Through working with others, children establish relationships with their peers and develop a sense of mutual obligation to help and learn from one another (Sato, 2004). Research on Japanese preschools describes how teachers create an environment where children voluntarily learn social skills and values in their daily lives (e.g., Lewis, 1995; Peak, 1991; Tobin et al., 1989; Tobin et al., 2009). For example, Tobin and colleagues (1989) observed that when children misbehaved and had conflicts with peers, their classroom teachers did not necessarily intervene immediately or directly. Teachers observed, watched over children carefully as protective figures, stood back, and waited for them to respond. Their *mimamori* created the opportunity for children to collaboratively solve their own problems. Teachers viewed their primary role to include creating opportunities for children to collaboratively solve their own problems. A U.S. child who attended a Japanese elementary school for 4 months described Japanese children's behaviors, "If American kids acted like that, they'd all get sent to the principal's office everyday" (Lewis, 1995, p. 205). Rather than punishing children, teachers used noisy and frequently disruptive behaviors in their classrooms to guide all children in monitoring their own behaviors, learning how to solve problems, and taking responsibilities for their own actions.

Thus, the practice of providing formal, individualized services to children with developmental disabilities presents a challenge for Japanese parents and educators. They must balance traditional socialization and educational practices of rearing and educating children within peer groups and concerns about stigmatization with new requirements to provide formal, individualized special education services. To achieve the goals of both socializing children into Japanese society and providing special education services, adults must help children to utilize services while remaining fully integrated into peer groups. Avoiding stigmatization is central. Given the emphasis of Japanese culture on interpersonal relationships (Dekovic, Engels, Shirai, DeKort, & Anker, 2002), problematic peer relationships can be a devastating experience for children (Hosaka, 2005; Kawabata, Nicki, & Hamaguchi, 2010; Markus & Kitayama, 1991). In Japan, where "self" tends to be understood in relation to social relationships, failure to connect to people may be experienced as a "nightmare" (Markus & Kitayama, 1991; *see also* Lebra, 1976).

In this book, we examine Japanese educational policies, cultural beliefs about disability, and socialization practices as they impact the implementation of formal special education services. Chapter 2 describes how we approached these issues from the perspectives and experiences of children, their parents, and educators. Chapter 3 provides historical and cultural contexts for the Japanese transition into the new special education system. In Chapter 4, we turn to children's everyday experiences at Greenleaf Elementary School. This chapter also focuses on the developmental contexts in which Japanese educational goals, practices, and policies are instantiated at Greenleaf Elementary School, including some challenges faced by children with disabilities and support available for them. Chapters 5 and 6 describe how Japanese adults and children creatively addressed the "dilemma of difference" created when children received necessary educational support that was different from that of their peers and was potentially stigmatizing (*see also* Minow, 1990). Chapter 7 then focuses on how children with disabilities experienced their disabilities and special education services through case studies of three children. In Chapter 8, we conclude with overall discussions and some ideas of how Japanese and U.S. educators can learn from one another.

Notes

1. Japanese teachers, including school nurses and other educators, are referred to as *sensei* (teacher).
2. By "mild," we do not mean to imply that the challenges these children face are insignificant; rather, we are simply referring to the relative severity of these disabilities.

3. After special education reforms in 2007, the new system of Japanese special education is referred to as "special needs education." In this book, we also use "special education" to refer to "special needs education" (*see* more detailed description of the reforms in Chapter 3).

4. In the DSM-IV-TR, Asperger's syndrome was listed as one category of Pervasive Developmental Disorders along with Autistic Disorders. In the DSM-5, Asperger's syndrome and Autistic Disorders are integrated into one category: Autism Spectrum Disorders.

5. Note that the Japanese definition of "Developmental disabilities" differs from that in the DSM-5 and ICD-10. For example, it does not include global intellectual disabilities. In this book, developmental disabilities refer to the Japanese definition unless otherwise specified.

6. We are grateful to Peggy Miller for the insights expressed in this paragraph.

7. All place and participant names used in this book are pseudonyms.

8. The official English translation of the Ministry until 2000 was "Ministry of Education, Science, and Culture." The Ministry was combined with the Science and Technology Agency in 2001, and currently is known as "Ministry of Education, Culture, Sports, Science and Technology." In this book, we refer to the Ministry as the "Ministry of Education."

9. Some information in this book was obtained from the website of, or publication by, the local board of education for our research site. To maintain confidentiality of the research site, we have excluded these information sources from the reference list of this study.

10. This episode is in textbooks and used for moral education in Japanese public schools. For example, a fourth grade classroom teacher used this "rule" to discuss attitudes toward people with disabilities when Misa visited their classroom as a guest teacher and shared her experiences of being in a wheelchair. We will describe children's responses to such rules in Chapter 6.

11. The original Japanese word for "physically and mentally" combines the Japanese word for "body" and *kokoro*.

2 RESEARCH PROGRAM

Child's drawing showing Misa in her wheelchair in the second grade classroom.[1]

Children's curiosity about my wheelchair helped me to initiate and establish relationships with them. Many older children asked me why I used a wheelchair, but younger children seemed more interested in the wheelchair itself. In the second grade hallway, children excitedly pushed me in my wheelchair, but had difficulty steering straight: "Watch out, we will hit the wall!" Even before I had entered their classroom, first graders immediately surrounded me as soon as they saw me in the hallway. One child requested, "Show me your driver's license [for a wheelchair]," and expressed concern that I did not have one. Several children spontaneously shared their own experiences of disabilities or difficulties. Rather than actively asking questions, I waited for children's reactions to my wheelchair and listened to how they related it to their own experiences. (From Misa's field note)

This excerpt from Misa's field note illustrates children's active co-construction of the meaning of disability during their everyday interactions at school. It also illustrates a "reactive strategy" to field research (Corsaro, 1997, 2003) on socially sensitive issues. The issue of "disability" in Japan is fraught with complexity. Stigma associated with disability also can be an obstacle to examining individuals' beliefs, experiences, and perceptions. To address these challenges, Misa first allowed children to approach her, ask her questions about her disability and wheelchair, and spontaneously react including sharing stories of their own difficulties before she ventured to ask any questions of her own. In this chapter, we discuss some methodological implications of a sociocultural developmental perspective of children's disabilities, the implementation of the ethnographic research, and Misa's reflections on her experiences collecting data on a culturally sensitive topic. We also consider the important, but too often minimal, role of scholars with disabilities in the field of disability studies and special education, including ethical issues in the elicitation of narratives describing stressful, and potentially traumatic, events.

Understanding the Experiences of Individuals With Disabilities

We will examine the issues of stigma and disability through the perspectives and experiences of Japanese children with developmental disabilities, their parents, and educators. In many cultures, disability is a sensitive issue to openly discuss and explore, in part, because of the stigma attached to disabilities (e.g., Goffman, 1963; Kock et al., 2012; Olney, Kenedy, Brockelman, & Newsom, 2004) and concerns about the potentially negative impact of sharing traumatic experiences. Therefore, individuals with disabilities may not necessarily welcome the opportunity to tell their stories. They may intentionally leave out central aspects of their experiences or choose to remain silent altogether. Yet understanding their beliefs and experiences is critical to providing relevant, effective, and culturally sensitive support.

The challenges faced by individuals with disabilities are complex, and the meaning of these experiences may be difficult to communicate directly. For example, children with disabilities may require accommodations to enjoy and fully participate in school activities. Yet receiving accommodations may make children feel that they are different from other children (Minow, 1990). Children may express their stress, ambiguity, and confusion indirectly in their stories, play, humor, and rituals (Clark, 2003). As we will discuss in Chapter 7, one of our participant children expressed and coped with stress through pretend play. If adults attend to children's implicit messages, they may be able both to give children opportunities to express their struggles more directly and to provide necessary support.

In addition, appropriate social distance and relationships may be critical to expressing and understanding socially difficult and emotional experiences. For example, some stories remain untold because individuals choose to remain silent in certain contexts, such as in their families. Their concerns are for family members, including their reaction to the stories, their impact on their relationships, and the extra burden secret stories may place on family members. For example, a Taiwanese grandmother, who had remarried in violation of cultural norms, kept stories about her deceased first husband secret for years until she told an ethnographer. During important transitions in her life, her first husband appeared in her dreams. She felt that these stories would not be appreciated by her family members. The researcher, however, was an outsider, so the grandmother did not have to worry about such consequences and felt comfortable in telling her stories of her first husband (e.g., Miller, Fung, & Koven, 2007).

Likewise, in some cultures, disability stories may be a type of secret story. In Jegatheesan, Fowler, and Miller's (2010) research with South Asian Muslim immigrants in the United States, parents expressed hesitation in disclosing their children's diagnoses of autism to extended family members. They were especially concerned about the possible negative impact on elderly grandparents' health. In Asian countries where people are sensitive to differences from others and group harmony is valued (Chan, 1998; Tachibana & Watanabe, 2004), telling one's own or a family member's disability story in public can highlight the differences of individuals with disabilities and suggest that they are not fully competent community members. This can bring shame to the family and damage their relationships with other extended family and community members.

Children with disabilities also may be sensitive to how their experiences influence their relationships with family members, and they may choose to remain silent about their experiences to maintain family roles. Children sometimes feel that they can handle their experiences and feelings better than their parents, especially if parents become overprotective or overwhelmed by hearing their stories (Clark, 2003). For example, an 8-year-old child understood her terminal illness and felt protective of her parents and older brother who would grieve her death (Deford, 1997). Children may know much more than adults think they do and have the ability to express their feelings and experiences. Researchers from outside may be able to provide more opportunities for them to express their feelings and experiences than family members and friends with whom children have close relationships.

Timing also is important in the telling of traumatic experiences. Stories about disabilities may cause emotional reactions such as fear, anger, shock, and sorrow in those with disabilities and others (Charmaz, 2002). Yet the meanings of traumatic experiences may change over time, and silenced stories may eventually become tellable. Portelli (2003) interviewed people who witnessed the massacre in Rome at the end of World War II. One of the participants described that it was the worst experience of his life. Now, he talks about those times with friends to share and remember their experiences. In addition to adjustment to a traumatic loss, people who acquire disabilities have to accept their disabilities and re-learn skills required in their daily lives. Parents of children with disabilities also have to make psychological adjustments and additional efforts to find necessary support for their children (Cohen & Napolitano, 2007). Children and parents may need time to remain silent until they internalize their past experiences and feel that they are no longer in a crisis situation.

Thinking back over their past experiences and re-organizing their stories can help people to cope with past traumatic experiences (Steedman, 1986). Every person has had experiences that have important meanings for them, such as experiences that determined their future paths. At these turning points, people sometimes leave behind "unfinished business," especially when they were not satisfied with the decisions they made. Acquiring a disability or discovering that one's child has a disability can be such a turning point. Individuals have to make decisions about how to cope with disabilities. Their prior desires may not be fulfilled and may have to be adjusted within the available resources and abilities (Cohen & Napolitano, 2007). Memories and emotional reactions to these experiences may come up years later. Steedman (1986) notes that writing down one's own history makes it possible to understand how each experience is connected and to learn about the self. In the same way, thinking back about their past and telling their stories may help people with disabilities and their family members to comprehend, internalize, and make peace with past painful experiences.

Similarly, children with disabilities may benefit from expressing their feelings and experiences. Unless children with disabilities and their parents are asked to share their experiences, their voices may remain silent, especially if children's disabilities are less visible as are "developmental disabilities." If adults and peers do not have sufficient knowledge and resources, then the needs and confusion of children with mild cognitive and behavioral disabilities may not be noticed unless someone creates opportunities for them to speak up. Research participation is one way to give public voice to the experiences and perspectives of these children, their parents, and educators.

Methodological Issues in the Sociocultural, Developmental Study of Disability

Given that asking questions about disabilities can cause emotional distress, the ethical study of individuals' experiences of "disabilities" raises methodological issues. To hear the narratives of Japanese children with disabilities, their parents, and educators, as well as be allowed to participate in their everyday lives, the methods we employ must be sensitive to Japanese cultural perspectives on disability.

Children with disabilities and their families may choose to communicate their stories to audiences whom they perceive as capable of understanding their experiences and who will not deny or ridicule their narratives (Charmaz, 2002), especially in Japan where people are sensitive to other people's responses. If they think that researchers are not able to understand the difficulties they are experiencing, then they may speak only briefly, or not at all. To hear their stories and interpret silence, researchers may have to develop relationships with participants, gain trust, and let them know that they can understand their stories. Sharing similar experiences with participants may help us to establish trusting relationships.

If researchers exploring disability stories have disabilities, their own personal experiences of disability provide them with unique opportunities to hear participants' disability stories and explore their perceptions and experiences of disability (Tregaskis & Goodley, 2005). For example, they may be especially sensitive to implicit messages regarding hardships and be able to interpret and explore them further. This sensitivity and empathy also makes it possible to recognize when the interview has become intrusive, and make an ethical decision whether to continue (e.g., Stake, 2010). Yet relatively few researchers with disabilities seem to use their personal experiences to develop studies of the meaning and experience of disabilities (Tregaskis & Goodley, 2005; *see also* Green, Davis, Karshmer, Marsh, & Straight, 2005; Peters, 2010; Ware, 2002). In this study, our first-hand experiences as an individual with a disability (Misa) and a parent of a child with a disability (Wendy) helped us to hear the voices of children with disabilities and their parents and also provided insider perspectives helpful to understanding and interpreting their experiences.

Implementation of the Ethnographic Research

We used ethnographic methods to examine the everyday experiences of Japanese children with developmental disabilities, their parents, and educators. We first considered new social and educational policies pertaining to disability and special education focusing on how the sociocultural and historical contexts of twenty-first century Japan have shaped such policies. We reviewed Japanese governmental and local documents describing relevant history and law produced during a period of transition into a formal special education system for children with developmental disabilities. This cultural analysis of policy focused on the timing of the implementation of new policies in relation to major historical events and societal transitions, cultural understandings of new disability categories, and education services for children with developmental disabilities. This analysis allowed us to consider how the formulation and implementation of formal, national policies were constrained by cultural context including traditional Japanese educational and socialization goals and practices and parental sensitivity to stigma as well as how policies were translated into local practices at Greenleaf Elementary School.

The field research component of our study spanned two school years and broadly considered how national educational policies and local cultural context intersect in children's everyday lives at school. We examined how educators, children, and their parents navigated their way through the transition to the new support system. Ethnographic field methods allowed us to engage in children's lives at school and gain an understanding of practices, challenges, and successes that they and their educators and parents were experiencing. Our focus on routine, everyday practices provided us with opportunities to examine how children and adults co-construct the meanings of disability in their everyday interactions (*see* Clark, 2010; Corsaro, 2003; Miller, Hengst, & Want, 2003) and obtain a deeper understanding of the "world" of Japanese children with developmental disabilities at Greenleaf Elementary School (e.g., Duncan, Huston, & Weisner, 2007; Garcia Coll & Marks, 2008, Miller, Hengst, & Want, 2003; Weisner, 2005).

Our research was enhanced through a combination of insider and outsider perspectives. Misa's participation as a volunteer teaching assistant provided her with a unique opportunity to learn about the school as an insider. Clear expectations and responsibilities as a teaching assistant also provided her with a place to belong and accordingly made it possible to observe and communicate with children and adults in natural settings, which was critical to understanding participants' own experiences (e.g., Briggs, 1986). Through her role as teaching assistant, Misa also was able to follow up with three children for longitudinal case study. This longitudinal design allowed us to observe how children perceived transitions into a special education classroom, how they adjusted to these new environments (including their relationships with peers and educators), and the ways that their parents and educators facilitated and supported their transitions.

Further, our bicultural experiences allowed us to move back-and-forth among a variety of insider and outsider perspectives.[2] Misa and Wendy have both insider and outsider perspectives in interpreting the experiences of Japanese children and their parents at school. As insiders we live effortlessly within a set of taken-for-granted premises but may have difficulty seeing or articulating these premises. As outsiders we may engage in the process termed "creative understanding" by Bakhtin (Morson & Emerson, 1990) in which we locate ourselves outside of the group to identify cultural "blind spots"—that is, patterns of beliefs, thoughts, behaviors, and so forth that insiders may take for granted. At the same time, a cultural outsider cannot flexibly enact, alter, or contextualize these premises. For example, in previous research on Japanese child welfare (*see* Bamba & Haight, 2011), Wendy's outsider perspective allowed her to identify "*Ibasho*"[3] as relevant to socialization, but its meaning was interpretable only in close collaboration with Sachiko Bamba, a cultural insider. It is through the repeated back-and-forth of insider and outside perspectives that clear vision is achieved. We do this through discussion with one another but also through our own reflections from our own multiple perspectives. In this book, we seek a deeper and more complete understanding of Japanese beliefs, practices, and experiences related to disability through an interaction of insider and outsider perspectives.

Cultural Analysis of Policy

Our analyses of policy primarily involved a systematic review of Japanese government documents on special education and local documents specifying how national laws were translated into practice in the particular context of Greenleaf Elementary School. Most documents we reviewed were available only in Japanese. Misa first summarized the documents in English and then discussed them with Wendy. Through this process we considered the cultural and historical contexts of the special education reforms and integrated cultural understandings of disabilities into our policy analysis.

First, we reviewed laws that determine special education in Japan, as well as the history and policies related to special education services for children with developmental disabilities. These documents were available through websites and publications by the government offices, such as the Ministry of Education and the Ministry of Health, Labour and Welfare. They included laws, regulations, notices, and announcements issued by the Ministries; research reports submitted to the Ministry of Education; publications summarizing historical contexts of special education; and the national curriculum standards for general and special education.

Second, we reviewed guidelines and instruction manuals related to special education established by the local board of education of the city in which Greenleaf Elementary School is located, including future plans and goals for special education, classroom management guidelines for special education classroom teachers, guidelines to create individualized education programs, and curriculum standards. These materials were provided by the principal of Greenleaf Elementary School and the local board of education or obtained from the website of the local board of education. Field notes also described discussions with individuals outside of Greenleaf Elementary School, such as educators in other schools and a staff member of the local board of education. Finally, information about Greenleaf Elementary School was obtained from educators as well as the school's web site including mission statements, goals, funding, and procedures to implement individualized support for children with developmental disabilities.

Field Research

Site

This research was conducted in "Riverside City,[4]" which has a population of more than 1 million. Within the city, the same local government serves several distinct areas including business and industrial districts, newly developed residential areas, and traditional areas. The local board of education takes the leadership role in all public schools within the city. In traditional areas, many families have resided in their homes for generations. People are expected to help one another, and raising children is viewed as a community responsibility. Although more people are leaving their parents' homes to raise their own families, multigenerational households remain common, and those who have left retain their places in the community and return for family gatherings. In contrast, the majority of residents in newly developed residential areas live in nuclear families. These areas were created over the past 10 to 30 years as a result of industrialization and urbanization. Because these areas are new and include residents from other cities, connections between community members typically are less strong than in traditional areas.

Riverside City was selected for our research for a variety of reasons. Riverside City is one of the cities recognized by Japanese educators as providing high-quality special education services. Within the city, almost all public elementary schools have at least one special education classroom, which is not yet typical in many other cities. On a more practical level, Misa's parents' house is located in this city, and she stayed there during the period of data collection. In addition, she had attended school in this city, which helped her to initiate conversations and establish relationships with some of the educators. They knew the elementary school she graduated from, and some of them knew the surrounding community. Some experienced educators also recognized Misa as a "child" who grew up in the city, rather than a researcher from the United States.

This study focuses on children who attend general public elementary schools. Most Japanese children, including those with "developmental disabilities," attend public schools. Only 0.3% and 1% of all elementary school-aged children attend national or private elementary schools, respectively (Ministry of Education, 2012b). These schools typically have entrance exams and may develop their own curriculum beyond what is required for public schools. As of 2011, only 8 of 74 national elementary schools and 1 of 216 private elementary schools had special education classrooms. In contrast, 73% of public elementary schools had special education classrooms (Ministry of Education, 2012b).

Greenleaf Elementary School was identified with the help of the local board of education as the primary research site of this study. It met national standards for elementary schools (Ministry of Education, 2002d), was implementing newly introduced educational services for children with developmental disabilities, and had a special education classroom. Another reason for choosing this site was its accessibility to Misa's wheelchair. Japanese public schools usually are two to four stories with classrooms on the upper floors. Elevators or accessible entrances are not yet common. Recently, the needs of children with physical disabilities have been recognized, and several schools have remodeled their buildings as needed when children with physical disabilities enroll. In Riverside City, as of 2004, about 10% of elementary schools had elevators in their school buildings.

Greenleaf Elementary School is located in the traditional area near the borderline of Riverside City and an adjacent city. This school was one of the smaller schools in Riverside City, enrolling about 200 children from first through sixth grades. Each grade level had one classroom of 30 to 37 children, with the exception of second grade, which had two classrooms of about 20 children[5]. Our field research was conducted in 2009 to 2010, the third and fourth school years during which formal special education services for children with developmental disabilities were being implemented at Greenleaf Elementary School. During this time, five to seven children with disabilities from second to sixth grades received services from two full-time classroom teachers in a special education classroom, "The Rainbow Room." A special support room,[6] "The Challenge Room," was used weekly by children from general education classrooms who needed extra help and daily by several children with developmental disabilities who had interpersonal problems. The Challenge Room was staffed by a part-time teacher and teaching assistants. Educators who teach in the Challenge and Rainbow Rooms participate in workshops and trainings for educating children with developmental disabilities but do not necessarily hold special education certificates[7]. During the two school years this study was conducted, there was one teacher who held a special education certificate. This teacher taught children in both general and special education classrooms. Children in the Rainbow and Challenge rooms maintained membership in their general education classrooms, participating as much as possible with their typically developing peers.

Greenleaf Elementary School includes a school building, gym, swimming pool, large playground, flower and vegetable gardens, animal cage, and fish pond. It is enclosed by walls and fences. The playground has a free space with soccer ball goals, basketball poles, and other equipment such as a climbing pole and is also used as a track during physical education classes. There is a gate near the school building that, for security reasons, is open only during children's arrival and dismissal times. During other times, visitors use an intercom to call the staff office for entrance. There are security cameras around the gate so that staff members can monitor people who visit and leave the school (*see* Fig. 2.1).

The first floor of the main building is used for administrative offices (*see* Fig. 2.2). The principal's office, a staff room, a school nurse's office, a business office, and a locker room for staff members are located on the west side. About half of the east side is occupied by the school kitchen. The remaining area includes a printing office, a studio with audio and video equipment for in-school announcements, a counseling room, and an office for a parent volunteer group, called "Team Greenleaf." (*See* Chapter 4 for more detailed description of Team Greenleaf.) Parents frequently gathered and worked in this office or another office for the parent and teacher association (PTA) located on the fourth floor.

There is an elevator between the east and west sides of the building. This school building did not have an elevator when it was built originally in the 1970s. The elevator was installed several years ago to accommodate a first grader with a physical disability. Teachers and other staff members frequently use the elevator to go to classrooms, but children are not allowed to use it without permission. Children with whom Misa was working sometimes accompanied her in the elevator. Other children who saw these children coming out from the elevator with Misa sometimes asked her if they could ride

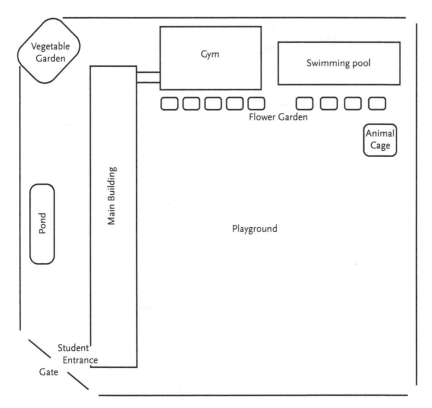

Vegetable
Garden

Gym

Swimming pool

Flower Garden

Animal
Cage

Main Building

Pond

Playground

Student
Entrance

Gate

FIGURE 2.1 Greenleaf Elementary School

the elevator too, and she had to handle the situation as a "teacher," tactfully refusing such requests.

The second, third, and fourth floors of the school building are used for classrooms, including general education classrooms; the Rainbow and Challenge rooms; and special rooms for science, crafts, home economics, and music. Classrooms are arranged so that children in the Rainbow and Challenge rooms are able to interact with other children in general education classrooms. Libraries are located on the second and third floors. The library on the second floor mainly has fictional books, and the library on the third floor has nonfiction (science, history, and reference books including a children's encyclopedia to be used for research projects). In addition, there is a classroom for small group instruction, a computer room, and an English classroom. The computer room is used for classroom instruction as needed, as well as club activities. During the 2009–2010 school year, the small group instruction room was primarily used for math instruction, as Math was taught

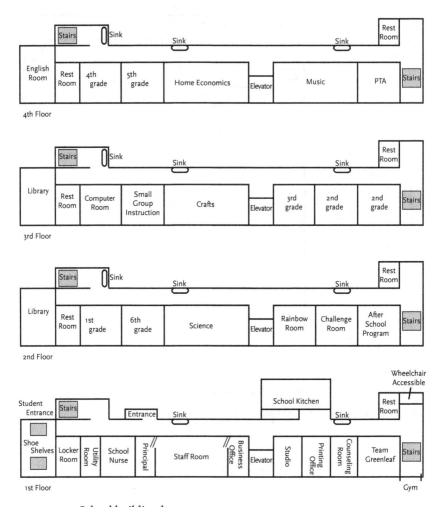

FIGURE 2.2 School building layout

in small groups in several grade levels. Either a general education classroom or the English classroom is used for English instruction, depending on the day's activities. The English classroom does not have desks and chairs and is used for a variety of activities involving music, dance, and games (*see* Fig. 2.2).

During the second school year of data collection, the classroom arrangement changed. In particular, the Rainbow Room expanded into the room next door (the former Challenge Room) as the number of children had increased. From April (the new school year), a counseling room located on the first floor was used as the Challenge Room, and the same part-time teacher continued to teach small groups of children there once a week.

Participants

A director of special education from the board of education introduced Misa to the principal of Greenleaf Elementary School. As suggested by the director, she visited the school one day in June, 2009 to observe the children during a school day in her role as graduate student from the United States without mentioning this study. She observed several classrooms, including those with children with developmental disabilities, and ate school lunch with children in a classroom. After observing the school and sharing information with the principal about schools in the United States, she explained the study and obtained permission to conduct it at Greenleaf Elementary School. When the principal heard that Misa would like to interview educators, children, and their parents, she suggested that she work as a daily volunteer. The principal reasoned that it would be easier to introduce the research project to children and parents if they first got to know Misa as a teaching assistant. Because the principal was looking for a teaching assistant to work with children in the Challenge Room, Misa began working as a volunteer teaching assistant 2 days after her first visit. In addition, Misa asked the principal to explain to parents and educators that observations would be conducted during the period of the study.

The principal also helped identify and introduced Misa to individual participants. Fifteen of the 17 educators at Greenleaf Elementary School participated in individual interviews. Two teachers did not participate because of their busy schedules. Sano *sensei*, the special education coordinator, served as a primary informant. She was an experienced teacher who also worked full time as the "school nurse," a position that involved overseeing children's health and their physical and mental development, providing health education, and referring children to appropriate health-care agencies. Parent participants were nominated by the principal. She was concerned that study participation might have a negative psychological impact on some parents who had not yet fully accepted their children's disabilities and needs for special support. She restricted her referrals to parents whom she viewed as having accepted their children's disabilities or "difficulties." Parents of three children with developmental disabilities were recruited. Their children, Dai, Kakeru, and Yusuke, were also selected for in-depth case studies. In terms of ethnicity and social class, these three middle-class families were similar to the other families whose children attended Greenleaf Elementary School.

At the beginning of data collection, Dai was 8 years old. He had a diagnosis of high-functioning autism. Until third grade, he participated full time in his general education classroom. In third grade, he began to have interpersonal problems with peers and struggled with increasing academic demands. He could express himself verbally but had difficulties in "reading" other people's thoughts and emotions. In addition, he frequently used polite language, which sometimes made him appear to be reading aloud from a book. He could take the initiative to expand activities he was interested in but was cautious about trying anything new. When he received appropriate support, he functioned well at school. During the study, Dai transferred to the Challenge Room and subsequently to the Rainbow Room. He retained his seat in his general education classroom but because of interpersonal difficulties preferred the Challenge or Rainbow Room. Yet he was always welcomed by peers and his classroom teacher when he returned to his general education classroom.

At the beginning of the study, Kakeru was 7 years old. He also had high-functioning autism. He studied full time in his second grade classroom with support provided by his classroom teacher who held a special education certificate. During the second semester, he began to study at the Challenge Room once a week. He was proud of his extensive knowledge of "bugs," a skill other second graders acknowledged and valued. This status within his peer group motivated Kakeru to work, study, and play with friends in his general education classroom. Yet he had difficulties in paying attention to others and needed assistance in following directions and staying on task. His behaviors in the classroom, such as talking at inappropriate times, could be distracting to others, and he began to notice that these behaviors made him different from other children. With the support of his parents and his second grade classroom teacher, Kakeru decided to transfer to the Rainbow Room in third grade.

At the beginning of data collection, Yusuke was 10 years old. He had a learning disability that made it difficult for him to decode written text and calculate and speech problems (stuttering). He went to a resource room in Parkside Elementary School[8] once a week to receive individualized support for his speech problems. He knew that he could not read, write, and do arithmetic at the level of his peers. When studying in his general education classroom, he lost motivation and described himself as "hopeless." For several months in fourth grade, he refused to go to school. When he came back to school, he studied at the school nurse's office, a counseling room, or the principal's office. In fifth grade, Yusuke began to view himself more positively, as he began playing and studying with other children in the Rainbow and the Challenge rooms. With support provided by educators and his parents, he decided to transfer to the Rainbow Room. He also retained a seat in his general education classroom, participating there with his peers mainly during lunchtime, social studies, science, music, and other activities in which his functioning more closely resembled that of his peers.

Procedures

Misa collected the field data in three waves: the summer of 2009 (6 weeks), the winter of 2010 (5 weeks), and the summer of 2010 (5 weeks).

Field entry. The principal introduced Misa to the children on her first day during the morning meeting. Morning meetings and activities with all children from first through sixth grades occurred every Monday and occasionally on Friday. At the end of the meeting, the principal introduced Misa as a student from the University of Illinois in the United States who had come to Greenleaf Elementary School to learn about a Japanese elementary school. She told children that Misa would attend school every day until the summer break as a teaching assistant. Misa then introduced herself and, as suggested by Sano *sensei*, encouraged children to ask her questions about her wheelchair and the United States when they saw her during recess and breaks. The principal also officially introduced the Challenge Room, which had been newly created at the beginning of the school year in April. The principal explained that the Challenge Room was a place where children could study one-on-one with a teacher when they had something difficult to understand[9].

At the beginning of the following week, the principal officially introduced Misa to educators during an in-school workshop on autism spectrum disorders and other disabilities that cause social and learning difficulties. The principal indicated that Misa had studied special education in the United States and would work as a teaching assistant primarily for children in the Challenge Room until the summer break.

During the first wave of data collection, children asked Misa many questions, mostly about her wheelchair, whenever possible. Some children even asked her questions during classroom instruction, and she had to tell them to ask her after class. As children became accustomed to her wheelchair, Misa was able to enter their classrooms without distracting them from classroom activities. Classroom teachers also encouraged children to ask Misa questions. This made it easier for Misa to initiate conversations with children and establish relationships.

Participant observation. Misa conducted participant observation as a teaching assistant for children with developmental disabilities for a total of 16 weeks across two school years. Her daily field notes focused on children's interactions with peers, their parents, and educators during their routine activities at school. Informal conversations related to research questions with educators, children, and their parents also were described in field notes.

Misa's role as teaching assistant. Misa typically arrived at school around 9 a.m. and stayed until 4 p.m. or 5 p.m. She spent her time in classrooms and sometimes in the staff room, where teachers had their own desks. In addition to her primary assignment in the Challenge Room, she assisted in the Rainbow Room. During the second and third waves of data collection, she also served as a teaching assistant in all general education classrooms from first through sixth grades. She assisted in Math, Japanese Language, crafts, English, international studies, integrated studies, social studies, science, home economics, music, and moral education. In these classrooms, her roles varied from moving around the classroom to help children who were struggling to working one-on-one with children identified by teachers.

After children went home, Misa wrote in the daily log for teaching assistants describing what she had done during each class period, her reflections, and any questions to the principal and the special education coordinator, Sano *sensei*. Occasionally, she discussed the children with Sano *sensei* and asked for suggestions. The principal and Sano *sensei* read the daily log and wrote comments and suggestions as needed. During the first wave of data collection, a copy of this daily log was filed in the Challenge Room folders of Yusuke and Dai and circulated on a daily basis to teachers involved in providing support for them, including their general education classroom teachers. These folders were prepared so that all educators involved in supporting Yusuke and Dai could share information. As Yusuke and Dai transitioned into the Rainbow Room at the end of the first wave of data collection, Misa's role as a teaching assistant shifted to assisting in general education classrooms. This allowed her to expand her observations to children in general education classrooms while following up with Yusuke and Dai.

Misa's role as guest teacher. During the second wave of data collection, educators and parents asked Misa to talk with children about her experiences in a wheelchair. Sano *sensei* and Yusuke's mother asked her to talk with him, individually, because he was beginning to suspect that he might have some sort of disability. Misa had worked with Yusuke individually as a teaching assistant, but had not talked with him about "disability." The principal also asked Misa to visit each classroom from first through sixth grades as a guest teacher to talk about her experiences in a wheelchair as part of "moral education," a required class described in the National Curriculum Standard. One of the goals of the year was learning about human rights, and the principal requested that Misa visit the classrooms to share her experiences in a wheelchair. The principal believed that it would be a good opportunity for children to hear from someone who actually had experiences coping with a disability. Each visit was about 45 minutes. After she shared her experiences briefly, children asked her questions. She brought extra wheelchairs to several classrooms, and children enjoyed "riding" in them. After the visits, children gave her reflection letters. This book includes some of the letters, drawings, and discussions with children.

Individual interviews. Most Japanese people are not familiar with individual interviews, so it is especially important to create an environment and atmosphere in which they feel comfortable and to ask questions in a way in which they do not feel obligated to answer (e.g., *see* Briggs, 1986; Miller, Hengst, & Wang, 2003). Misa made the interviews conversational and asked questions whenever appropriate during or after routine activities, such as when participants spontaneously brought up issues related to our research questions. When questions were asked during daily activities and conversations, it was not possible to audio-record participants' responses. In such cases, Misa had to rely on notes taken during or after the conversations.

Misa also did not interview participants until she had established relationships with them and learned specific terms used at school—for example, the names they used to refer to their classrooms and terms regarding types of support for children with developmental disabilities. During the first 3 weeks, Misa focused on her role as a teaching assistant and on establishing relationships with children, their parents, and educators. She did not actively collect data by asking questions or interviewing but kept field notes regarding her informal communications and observations of daily interactions with and among children, parents, and educators. During their conversations, Misa made sure that her questions were related to her role as a teaching assistant, not as a researcher. In the fourth week, Misa began interviewing adults and children individually.

Interviews with adults. Individual interviews with parents and educators were semi-structured and lasted from 30 to 60 minutes. They were conducted in a private location at school. The following issues were discussed: (1) participants' beliefs about, and reactions to, children's disabilities; (2) participants' experiences in special education including with the new system; (3) how beliefs about developmental disabilities and societal responses affect the lives of children at home and school, including children's relationships with their peers; (4) challenges faced by children with developmental disabilities, their educators, and parents; and (5) effective ways to handle these challenges. All but two interviews were audio-recorded. One interview with an educator was conducted through e-mail and supplemented with field notes describing informal daily conversations. A second interview was not recorded because it would have been an inappropriate request given that this educator was significantly older than Misa and serving as her supervisor. Rather, field notes described informal conversations with him regarding children with disabilities and support for these children.

During the second and third wave of data collection, Misa asked follow-up questions informally to parents and some educators. Their responses were described in her field notes.

Interviews with children. Individual interviews with children focused on the services they received, why they received them, and how they felt about them. Because they did not know they had "disabilities" or received "special education" services, Misa did not use these terms during the interviews. Rather, she used "difficulties" and referred to the "Challenge" and "Rainbow" rooms. By the time Misa interviewed children, they had become used to talking with her individually. She framed questions for them as an extension of their daily conversations. These interviews were conducted in the Challenge Room, where she usually spent time with them.

During the first wave of data collection, formal interviews were conducted with Yusuke and Dai. Misa had been working with them since her first week at Greenleaf Elementary School and talked with their parents on a daily basis. She was able to arrange the interviews easily and the principal also allowed her to interview them when she worked with them individually. Formal individual child interviews lasted approximately 10 minutes. Misa recorded the interview with Dai, who started and stopped the recording so that he was able to have control over it. The interview with Yusuke, who stuttered, was not recorded because his mother indicated that in the past he had been distressed to hear his recorded voice.

The third child participating in the case study, Kakeru, was informally interviewed during the second wave of data collection when he worked with Misa, individually, at the Challenge Room. During the first wave of data collection, he studied full time in his general education classroom. Misa observed him in his classroom and occasionally talked and interacted with him. She did not, however, have an opportunity to talk with him individually for the interview without "singling" him out. Rather, she asked the principal and Sano *sensei* for permission to observe and work with him in his classroom as a teaching assistant. Misa kept a record of communications with him and observations in her field notes.

Misa took notes of everyday conversations she had with all three children as much as possible during her observations and included these in daily field notes. The children talked to educators and teaching assistants about what they thought about school much more during daily activities and interactions than during the formal interviews. Misa's dual roles as a teaching assistant and a researcher allowed her an opportunity to capture children's voices in their everyday interactions at school (e.g., Clark, 2010; *see also* Paley, 1990, 1993). Input from children largely comes from Misa's field notes.

Review of case records. The principal shared with Misa the evaluations used to determine eligibility for special education services of the three children who served as primary participants. Misa took notes as needed, including on children's diagnoses. In addition, when working individually with these three children, Misa took notes about the materials they were working on, their level of understanding, and comments from their classroom teachers and parents. Misa's daily logs as a teaching assistant, which were kept separately from her field notes, also involved comments and responses from the principal and Sano *sensei* regarding children's problems and progress and suggestions for Misa to handle situations she faced in classrooms.

Analysis of Field Data

Recorded interviews were transcribed verbatim. Analyses of transcribed interviews, field notes, and school records were conducted in Japanese by Misa. Using analytic induction techniques (Goets & LeCompte, 1981; Lincoln & Guba, 1985), the meanings of participants' experiences and beliefs were interpreted through repeated readings of the transcribed interviews and field notes. Themes were identified from recurring topics in field notes and during interviews. Negative cases were used to expand and revise initial interpretations. Misa's interpretations as an outsider frequently identified differences from U.S. practices, which allowed us to reflect on both Japanese and U.S. practices, raise additional questions, and examine further the experiences of Japanese children, their parents, and educators. Discussions with Wendy also raised issues for further study that were taken for granted by Japanese cultural insiders, including education for "*kokoro*" and the roles of peer relationships in education.

Attempts were made to enhance the credibility of the interpretations of participants' experiences and beliefs. First, the credibility of Misa's interpretations was critiqued by a Japanese Master of Social Work (MSW) student in the United States who had practice experience as a social worker for individuals with disabilities in Japan and through discussions with Wendy. Further, feedback from individuals who had professional and/or academic experiences in the field of school social work or special education in Japan critiqued the credibility of interpretations regarding Japanese educational policies and practices. The adequacy of the Japanese-English translation of illustrative excerpts also was critiqued. In addition, this study was conducted across two school years. This prolonged engagement enabled Misa to establish and maintain trusting relationships with participants and to gain an understanding of the context. It also allowed ample opportunities to clarify, support, or discount themes identified in preliminary analyses. In addition, a summary of the findings was shared with some of the participants. Their feedback was used to strengthen interpretations from their perspectives. Finally, the use of multiple data sources (children, parents, and educators) as well as the use of multiple methods (interviews and observations) allowed for triangulation and expansion of understanding.

Misa's Reflections: The Use of My Wheelchair As a Tool to Hear Children's Stories

My role as a teaching assistant and use of a wheelchair offered me advantages in hearing children's stories. First, elementary school teachers in Japan are considered to be the "mothers" of children at school. Yet they also are adult authority figures that, as Fine and Sandstorm (1998) articulated, can be an impediment to gaining access to children's experiences (*see also* Clark, 2010). As a teaching assistant, I also was viewed as a nurturing individual but had much less authority than did classroom teachers. Also, as I sat in a wheelchair, I was face-to-face with children. They freely interacted with me as a friend, as well as a teacher.

Nevertheless, I also faced several challenges in addressing children's "disabilities." Many children with developmental disabilities were aware that they experienced different struggles than their peers, but they did not necessarily consider these "disabilities." Further, educators were very careful about bringing up children's disabilities with parents who had not noticed or accepted their children's disabilities and need for special education services. The principal also suggested that I use a term "difficulties," rather than disabilities, when talking with parents and children.

In this context, I had to be careful about asking participants about children's "difficulties." To initiate and establish relationships with children, their parents, and educators and to encourage their voluntary participation, I used participants' curiosity. My previous experience in both the United States and Japan suggested that people, especially children, are interested in and curious about my wheelchair. For example, when I visited elementary schools, children approached me to look at my wheelchair and ask questions. Japanese children, who have more time unsupervised by adults at school than U.S. children, had many opportunities to interact with me, for example, during recess, breaks, and lunchtime. Yet whenever possible, U.S. children also sought me out to ask about my wheelchair during less structured activities. In other words, my wheelchair was a tool that enabled me to interact with children and hear their stories and experiences. In addition, I prepared materials, including a toy wheelchair to facilitate conversations with children about their own stories and experiences. I also developed interview protocols involving my personal stories that may help children to reflect on their own difficulties. Creating the protocols also helped me to reflect on my experiences and to decide when, what, and how much to disclose (Dickson-Swift, James, Kippen, & Liamputton, 2007).

Still, I was concerned about the extent to which children would connect my experiences to their own because they had different disabilities than me. On the other hand, I was encouraged by Clark's (2003) account of the ability of children to reflect on their own experiences after hearing of other's challenges. For example, Clark (2003) described her asthma when interviewing children with diabetes to let children know that they had a shared concern—their illnesses. In addition, by revealing that she did not have the same experiences as the children and that she wanted to learn from them about their experiences, she helped to motivate them to tell their stories.

Once I went to Greenleaf Elementary School, I found that I did not have to use the prepared materials because my wheelchair itself made a strong impression on children. Even before I attempted to interact with children, they came to ask about my wheelchair. The opening vignette of this chapter illustrates children's curiosity. Even if they did not remember my name, as soon as children saw my wheelchair, they came to see how the wheelchair worked and asked questions. My wheelchair and stories also created a safe environment for some children to express their needs and struggles and share their experiences of overcoming hardships. Overall, my wheelchair helped me to initiate interactions and conversations with children and hear their stories about difficulties they had experienced in the past.

I had three different types of interactions with children—specifically, interactions in less structured settings, such as during lunch, recess, and 5-minute breaks between classes when I visited classrooms as a teaching assistant; structured and official conversations with children when I visited their classrooms as a guest teacher who shared experiences about life in a wheelchair; and conversations with children in a structured and individual setting. In all of these settings, children shared what they thought about wheelchairs. Several children also volunteered their own stories of handling a variety of difficulties.

Individual Informal Interactions

Dyson (2003) described children's movement back and forth between their official and unofficial social worlds. They modify what they have learned in the unofficial world of family and friends to interact appropriately with their peers and teachers in the official world of school. Japanese first graders initially used their knowledge of the unofficial world to make sense of my presence in their classroom. When they first saw me, they did not consider me as a person who belonged to the "official" world of school, although they recognized other adults as either teachers or parent volunteers who helped them. One child actually looked at my wheelchair and asked me, "Can you really teach?" Once a classroom teacher introduced me as a teaching assistant and started giving instruction, children treated me as a person who would help them in the official world of school. Yet my wheelchair was always on the borderline between their official and unofficial worlds, and stories about my wheelchair usually belonged to the unofficial world, limited to recess or breaks. In the unofficial world, children freely asked about me and my wheelchair.

Whenever I visited their classrooms, children came to me to ask questions. Generally, younger children were curious about my wheelchair itself—for example, how it works—and asked me questions without hesitation. Older children were more cautious. For example, second graders first asked me if they could push me around the hallway, but first graders touched my wheelchair before asking for my permission. Older children also were more curious about the reasons I was in a wheelchair. They did not come to see me as soon as I entered their classrooms as younger children did. They came to ask questions once they got used to my presence. Several children told me about their grandparents who were in wheelchairs and showed me how they helped by pushing my wheelchair around. There also were children who asked me if I needed help.

Although many children were curious about how my wheelchair works, several children told me about their "difficulties" and "disabilities." For example, a first grade boy sitting next to me during lunch asked about my wheelchair, "Do you have a disability? I have a disability, my leg is . . ." and shared his experiences of being in a hospital and using a wheelchair. His disability was not readily apparent, but he wore shoes slightly different from other children. It surprised me, because I did not expect a first grader to know the term "disability" and use it correctly. He also used the term without any hesitation. He was the only child who used "disability" to refer to his own "difficulties." There was another child who used "disability" to refer to children in a special education classroom but described his own learning disability as "difficulties."

Interactions in Structured and Official Settings

My wheelchair stories became official when, at the request of the principal, I visited children's classrooms as a guest teacher to discuss life in a wheelchair. When I visited as a guest teacher, children "officially" asked me questions and wrote letters to me. The principal believed that children learn more from listening to people who actually have experienced difficulties than only reading books. What surprised her was that some children reflected on their own difficulties and shared their experiences with peers.

Younger children asked more about how my wheelchair works and how I perform daily activities, such as cooking, grocery shopping, and driving a car. Children in one classroom were curious about restrooms for people with disabilities. I told them that there was one in the school building that was accessible to people in wheelchairs. Immediately, one child responded and shared with the class that she had used this restroom. A few days after I visited their classroom, I heard from one of the educators that a group of children went to check on and observe the restroom.

When I visited a sixth grade classroom, children shared their own experiences of when they had problems. After several children asked about my experiences, one child shared her story of how she handled other children's responses when she had a bruise on her face. This child's story and my wheelchair stories eventually created a safe environment to share personal experiences, and other children began to share their own stories. One child shared her thoughts about her sister with a physical disability. There were several children who asked me what I would do if I felt down. Others asked if there were times I felt like throwing everything away, avoiding everything, and hiding from everyone. I discussed how boring my life was when I felt like that and shared some of my coping strategies. In their letters, they shared some other experiences with me and asked more questions. Later, their classroom teacher told me that he was surprised that children shared so much of their own experiences in the classroom. Usually, the class is quiet and children are reluctant to answer his questions. Not only children who shared their experiences, but also children who listened to other children, seemed to learn about their peers in this safe environment.

Even younger children with disabilities asked me questions reflecting their own experiences. For example, a first grade boy with autism spectrum disorder asked, "It must be hard [to do everything in a wheelchair]. Why do you want to?" I told him that it is actually hard, but if I do my best, I can have good experiences that make me happy. Letters children wrote to me after the class illustrated their curiosity about my wheelchair and stories I shared with them and how much they enjoyed learning things that interested them.

Individual Communication in a Structured Setting

During my stay at Greenleaf Elementary School, Yusuke, a fifth grade boy with a learning disability, began suspecting that he had "difficulty in learning."

Upon the request of a special education coordinator and his mother, I talked with him individually about my wheelchair. Yusuke was frustrated because although he was working very hard on reading and writing, he still was behind his peers. The special education coordinator explained to me that his disability and my disability were different, but he might be able to learn something from my experiences.

By the time I spoke with him, he had already heard from his mother about his "difficulties," although she did not use the term "learning disabilities." After both of us shared our stories, I asked him if there was something he'd like to talk about or that he found similar to me. He indicated that we both had problems we had to deal with. Although my disability and his disability were different, both of us have difficulties and need assistance in performing daily activities. For him, assistance is needed in learning how to write and read, and for me a wheelchair is needed to move around. Before this meeting, several teachers indicated that it might be too difficult for children of his age to make the connection between my difficulties and their own. As with other children who heard my stories and reflected on their own past experiences, Yusuke found similarities between us.

The Thoughtful Use of Self-Disclosure

If thoughtfully used, self-disclosure can help to create a safe environment and facilitate participants' sharing of sensitive experiences. Self-disclosure of a researcher's personal experiences can be a useful tool in establishing relationships with participants and hearing their stories. The use of researchers' self-disclosures, however, must be thoughtful, carefully considered, and responsive to complex ethical issues, especially when the research focus is on emotionally challenging experiences, such as disability.

Research on Disability by a Researcher With a Disability

The existing literature suggests the potential use of researchers' experiences of their disabilities as a way of eliciting the experiences of individuals with disabilities. Their previous personal experiences, including fear and pain related to disabilities, are useful in analyzing and interpreting the experiences of research participants. They can understand the experiences of oppression and discrimination "instinctively," which is a useful resource for researchers involved in disability studies (e.g., Tregaskis & Goodley, 2005). For example, while hearing children's experiences of struggles, my first-hand experiences of coping with a disability helped me to identify and interpret participants' implicit messages and consider if or how I might examine further their experiences.

In addition to analyzing and interpreting participants' experiences, researchers' personal experiences of disability can be used in other phases of the research, including data collection. In qualitative studies, disclosure of researcher's experiences is generally useful in developing equal relationships with participants, building rapport, and facilitating participants' sharing of experiences (Abell, Locke, Condor, Gibson, Stevenson, 2006; Linde, 1993). Therefore, it is reasonable for researchers with disabilities to share their disability stories when exploring participants' experiences of disability, if done carefully. I intentionally refrained from sharing my experiences unless I was asked. Nevertheless, children, educators, and their parents gave me opportunities to share my experiences, which facilitated the voluntary sharing of their personal experiences of coping with difficulties.

In her book about American life stories, Linde (1993) explains that sharing one's life story is a process involved in the development of personal relationships, such as close friendships. In a research setting, participants' perceptions of relationships with researchers, such as degree of intimacy, also influence their decisions of which story to tell. Researchers from universities may be viewed as outsiders by participants who are in vulnerable situations because of differences in social, economical, and cultural status; age, and so forth. They may feel that their relationships are not equal. If researchers disclose their personal experiences, then it may help participants feel closer to the researchers and make it easier to talk with them about their experiences (Abell et al., 2006; Dickson-Swift et al., 2007). For example, although I know Japanese culture, I was a researcher from a university in the United States. Without showing children and educators that we share something in common (e.g., the same cultural background), it would have been difficult to establish relationships with them.

The similar experiences of researchers and participants can facilitate the establishment of trusting relationships and create a safe, secure environment for participants to share their own experiences, as my wheelchair stories did. When they feel secure and know that researchers are capable of understanding them, participants' further disclosure can be supported (Dickson-Swift et al., 2007; Linde, 1993). When introducing herself, Clark (2003) told her participant children with chronic illnesses that she had asthma. Although her experiences as an adult were different from those of these children, it was important for children to learn that they had something in common to initiate their relationships. Even if researchers' stories are not directly related to participants' experiences, their stories may be useful. Indeed, children made connections between my experiences in a wheelchair to their own experiences of handling difficulties. Many children reflected on their own experiences and found something similar, including their grandparents' wheelchairs and their own difficulties. A wheelchair is just one example of the things we had in common that eventually became a chance for us to share experiences more directly. A safe environment is created to share sensitive, personal experiences.

Listening to other people's stories also reminds us of our own stories (Clandinin & Connelly, 2000). As an individual with a disability, it is not unusual to remember similar experiences while hearing other people's disability stories. Sharing such stories with participants may encourage them to elaborate their stories. They may remember their stories by hearing researchers' stories. In other words, researchers' own stories may be useful in introducing new topics, especially when asking about sensitive issues, such as disability. Researchers can ask about sensitive issues indirectly by sharing related experiences.

Methodological Implications for Research

Self-disclosure can be used in research broadly focusing on sensitive issues, including children's disabilities and illnesses, traumatic experiences, and culturally and socially challenging experiences. How and what to self-disclose may also vary across cultural contexts. Examples of the use of my wheelchair narratives suggest the importance of careful consideration of how to address sensitive and challenging issues in a culturally appropriate manner. In a Japanese culture in which individuals are expected to sense what others are feeling and thinking rather than to express their own emotions and thoughts (e.g., Azuma, 1994; Shweder et al., 2006), self-disclosure initiated by researchers may be perceived as excessive or inappropriate. By waiting for participants to ask questions, I was able to share stories they wanted to hear and to initiate conversations in a way that they felt comfortable. This strategy may also be used in other studies, for example with people from cultural backgrounds different from researchers.

Ethical Issues

The personal stories of researchers, however, may affect participants' responses in unintended ways. Telling and hearing stories may cause risks for both participants and researchers. There may be psychological consequences as a result of remembering painful experiences and feelings associated with disabilities, such as anxieties and fears, which usually do not come up in daily life (Tregaskis & Goodley, 2005). It should be the participants who decide if they tell their stories. Therefore, it is necessary to pay attention to participants' verbal and nonverbal behaviors and implicit meanings of their stories to minimize negative consequences for them. Participants also should be informed ahead of time that they will be invited to share their stories but that they do not have to do so.

Further, researchers with disabilities must consider carefully and make a personal decision regarding any sharing of their own stories to protect themselves from accidental and unexpected disclosures. One of the ways to prevent psychological consequences for researchers may be preparing stories before meeting with participants. Individual interviews with researchers in the field of healthcare showed that accidental disclosures made some researchers feel confused and out of control. There also were researchers who were not comfortable with disclosing their experiences during interviews with participants (Dickson-Swift et al., 2007). These responses suggest that it may be better if researchers plan the level of disclosure before meeting with participants, especially when the research focuses on sensitive issues including disabilities.

Self-disclosure that is excessive, directive, evaluative, or too brief may lead participants to remain silent, to respond in a way consistent with what researchers expect, or may cause misinterpretations and misunderstandings (Abell et al., 2006; Charmaz, 2002; Dickson-Swift et al., 2007). Researchers should critically evaluate the possible effects of revealing their own stories on participants, and any unnecessary and irrelevant disclosure should be avoided (Poindexter, 2003). For example, excessive disclosure may give participants an impression that researchers are trying to attract their attention and support and may prevent the development of equal relationships. Because the purpose of the interviews generally is to hear participants' experiences, researchers' stories have to be used carefully, so that they facilitate but do not interrupt participants' accounts. It may be helpful for researchers to describe how they came to know about particular disabilities by using their own experiences, so that participants understand that they share something in common. Inviting participants to ask questions may also be effective in making sure that they understand the researchers' stories.

Interviewing is a series of interactions between participants and researchers. It may be necessary to decide how much to disclose depending on participants' responses during the interview. If researchers have at least considered which story has the potential to lead participants' responses, a strategic, thoughtful, and deliberate plan can be made. In addition, leading effects may be reduced if researchers spend enough time with participants to hear the same stories several times (Lincoln & Guba, 1985). Stories may have several versions, but the core message of the stories should be maintained.

Discussion

Our methodological strategy is ethnographic. It can be located in an evolving methodological conversation about how to obtain a deeper and more complex understanding of children in cultural context (e.g., Miller, Fung, Lin, Chen & Boldt, 2012) as well as a burgeoning ethnographic base of work describing children's worlds and perspectives (e.g., Briggs, 1998; Corsaro, 2003; Miller, Hengst, & Wang, 2003). An important feature of the current research is its systematic use of our multiple insider-outsider perspectives and the thoughtful use of self-disclosure shaped to a Japanese cultural context. Another important feature of this research is its focus on the cultural analysis of policy. How culture informs policy decisions and guides and constrains its implementation on the ground is an issue gaining recognition in ethnographic studies (e.g., Duncan, Huston, & Weisner, 2006; Gracia Coll & Marks, 2008). In addition, our methodological approach flows from our emphasis on socially sensitive topics. Although ethnographic work on issues involving stigma is complex, it also is critical to hearing and understanding the perspectives of those with disabilities so that effective policies and practices may be designed and enhanced.

In conclusion, our use of policy analysis and ethnographic field methods allow an interpretation of the meanings of social behavior and everyday experiences from the participants' perspectives as situated within a broader context of beliefs, practices (e.g., Hymes, 1982) and policy. Everyday behaviors and conversations are embedded within specific sociocultural-historical contexts (Bakhtin, 1981; Morson & Emerson, 1990). Without an understanding of these contexts, our understanding of external behavior and verbal communications is limited. Thus, intertwining cultural analysis of policy with ethnographic methods allows the identification of the beliefs and practices inherent in everyday life, interpretation of what such shared beliefs and practices may mean to the participants themselves, observation of processes of change in beliefs and behaviors over time (e.g., see Gaskins, Miller & Corsaro, 1992; Jessor, Colby & Shweder, 1996; Rogoff, 2003), and the contextualization of such beliefs and practices within national policy systems. Ethnographic methods provide us with opportunities to hear the voices of individuals with disabilities and understand their experiences: how they think and feel about their disabilities, the way they cope with difficulties associated with their disabilities, and how they integrate their difficulties into their daily lives and interactions with others (Lutz & Bowers, 2005; Phillips, 1990).

Notes

1. When Misa visited general education classrooms to share her experiences in a wheelchair, she brought extra wheelchairs to several classrooms. Children enjoyed "riding" on and pushing them.

2. Thanks to Peggy Miller for the insights expressed in this paragraph.

3. "*Ibasho*" is literally translated as a "place to belong," and connotes a place where one feels cozy, at home, fully accepted, and able to express oneself fully. It is considered to be basic to mental health and well-being throughout the lifespan.

4. To maintain confidentiality of the research site, details of the city have been modified.

5. The national law specifies that in general education classrooms, 1 classroom teacher is assigned for every 40 children. The law also provides the standard to calculate the number of educators assigned to each school depending on the number and types of classrooms, either special or general education classrooms (Ministry of Internal Affairs and Communications, 2011a). The latest amendment in 2011 decreased the maximum classroom size for first graders to 35 (Ministry of Education, 2011b).

6. Currently, instruction in special support rooms is not considered "special education" in Japan. Special support rooms are usually staffed by classroom teachers during their planning time, part-time teachers, or teaching assistants.

7. Under the law that determines teacher certification, educators who teach in classrooms at special education schools are required to hold a special education certificate of their specialization, such as hearing and visual impairments, intellectual disabilities, and physical disabilities, in addition to a general teaching certificate. However, schools are allowed to postpone implementing this requirement (Ministry of Internal Affairs and Communication, 2008b). During the 2011-2012 school year, 70% of educators at special education schools held special education certificates for the disabilities that children they worked with had (Ministry of Education, 2012a). Further, the law does not require certification for teaching in special education classrooms at general public schools. It is typical that children in special education classrooms are taught by teachers who only have a regular teaching certificate.

8. Children may receive special education services at resource rooms in other schools when their schools do not offer needed services.

9. Any child experiencing difficulties in learning in a general education classroom may be referred to receive small group or individual instruction at the Challenge Room. The only requirement during this school year was parental permission.

3 THE HISTORY AND POLICIES OF JAPANESE SPECIAL EDUCATION

Challenge Room

During an interview, Kikuchi *sensei*, the assistant principal, reflected on the children he had taught during his 20-year teaching career and changes in the way certain difficulties were understood and handled: "Thinking of all of the fifth and sixth graders I have ever taught, there were many different types of children... Now, we've started recognizing the importance of special education, and also there are workshops available, though it is said that Japan is behind in terms of such [supports for children]. These children are cared for now... I'd seen such children [in my classrooms over the years]. There was always one or two in a classroom who, I now think, that kid might have been one of them... In those days, maybe the same as when we were children, we treated these children as a fidgety (*ochitsuki-no-nai*) kid or like that, and so, [we] scolded them or let them repeat [until they understood], and I did the same. So, when thinking of that, I feel I'm sorry about what I've done, and if I could see those kids again, I know it's impossible, but I'd be able to [treat them] differently."

This chapter describes Japanese educational policies and history related to special education and considers factors that contributed to the recent implementation of formal special education services for children with "developmental disabilities." Compared with disabilities involving mobility, hearing, and vision; learning disabilities, ADHD, high-functioning autism, and Asperger's syndrome have only recently been recognized as disabilities across the world. The term "learning disability," for example, was first used by U.S. scholar Samuel Kirk in 1962 to refer to children who did not fit into the traditional categories of disabilities, such as general intellectual disabilities, but showed delay in development of language, speech, reading, or communication skills. After a series of discussions with scholars and parent groups, the label of learning disabilities became widely known and was included as one of the disability categories for U.S. special education when P.L. 94-142 was passed in 1975 (e.g., Kirk, 1977; Kirk & Kirk, 1983). Later, children with autism and ADHD became formally eligible for special education in 1991 and 1997, respectively (e.g., Smith, 2007).

In contrast, the Japanese government did not begin implementing a system of formal, individualized special education services for children with developmental disabilities until 2007. This system was implemented only after extensive study, deliberation, and exchange of opinions between the government, scholars, and organizations such as parent support groups. Although some Japanese scholars had learned about the new category of learning disabilities in the United States, it was not given much attention in Japanese public education until the 1990s (e.g., Kadomoto, 1990). Indeed, it took nearly three decades to begin implementing the new system after the need for specialized support for children who were struggling in general education classrooms was first reported in 1978 (National Institute of Special Needs Education, 1978).

Special education services had long been provided for Japanese children who required intensive support—for example, resulting from significant hearing and visual impairments and global intellectual disabilities—in special education classrooms and schools. Children with conditions falling under the new category of "developmental disabilities" were, as Kikuchi *sensei* described, included in general education classrooms where they received support, as needed, from classroom teachers and peers. In this sense, Japanese special education was characterized by two extremes: full support but in a segregated setting or full inclusion in general education classrooms without individualized support by specialists.

Prior to 2007, educators worked with children who were struggling socially or academically without differentiating the source of those struggles as caused by "disabilities" or other issues. In our interviews, teachers who had been teaching for more than 20 years stated that they had previously treated children currently identified as having "developmental disabilities" as just one of many children who are selfish (*waga-mama*), uncooperative (*katte-na*), "a little bit different," unable to sit still, slow learners, and so forth. During the 1990s, the presence of children whose struggles within general education classrooms were attributed to mild cognitive and behavioral disabilities such as learning disabilities, ADHD, and high-functioning autism received wider public attention through various publications and other media. These children eventually came to be categorized together as having "mild developmental disabilities." One classroom teacher, Sekine *sensei*, described the recent change in perceptions regarding these children:

> ...There must have been these children for a long time, but well, there were more children[1], and [children with mild disabilities such as high functioning autism] lived well in their own ways in that environment. I mean, [other children] might have thought that they were somewhat different, but they grew up together [and understood them]. But now, I feel the educational environment has been changing. [For example], there are the *names* of disabilities describing characteristics of these children, and parents also have knowledge and read many books, and some of the children actually have diagnoses...I might have been interacting with [this kind of child] for long years, but it's been about 10 years since I came to feel strongly, "this kid is this kind."

Although educators had been providing support for children with developmental disabilities in their classrooms using available resources, without a formal system of support, as Kikuchi *sensei* stated, services available for them were limited. Some of these children may have struggled to find their *Ibasho*, a place where they felt comfortable and accepted at school, with peer relationships, or to achieve academically. Under the new special education system, children with developmental disabilities are given an opportunity to receive more specialized support. These opportunities, however, may come at the cost of highlighting their differences from their peers.

The special education reform also has created challenges for educators, including experienced teachers, who must integrate individualized services with traditional Japanese education within peer groups while minimizing the risk of stigmatization to children with developmental disabilities. As Kikuchi *sensei* described, workshops are available for educators who are currently teaching, but it may be difficult for those who have established their teaching styles to adjust to the new requirements. Sekine *sensei* shared her thoughts, "Because the society keeps changing, I have to hang on and catch up with it...If I say, 'It's ok,' or 'That's enough [learning for me],' I think it's time to quit teaching."

In this chapter, we consider the social and historical factors within and outside of Japan that impacted the understanding of children's disabilities in Japanese society and the timing of the implementation of special education services for children with mild cognitive and behavioral disabilities. In particular, how was the new category of "developmental disabilities" culturally constructed? Why was the Japanese government, typically noted as progressive in its early and elementary school education policies, slow relative to other modern societies in implementing formal special education services for children with mild cognitive and behavioral disabilities? Part of the answer to these questions, no doubt, lies in the traditional Japanese socialization priorities and practices discussed in Chapter One. In this chapter, we consider how the implementation of special education for children with "developmental disabilities" is situated within the broader historical and educational policy contexts of Japanese education.

History of Special Education for Children With Developmental Disabilities

The Emergence of Special Education Classrooms

Some special education classrooms for Japanese children "underachieving" in traditional academic settings emerged in the late nineteenth and early twentieth centuries after Japan opened up to communication with other societies. Nevertheless, educational opportunities for children with disabilities remained limited because of a tradition of exempting children from "compulsory" education for various reasons. Since the Legislation of Elementary Schools, the basis of the contemporary compulsory elementary education, was enacted in 1886, parents have been allowed to request local governments to exempt their children from attending school for certain periods of time because of illness and family problems such as poverty (Ministry of Education, 1981). The result was that many children, including those with disabilities, did not receive a formal education. Today, the notion of "exemption from education" continues to exist in laws regarding compulsory education (Ministry of Internal Affairs and Communication, 2007), but only a very few children are actually exempted (Ministry of Education, 2003).

The exclusion or exemption of children with disabilities from education in nineteenth century Japan was consistent with contemporaneous beliefs and practices more generally related to individuals with disabilities. Before the modern education system was established in the 1870s and 1880s, individuals with disabilities tended to be classified as "useless." Once they were classified as "useless," they might be given an opportunity to become "useful" through specialized training and education.[2] Yet the underlying belief was that people who were "useless" should be excluded from society. As they learned about special education in Western countries, some Japanese scholars and government leaders began to emphasize the importance of providing educational and training opportunities for individuals with disabilities (Nakamura & Arakawa, 2003; Sugawara, 2011). The Legislation of Elementary Schools was successful in securing the opportunity for children with disabilities to receive a public education, but stigmatizing beliefs about disability persisted.

Contemporary special education in Japan emerged in the late 1870s as schools for children with vision and hearing impairments. These schools were described for the first time in law in the 1890 second amendment of the Legislation of Elementary Schools (Ueno & Hanakuma, 2006; Ministry of Education, 1981). Special education for "blind" and "deaf" children emerged earlier and followed a slightly different path than education of children with other disabilities, in part because there were strong advocates for education for children with these impairments (Nakamura & Arakawa, 2003).

Special education for children with other disabilities began in special education classrooms within general public schools. The first such special education classroom for children who were underachieving in a traditional academic setting was established in 1890. From a twenty-first century perspective, these "underachieving" children may have had learning disabilities, ADHD, and other less visible and relatively specific disabilities (Murakami & Meyer, 2010). As the number of special education classrooms increased, such classrooms were opened to children with more global intellectual disabilities who otherwise might not have attended general public schools (e.g., Murakami & Meyer, 2010; Ueno & Hanakuma, 2006). In 1907, the government officially recommended the establishment of classrooms for children with intellectual disabilities and vision and hearing impairments at teachers' training colleges[3]. One of the purposes of these classrooms was to conduct research on how to educate these children (Third Amendment of the Legislation of Elementary Schools; Ministry of Education, 1981). Because of financial constraints and other factors, support from the Ministry of Education did not last long, and many schools had to close their special education classrooms (Murakami & Meyer, 2010; Nakamura & Arakawa, 2003).

After World War I, economic conditions improved and the general public became increasingly aware of democracy. People became empowered to advocate for change, including toward the treatment of individuals with disabilities.

For example, groups of educators emphasized children's rights and established guidelines to facilitate individual children's learning based on their abilities. Gradually, Japanese governmental policies shifted from providing "charity to the disabled," which was stigmatized, toward creating a social welfare system focused on prevention and the recognition of the rights of all citizens to receive whatever particular supports they required to function and contribute to society. Along with this shift, the Ministry of Education began to promote special education classrooms. As a result, a number of special education classrooms increased again in the 1920s up to 463, nationally. Yet the belief that children with disabilities should be taught in segregated classrooms, isolated from other children and the broader society, persisted (Nakamura & Arakawa, 2003).

Despite the continuous effort made by the Ministry of Education, by 1931, the number of special education classrooms had decreased to 100. These losses resulted, in part, from the economic crisis in the early 1930s[4]. They also reflected the shift toward militarism within Japan and concurrent devaluing of individuals with physical limitations (Nakamura & Aarakawa, 2003).

During Japan's involvement in World War II (1941–1945), special education classrooms remained few in number. In 1941, The Ministry of Education strongly recommended the creation of special education classrooms when the "Legislation of Elementary Schools" was replaced as the "Legislation of National Schools." This law was not fully implemented during the war (Ministry of Education, 1981) despite an increasing need for classrooms for children who were "weak" including those suffering from infectious diseases, such as tuberculosis. In 1942, 96% of 1616 special education classrooms, nationally, were for children with illnesses who were "weak" (Nishimaki, 2005). During this period, children with disabilities were looked down on as "non-people." The exceptions were some children enrolled in "blind" and "deaf" schools who were able to contribute to the war effort through physical work.

Toward the end of the war, the very existence of public education was threatened, and even more special education classrooms were closed (Ministry of Education, 1981; Nakamura & Arakawa, 2003). Older children went to work to contribute to the war effort, younger children moved to safer, rural areas, and educators were drafted into military service. After World War II, not only special education but the Japanese education system as a whole required extensive reform.

Post-World War II Educational Reform

Following World War II, Japanese education underwent major reforms. The Fundamental Law of Education and the School Education Law were passed and enacted in 1947. These laws, along with the new constitution of Japan, were created while Japan was occupied by the Allied Powers led by the United States. This educational reform movement is the basis of the current educational system. It also created confusions and complications. The educational reform movement included concepts that varied from traditional Japanese practices including the equal access to education as a "right," not as a privilege "allowed by the emperor." On a practical level, there was a lack of resources to implement reforms (Ministry of Education, 1992). These challenges likely contributed to the Japanese government's relatively slow implementation of formal special education for children with developmental disabilities. For example, during the 1970s, when Western countries, including the United States, began to recognize the unique needs of children with learning disabilities and provide special education services for them, the Japanese government's priority still was to establish compulsory special education for children with severe disabilities who were excluded from public education.

The major components of Japanese post-World War II educational reforms included (1) equal access to education and gender equality, including support for children from low-income families and special education for children with disabilities; (2) the establishment of a "single line" educational system consisting of elementary, junior high, high school, and college education; (3) free compulsory education through junior high school (ninth grade); and (4) "personality education" (Ministry of Education, 1992, 2001b). Personality education involves "Education that raises individuals who care for truth and justice, respect personal values, set a high value on labor and responsibility, and are independent and healthy physically and mentally as members of a peaceful nation and society" (*see* Article 1 of the Fundamental Law of Education of 1947[5]) (Ministry of Education, 2010a).

The holistic educational philosophy reflected in personality education remains a cornerstone of contemporary Japanese elementary education. This broad approach to supporting children's development is consistent with the values reflected in Japanese social and child welfare policies.[6] These polices focus on prevention and support for the healthy mental and physical development of all Japanese children (Ministry of Internal Affairs Communication, 2008a; *see also* Bamba & Haight, 2011). Yet the inclusion of children with disabilities has proven to be challenging.

In 1947, the School Education Law set out the framework and requirements for preschool, compulsory, and higher education (Ministry of Internal Affairs and Communication, 2007; Ministry of Education, 1981). It indicated that special education services were to be provided at special education schools or special education classrooms in general public schools (National Archives of

Japan, 1947). Elementary, junior high, and high schools were to create special education classrooms for children with "abnormal personality," "mental retardation," [7] language disabilities, health impairments, and other problems affecting school learning (Ministry of Education, 1953; National Archives of Japan, 1947).

Given limited governmental resources, by 1953, only about 800 special education classrooms existed across the country (Ministry of Education, 1953). Many children, especially those with moderate to severe disabilities, were left without specialized services or completely exempted from receiving public education. In 1957, the Ministry began providing financial assistance to cities that created new special education classrooms. By 1970, the number of special education classrooms for children with global intellectual disabilities at elementary and junior high schools increased to nearly 15,000 (Ministry of Education, 1981).[8]

During this period, the government's primary goal for special education was to make it compulsory for children with severe disabilities. When the School Education Law was passed in 1947, the obligation to establish special education schools, other than "blind" and "deaf" schools," was postponed[9] (Ministry of Education, 1981). The government originally postponed compulsory education at all special education schools, including "blind" and "deaf" schools, because of a lack of facilities and educators. This action was strongly opposed by well-organized and established advocate groups for compulsory deaf and blind education[10]. This movement was joined by parent support groups, and in 1948 the Ministry of Education finally secured funding to implement compulsory "blind" and "deaf" schools (Itagaki & Toki, 1993; Nakamura & Arakawa, 2003).

In contrast, very few special education schools existed for children with other disabilities. Their advocates were fewer and had fewer resources to push for the implementation of special education schools (Ministry of Education, 1981; Nakamura & Arakawa, 2003). Even the obligation to establish compulsory special education schools for children with severe disabilities, including intellectual disabilities, physical disabilities, and other health and emotional impairments was postponed for nearly three decades. Given the government's priority to provide special education to children with severe disabilities, this postponement also slowed down the implementation of special education services for children with milder, "developmental disabilities," who were already receiving a public education.

For more than a decade after the implementation of the School Education Law in 1947, the number of special education schools for children with severe disabilities (other than hearing and vision) remained low because of inadequate support from the national government (Nakamura & Arakawa, 2003). Thus, the only option for many children with severe disabilities was to receive support at special education classrooms in general public schools. As described above, however, there was also a lack of special education classrooms available for children with moderate disabilities. As a result, special education classrooms were usually "reserved" for children with moderate disabilities who did not require intensive support at special education schools. If children's disabilities were considered to be more severe, then their access to public education was frequently denied, and many of them were "exempted" from public education or had their school attendance "postponed" (Itagaki & Toki, 1993; Mogi, 1992) by parental request under the School Education Law (Ministry of Internal Affairs and Communication, 2007). To improve availability of public education to children with severe disabilities, in 1956, the national government made financial support available for local governments to create new special education schools. In 1973, the Ministry of Education (1992) issued a regulation to make special education schools for children with disabilities compulsory beginning in the 1979–1980 school year. The number of special education schools increased, and children with severe disabilities were given opportunities to receive a public education.

The Ministry of Education's responses to two reports on children with disabilities illustrates its prioritization of children with severe disabilities. In the late 1970s, an advisory committee to the Ministry of Education submitted two reports on special education services. One report focused on children with severe and/or multiple disabilities (National Institute of Special Needs Education, 1975) and the other on children with milder disabilities who were being educated in general education classrooms (National Institute of Special Needs Education, 1978). The report on severe disabilities was taken into consideration immediately. It led to the formation of new services for children who required intensive support outside of general public schools. This reform improved access to a public education for children with more severe disabilities. After 1979, the number of children who were exempted from or postponed school attendance decreased tremendously (from approximately 20,000 in 1972 to 10,000 in 1978, to 3,400 in 1979, to 1200 in 1991; Ministry of Education, 1992). However, it also resulted in a system of special education in which children with disabilities were segregated from their typically developing peers. This practice was counter to the practice of mainstreaming and inclusive education for children with disabilities[11] that had become recognized and accepted by many countries around the world[12] (e.g., Ministry of Education, 2010b).

Special Education for Children With Milder Disabilities in General Education Classrooms

The report on special education for children with milder disabilities (National Institute of Special Needs Education, 1978) eventually became the basis of current special education services for children with "developmental disabilities." Yet it was not discussed at the governmental level until a decade after its submission (National Institute of Special Needs Education, 1992; Tsuge, 2004). The report recommended the part-time use of special education classrooms for children with milder disabilities who were being educated in general education classrooms. The report further indicated the need for attention, including extra support, to children who were on the "borderline" of intellectual disabilities within general education classrooms. Tsuge (2004) noted that children on the borderline may include those with milder disabilities, currently referred to as developmental disabilities. These children might be able to keep up with their peers with informal support provided, for example, by classroom teachers and their peers but still be struggling in general education classrooms. Rather than studying in general education classrooms all day long without appropriate support, the report recommended that these children should have access to special education classrooms, as needed, within the local public schools. This report provided a direction for the future establishment of formal special education services for children with developmental disabilities.

Several studies have estimated the percentage of Japanese elementary and junior high school-aged children on the "borderline." During this time, Mogi (1992) estimated that at least 3% to 4% of elementary and junior high school-aged children had some sort of milder disability. Another study at 16 elementary schools and 16 junior high schools in one prefecture in 1994 also showed that approximately 3% of elementary school and junior high school children had learning difficulties (Abe, 1998). Yet only 1% of children were receiving services at special education schools or classrooms (e.g., Ueno & Hanakuma, 2006). The other 2% to 3% remained full-time in general education classrooms. Mogi further described that although these children were still able to learn in general education classrooms and make friends, without special attention in their classrooms, they fell behind academically. In addition, some may have developed low self-esteem and a dislike of school.

It was not until the 1990s that the special needs of children with developmental disabilities received wider public attention as a result of internal and external pressure on the Japanese government. In 1990, Japanese parents of children with learning disabilities formed a group to advocate for formal support for their children who were being educated in general education classrooms (National Association of Parents of Children with Learning Disabilities, 2013). Around this same time, the Japanese government also was pressured by a movement across the world to protect children's rights. This movement included the Convention on the Rights of the Child that identified appropriate education as a basic human right (United Nations, 1989). Next, the Standard Rules on the Equalization of Opportunities for Persons with Disabilities, which represents governments' moral and political commitments to take action for equal participation of people with disabilities, included that individuals with disabilities be provided with a public education in integrated settings (United Nations, 1993). Further, the Salamanca Statement called on governments to provide inclusive education (UNESCO, 1994).

A decade after the 1978 report on children with mild disabilities was submitted to the Japanese Ministry of Education, the need for a new system for children with milder disabilities that could provide them with the necessary support part-time in special education classrooms was indicated by the Extra Council of Education and the Council for Educational Curriculum (National Institute of Special Needs Education, 1992). By the 1990s, the special education system in Japan entered a period of reform (e.g., Abe, 1998). However, it was not until 2007 that special education services for children with "developmental disabilities" were fully implemented. The government spent more than a decade conducting a series of research studies to determine the needs of children with developmental disabilities and examine the best way to provide services to meet their needs.

Even in the 1980s, however, there was substantial variation across Japan in educational services for children with disabilities. Some local boards of education implemented special education services beyond that required by national laws. For example, in the late 1980s, several local boards of education in Tokyo implemented resource rooms at elementary schools. Children with autism spectrum disorders and emotional, visual, and other disabilities from general education classrooms received special education services at resource rooms several hours a week, while maintaining their membership in general education classrooms and receiving support from their classroom teachers and peers (Goldberg, 1989). Heyer (2008) also highlighted the experience of Ototake (1998; *see also* Chapter 1). Despite the severity of his physical disabilities, he received a public education through high school in general education classrooms. Once Ototake was accepted in general education classrooms, his teachers and peers recognized him as equal to the other children, and provided him with necessary support.

The accommodations experienced by Ototake, however, were not available at every school, and many children with less obvious challenges, including those with developmental disabilities, were struggling in general education classrooms or segregated in special education classrooms or schools. A research report on the needs for resource rooms submitted to the Ministry of Education in 1992 revealed that many children with disabilities who studied in self-contained special education classrooms also participated, part-time, in general education classrooms (National Institute of Special Needs Education, 1992). Yet part-time support was not available in special education classrooms for children with milder disabilities who were being educated in general education classrooms. If children required extra support, they had to transfer to special education classrooms, even though they did not need full-time special education support. The report identified this problem and stressed the need for instruction in resource rooms for children who required additional support to benefit fully from instruction in general education classrooms.

In response to increasing needs for extra support for children with mild disabilities in general education classrooms, an amendment to the enforcement regulation of the School Education Law was passed. Beginning in 1993, public schools began to create resources rooms, so that children with milder disabilities from general education classrooms could receive special education services part-time within local public schools[13] (Ministry of Education, 1993a, 1993b). During the same school year, the amendment of the law that determines the maximum classroom size and teacher assignment made it possible to assign extra teachers for team-teaching in general education classrooms (Ministry of Education, 1993a, 1999). These new policies facilitated the provision of individualized support for children with disabilities in general education classrooms.

The Emergence of "Developmental Disability"

The research report on resource rooms in 1992 also addressed the unique needs of children with learning disabilities and argued that they could benefit from services at resource rooms. Consequently, the Ministry of Education started a new research project on children with learning disabilities (Ministry of Education, 1992, 1993a). The interim and final reports of the research (Ministry of Education, 1995, 1999) defined learning disabilities for the first time at the governmental level, and criteria for the assessment of learning disabilities were proposed. According to the Ministry of Education, which has established criteria to assess children's eligibility to receive special education services, learning disabilities refer to:

> a deficit in understanding and using certain abilities including listening, speaking, reading, writing, doing mathematical calculations, and reasoning without delay in overall intellectual development. It is suggested that learning disabilities are caused by deficits in the central nervous system. Environmental factors and other disabilities including visual and hearing impairments, intellectual disabilities, and emotional disorders are not a direct cause of learning disabilities. (Ministry of Education, 1999)

In addition, several suggestions were made as to how to teach children with learning disabilities at general public schools, such as providing support by classroom teachers in their general education classrooms; team-teaching to provide individual and small group instruction within general education classrooms; providing support during noninstructional hours, including after school, by classroom teachers; and providing instruction at resource rooms (Ministry of Education, 1999).

Further, in 2001, an advisory committee assigned by the Ministry submitted a report entitled, "Future directions of special education in the 21st century: Specialized support that meets the needs of each child" (Ministry of Education, 2001a), which was a shift from support provided in segregated settings. This report underscored that special education had been targeting children in special education schools and classrooms, but support for children who required additional help in general education classrooms was not yet adequate. This report described the needs of children with ADHD and high-functioning autism for additional support as well as those with learning disabilities. After resource rooms were implemented in 1993, the need for additional support for children with these "new" disabilities was publicly indicated (e.g., Ministry of Education, 2001a; Ueno & Hanakuma, 2006). As a result, the report suggested that the government had to be actively involved in providing support for children with disabilities who were being educated in general education classrooms (Ministry of Education, 2001a). As new approaches for educating these children were discussed at the governmental and practice levels, learning disabilities, ADHD, and high-functioning autism eventually became known as "mild developmental disabilities" in Japanese society (e.g., Ueno & Hanakuma, 2006).

Disability Rights Movement

This special education reform was also part of a larger reform of Japanese policies and programs for people with disabilities. These reforms emerged, in part, from pressure by worldwide movements advocating for the rights of individuals with disabilities. For example, the Basic Programme for Persons with Disabilities was developed in 2002 by the Japanese government as a result of external pressure to promote normalization and inclusion of people with disabilities including the International Decade of Disabled Persons (1983–1992; United Nations, 2004) and the subsequent Asian and Pacific Decade of Disabled Persons (1993–2002, extended to 2012; Cabinet Office, the Government of Japan, 2010). The Program and its Five-Year Plan for implementation clearly described a need for educational reform involving formal special education services for children with learning disabilities, ADHD, and high-functioning autism and requested that the government develop guidelines for the educational reform by the end of the fiscal year 2004 (Cabinet Office, the Government of Japan, 2002a, 2002b).

The need for special education reform was clearly indicated by national research on children who required extra support in general education classrooms. In 2002, among 41,579 children in five areas across Japan, 6.3% were identified by their classroom teachers as exhibiting academic or behavioral difficulties (4.5%, academic only; 2.9%, behavioral only; 1.2%, both academic and behavioral; Ministry of Education, 2002a). Yet in the same time period, less than 1% were receiving special education services at resource rooms (0.89%) and special education classrooms (0.5%)[14] (Ministry of Education, 2006g). Consequently, special education reforms were proposed in the final report of the research project submitted to the Ministry, including for children who were struggling academically in general education classrooms (Ministry of Education, 2003). In this final report, definitions and criteria for the assessment of ADHD, Asperger's syndrome, and high-functioning autism were described for the first time in special education, along with the definition of learning disabilities described in the 1999 report (Ministry of Education, 1999). In the 2003 report, ADHD and autism were defined based on the Diagnostic and Statistical Manual of Mental Disorders (DSM) fourth edition by the American Psychiatric Association. In the Japanese special education system, ADHD was defined as:

> a disability causing impulsivity, hyperactivity, and/or a lack of attention that are not consistent with the age and the level of development of the child and that affect the child's participation in social activities

and educational performance. Symptoms of ADHD are usually present before the age of seven and are persistent. It is suggested that ADHD is caused by deficits in the central nervous system. (Ministry of Education, 2003)

High-functioning autism and Asperger's syndrome was defined as:

symptoms of high functioning autism are usually present before the age of three. High functioning autism refers to autism that is not associated with intellectual disabilities. Symptoms of autism, which is a disability causing behavior problems, include 1) difficulties in developing social relationships, 2) delay in language development, and 3) narrow interests and persistent preoccupation with certain things. Asperger's syndrome is not associated with intellectual disabilities or delay in language development. High functioning autism and Asperger's syndrome are categorized as pervasive developmental disorders [in DSM-IV]. (Ministry of Education, 2003)

Shift to Individualized Education

Reform in special education also was part of a larger movement to individualize Japanese education for all children. Until about 2002, it was common for teachers to present one lesson to the entire class (e.g., Shimizu, 1999). Around the time of special education reforms, public schools had begun to attend to the diverse needs of individual children within general education classrooms. For example, teachers began preparing multiple lessons for children functioning at different levels of ability. The amendment to the National Curriculum Standards for junior high and elementary schools in 1998 formally addressed the need to attend to children's individual needs in general education classrooms beginning in 2002.[15] It was amended again in 2003 and the requirement of providing individualized instruction was reinforced (Tsuge, 2004).

Recent changes in the educational needs of children, and parents' expectations for schools may also have facilitated this transition to individualized education. For example, one of the participant educators stated that the "environment where children grow up is different in terms of historical and societal backgrounds, so children also have changed." As a result of urbanization, children have lost many opportunities to learn basic interpersonal skills in the community and even within their families, which typically have fewer children than in the past. This teacher believes that 20 years ago, children were more patient (*shinbo-zuyoi*) and persistent in completing tasks. She feels that children currently are less mature and able to control themselves (*gaman-dekinai*) and more prone to express their dislike if things are not going their way. She speculates that this may be because their parents are more permissive. She also has observed changes in parents' attitudes; for example, parents may say, "Please respect my child as an individual," or, "Look at my child."

A retired teacher who had been volunteering for years at Greenleaf Elementary School, our research site, shared his views that not only are children less patient than in the past but that teachers' authority seems to be weakening. He explained that recently schools have needed to have volunteers working with children, because teachers cannot handle children; for example, "When children go out of the school, such as a field trip or just going to a park nearby, teachers need someone who can assist in directing children to walk in a straight line. But in the past, children used to be able to follow if a teacher said to walk in a line." Sano *sensei* also has observed changes over her career:

> It used to be that children came here [the school nurse's office] when they found it difficult [to be in their classroom], and took a rest for a while. [They knew] they would be understood [by me] without saying anything, and told me when [they were ready to] go back to their classrooms. The number of children like this was much lower during that time and no one said "special education" or things like that, but I came to realize that it was not enough [and I had to think of other ways to deal with these children]. I mean, it's getting busier in the field of education, and teachers keep telling children [to do this or that], and such children are more and more marginalized and struggling.

As a result of an increasing focus on individualized education, general education classroom teachers are now required to attend to the needs of children with diverse abilities in their classrooms. In 2003, the National Curriculum Standards provided several examples of instruction intended to meet the needs of children whose levels of understanding and abilities are diverse—for example, providing additional support for children who are struggling as well as preparing extra activities that require application of the learned materials for children who have completed assigned tasks (Tsuge, 2004). The amendment of the regulation of the law that determines the maximum classroom size and teacher assignment in 2002 further facilitated individualized instruction within general education classrooms by allowing schools to assign extra teachers to both general and special education classrooms when children who require additional support are identified (Ministry of Education, 2002c). From

2004, local governments were allowed to use funds provided by the national government more flexibly to hire extra educators[16] to assist in general and special education classrooms[17] (Ministry of Education, 2006f).

Formal Special Education Services for Children With Developmental Disabilities

Along with these amendments, the Ministry of Education began to prepare in 2004 to 2005 for major special education reform. As requested in the Five-Year Plan for the Basic Programme for Persons with Disabilities, the Ministry distributed a tentative guideline for educational reform in 2004, which involved suggestions described in the 2003 final report (Ministry of Education, 2004). In 2005, the Elementary and Lower Secondary Education subdivision of the Central Council for Education submitted a report to the Ministry regarding how to implement the new special education system (Ministry of Education, 2005c), which became the basis of this special education reform. The report described that the reform was to include a re-organization of the roles and functions of special education schools, establishment of special education services for children with milder disabilities in general education classrooms, and new requirements for teaching certifications for special education.

In 2006, one year before the formal implementation of the new system of special education, the enforcement regulation of the School Education Law was partially amended (Ministry of Education, 2006b). This amendment made it officially acceptable for children with learning disabilities and ADHD to receive services at resource rooms (Ministry of Education, 2006a, 2006b). Children with autism spectrum disorders had been receiving services under "emotional disorders," but autism was separated from emotional disorders in this amendment. These children are now eligible to receive instruction part-time at resource rooms[18] (Ministry of Education, 2006b).

In 2006, the Fundamental Law of Education was amended for the first time since it was passed in 1947 and a description of special education was added. This amendment makes it clear that it is the responsibility of the national and local governments to make sure that children receive necessary support for an appropriate public education (Ministry of Education, 2006c). The School Education Law and its regulations were amended again in 2006, and the new special education system, including services for children with learning disabilities and ADHD, started in the 2007–2008 school year (Ministry of Education, 2006d; 2007a).

In 2007, the Ministry of Education distributed a notice to local boards of education requiring public schools to introduce new staff positions and implement a broad array of procedures to provide formal special education services for children with disabilities who are being educated in general education classrooms. In summary, each school was to implement an in-school committee to establish a system to assess and discuss the needs of children, including those with disabilities. The principal of each school was to select an educator to serve as a special education coordinator. The duties of the special education coordinator include organizing in-school trainings and workshops on special education for educators and communicating and collaborating with other related agencies and with parents. Educators also were advised to work collaboratively with a special education coordinator within the school and parents and to be mindful of the importance of early intervention. The Ministry also recommended that educators in general public schools develop and utilize individualized education programs as needed (Ministry of Education, 2007a). An English translation of this notice is included in Appendix A.

The Support for Persons With Developmental Disabilities Act

The Support for Persons With Developmental Disabilities Act, passed in 2004 and enacted in 2005 (Ministry of Health, Labour and Welfare, 2004a), was the first law that defined "developmental disabilities" and addressed the national and local governments' responsibility to provide support for individuals with developmental disabilities[19]. The "developmental support" determined by the law includes "medical and educational support as well as social welfare that promotes their [individuals with developmental disabilities] appropriate psychological development and facilitates their social lives without any disturbance (Article 2-3)." A notice distributed before the implementation of this law under the names of both the Ministry of Education and the Ministry of Health, Labour and Welfare[20] underscores the importance of providing early and prompt intervention programs for individuals with developmental disabilities, as soon as children are diagnosed (Ministry of Education, 2005a).

Under this law, "developmental disabilities" are (Ministry of Health, Labour and Welfare, 2004a):

autism[21], Asperger's syndrome and other pervasive developmental disorders; learning disabilities; attention deficit hyperactivity disorders; and other related disabilities caused by deficits in brain functioning determined by the enforcement ordinance. Typically, symptoms of these disabilities are present since early childhood. (Article 2-1)

According to its enforcement ordinance (Ministry of Health, Labour and Welfare, 2004b) and regulation (Ministry of Health, Labour and Welfare, 2004c), other related disabilities include those involving language, motor coordination, psychological development, behavior, and emotions. In the notice distributed by the two Ministries in 2005, developmental disabilities also included epilepsy and other disorders caused by deficits in the central nervous system and the continuing effects of traumatic brain injury and cerebrovascular disorders (Ministry of Education, 2005a). The Ministry of Education (2005b) described how this law would impact public education. It also required school staff members to be educated to help them acquire specialized knowledge about developmental disabilities.

The Formal Use of "Developmental Disability" in Education

Before the Support for Persons with Disabilities Act was passed, learning disabilities, ADHD, and "high-functioning autism[22]" were presented as typical disabilities of children with additional needs who were being educated in general education classrooms. These disabilities were frequently grouped and referred to as "mild developmental disabilities" in Japanese society (Ueno & Hanakuma, 2006). The Ministry of Education emphasized these three categories of disabilities in its regulations, including enforcement regulations, notices, and announcements. As the broad definition of developmental disabilities in the Support for Persons with Developmental Disabilities Act suggests, however, these are not exhaustive and other disabilities can be included. Consequently, in 2007, the Ministry announced that it would use the term, "developmental disabilities," which was more familiar to Japanese people. The Ministry decided not to use "mild developmental disabilities" because of the ambiguity of its definition[23] (Ministry of Education, 2007b).

In its announcement, the Ministry acknowledged that the definition of developmental disabilities was only for political and administrative uses, and was not a clinical or academic definition (Ministry of Education, 2007b). For example, neither the DSM-5 by the American Psychiatric Association (APA, 2013) nor the ICD-10 by the World Health Organization (WHO, 2007) group listed these mild cognitive and behavioral disabilities as "developmental disabilities." In the United States, generally, developmental disabilities include disabilities involving more obvious impairment of children's physical and cognitive abilities—for example, severe and chronic disabilities involving mental and physical impairments that are present before age 22 years (U.S. Developmental Disabilities Assistance Bill of Rights Act of 2000; Department of Health and Human Services, 2000).

Support Under the New System of Special Education

The new system of Japanese special education is called *tokubetsu shien kyo-iku* (*tokubetu*: special, *shien*: support, help, *kyo-iku*: education). Although the official translation used by the Ministry of Education is "Special needs education," the literal meaning of *tokubetsu shien kyoiku* is "Special support education." Both translations mean that children should receive necessary support that meets their special needs. Before the amendment of the School Education Law in 2007, a special education school was called *Yogo gakko* (*yogo*: protective care, nursing; *gakko*: school), and a special education classroom was called *tokushu gakkyu* (*tokushu*: special, *gakkyu*: class, classroom). These terms connoted protection for children who were weak or handicapped because of illness and disabilities. The way to "protect," however, frequently was to provide educational services in isolation from other children in special education classrooms or special education schools. Therefore, the transition to *tokubetsu shien kyo-iku* was a large step toward promoting the individual rights of children with special needs in general public schools. In this book we will simply use the term "special education" to refer to *tokubetsu shien kyo-iku*.

Types of Placement

As of 2007, four types of placement for children with disabilities were available under the School Education Law and its regulations. They are special education schools, special education classrooms, resource rooms, and general education classrooms. Currently, only the services provided at resource rooms, special education classrooms, and special education schools are considered "special education" under the law. Children may also receive additional support at special support rooms and within their general education classrooms. Utilization of special support rooms is recommended by the government, although the law and its regulations do not specifically define special support rooms. Generally, children with developmental disabilities receive services in resource rooms, special support rooms, or within their general education classrooms. If they need more intensive support, they may receive support in special education classrooms.

A notice distributed to prefectural governors and local boards of education in 2002 by the Ministry of Education has been used as a guideline to determine children's placement. This notice describes the severity of disabilities and characteristics of children in special education schools, special education classrooms, and resource rooms under each of the disability categories (Ministry of Education, 2002b, 2006a). Placement determination for children with disabilities is made by considering the best interest of children with input from multiple professions, such as education, medicine, and psychology (Ministry of Education, 2002b). In addition, the enforcement ordinance of the School Education Law requires input from children's parents as well as a team of specialists before making a decision to place their children in special education schools (Article 18-2; Ministry of Internal Affairs and Communication, 2011c). Typically, parents of children with disabilities are provided with opportunities to discuss their children's placement with local boards of education, as well as administrators of general and special education schools. Based on the assessment, discussions, and parents' preferences, local boards of education make a final decision whether children attend general or special education schools. Procedures to place children in special education classrooms and resource rooms may vary by local boards of education. In Riverside City, parents' opinions and children's preferences are valued in this process (see subsequent chapters for more detailed descriptions).

Special education schools. The School Education Law determined that special education schools are for children with significant hearing impairments, visual impairments, intellectual disabilities, physical disabilities, or other health impairments (Ministry of Internal Affairs and Communication, 2007). These schools have a national curriculum standard set by the Ministry (Ministry of Education, 2009d). Children whose disabilities are severe enough to attend special education schools may attend general, local public schools, if the schools have an appropriate educational environment for them, including any necessary equipment and educators with the knowledge and skills to teach them (Ministry of Education, 2002b).

Special education classrooms and resource rooms. The School Education Law and its regulations describe that schools *can* create special education classrooms for children with disabilities, including intellectual disabilities, physical disabilities, low vision, hearing impairments, other health issues, language disabilities, and autism-emotional disorders (Ministry of Education, 2002b, 2009a; Ministry of Internal Affairs and Communication, 2007). For example, if a school has a child with an intellectual disability and a child with autism, the school may create two special education classrooms, one for intellectual disabilities, and the other for autism-emotional disorders. The maximum special education classroom size as determined by law is 8, substantially smaller than the maximum classroom size of 40 for general education classrooms[24] (Ministry of Internal Affairs and Communication 2011a). When schools determine that a classroom has a child who requires additional support, more teachers may be assigned to both general and special education classrooms (Ministry of Education, 2002c).

Instruction at resource rooms is described in the enforcement regulation of the School Education Law. As of 2011, disability categories eligible for this service are language disabilities, autism-emotional disorders, low vision, hearing impairment, learning disabilities, ADHD, and children with other disabilities who can benefit from receiving support at resource rooms (Ministry of Education, 1993b, 2002b, 2006a, 2006b). Services provided at resource rooms include academic instruction and skills that help children handle difficulties caused by their disabilities (Ministry of Education, 1993b, 2006b). Children may receive services in resource rooms in other schools when their schools do not have a resource room[25]. In this case, the notice in 2002 states that classroom teachers and teachers providing services at resource rooms have to exchange information on a regular basis and work with the children collaboratively (Ministry of Education, 2002b).

Unlike special education schools, there is no national curriculum standard determined by the Ministry of Education for special education classrooms and resource rooms. If appropriate, the enforcement regulation of the School Education Law allows schools to use specially designed curriculum for children in special education classrooms and resource rooms (Ministry of Internal Affairs and Communication, 2011b). In this case, educators have to consult and utilize the National Curriculum Standards for special education schools in addition to the National Curriculum Standard for general elementary, junior high, or high schools[26] (Ministry of Education, 2002b, 2009c).

Special support rooms. The utilization of special support rooms was suggested in the final report in 2003 (Ministry of Education, 2003), and the implementation of special support rooms was described in 2005 before the formal start of the new special education program (Ministry of Education, 2005c). In the 2005 report on special education reform submitted to the Ministry, a special support room was described as:

> a room where children in general education classrooms who have disabilities, including learning disabilities, ADHD, and high functioning autism, receive specialized instruction as needed. This support is in addition to that received in their general education classrooms, such as appropriate support from classroom teachers, team teaching, individual instruction, and accommodations depending on the level of understanding of content.

Although a special support room is not mentioned in either the School Education Law or its regulations, when the amendment of the School Education Law was passed, implementation of a special support room was included as a supplementary resolution (Ministry of Education, 2006e). However, there is no national guideline for the utilization of special support rooms. Cities and prefectures vary in how they utilize special support rooms.

In Riverside City, the location of our research site, resource rooms and special support rooms are clearly differentiated. A guideline created by the local board of education states that services at resource rooms "are provided based on individualized education programs that fit the characteristics [of each child]." In contrast, support provided at special support rooms is more flexible. The guideline describes a special support room as a place that has "a comfortable environment, which [teachers can use for] children to calm down emotionally, provide instruction that fits the characteristics [of each child], and assist children in fulfilling/enjoying learning and daily lives in their classrooms." The guideline lists three examples of the utilization of special support rooms: (1) learning in a way that fits the child's learning style, which facilitates motivation to learn by experiencing how fun it is to understand; (2) providing transitional support for children who are not comfortable with being in their general education classrooms; and (3) providing space for all children that increases the variety of their learning.

Ongoing Issues

Despite significant special education reforms, Japanese education faces several challenges. In 2006, the Convention on the Rights of Persons with Disabilities was adopted by the United Nations and came into force in 2008 (United Nations, 2006, 2010). Japan signed this convention in 2007 but as of 2012 had not ratified it (United Nations, 2013). The convention requires governments to provide children with disabilities with a public education through high school in inclusive settings (United Nations, 2006).

> (b) Persons with disabilities can access an inclusive, quality and free primary education and secondary education on an equal basis with others in the communities in which they live. (Article 24-2)

To meet the requirement, an advisory committee assigned by the Ministry of Education stressed the need of continuing emphasis on early identification and continuous intervention throughout public education (Ministry of Education, 2009b), including special education services in secondary education settings after children complete their compulsory education[27]. Yet special education and accommodations for individuals with developmental disabilities at the high school[28] and college levels are just beginning in Japan. One mother was concerned about her son's education after graduation from junior high school. Given that few general education high schools provide special education services, Yusuke may have to go to a special education high school, which may limit his future path.

Discussion

In 2007, the Japanese government implemented educational policies requiring formal, individualized special education programs in public schools for children with "developmental disabilities." These complex educational reforms only occurred following study, discussion, and reflection extending for decades. There are a number of complex, interacting factors that likely impacted these special education reforms and their slow implementation relative to other industrialized societies. First, mandates for educational reform following World War II were underfunded. Although some scholars stressed the needs of children with milder disabilities, given a lack of adequate resources, Japanese leaders choose to prioritize services for children with relatively severe disabilities. This focus may have contributed to a lack of awareness of milder disabilities among parents and educators. Awareness was heightened by support groups of Japanese parents whose children had developmental disabilities and were struggling in general education classrooms, as well as by international pressure to provide an appropriate, inclusive, basic education to all children as part of their human rights (United Nations, 1989, 1993; UNESCO, 1994).

Second, given that special education traditionally was provided in segregated settings, either in special education classrooms or schools, Japanese leaders may have been cautious in implementing changes to remove the "wall" between special and general education. These changes also have required changes in the educational system as a whole; for example, changes in teacher education as formal special education services for children with "developmental disabilities" requires bringing special education to general education classrooms.

Next, educators and researchers were concerned that creating new disability categories—especially labeling children who functioned well in many areas as having "disabilities"—and providing services to children outside of their peer group could lead to stigmatization. Kadomoto (1990) stressed that the new formal support system for children with learning disabilities and other mild disabilities had to be designed to provide appropriate support without stigmatization. Even after learning disabilities, ADHD, and autism spectrum disorders including Asperger's syndrome were defined at the governmental level in the late 1990s and the early 2000s, Tsuge (2004) cautioned that these definitions should not be used to label children or create new disabilities but as guides to providing the necessary support for each child.

There also were a number of positive social trends in Japan that facilitated the design and implementation of educational reforms impacting services for children with developmental disabilities. First, there were broader changes occurring in Japanese society to support individuals with disabilities including through medical and early intervention. This social trend resulted in the passages of the "Support for Persons with Disabilities Act," which further extended support for individuals with developmental disabilities beyond educational services. These changes reflected, and helped to change, people's understanding, valuing, and acceptance of the need to support children with developmental disabilities. In addition, Japanese education has increasingly recognized individual variation in the learning of typically developing children in general education classrooms. Traditionally, Japanese educators prepare one lesson for the entire class. Increasingly, they are planning multiple lessons to support the learning of children at various levels of understanding and academic skill. Providing individualized support for children with developmental disabilities is a logical extension of this trend.

Challenges to the Implementation of Special Education Reforms

As a result of the special educational reform, children with developmental disabilities are now able to receive individualized support. Yet providing formal, individualized services can present challenges for Japanese parents and educators. These laws determine frameworks of the new system of special education but do not provide specific procedures to assess the needs of children and plan and provide services to those who are struggling, which can cause confusion and delay in providing appropriate support. For example, some elements of the new special education system such as Individualized Education Programs (IEPs) are borrowed from special education in other countries, including the United States. In contrast to U.S. special education that has clear guidelines and requirements to develop IEPs for all children in special education (e.g., Department of Education, 2013; Illinois State Board of Education, 2009), the Japanese government has a more flexible approach and only recommends the use of IEPs for children with disabilities in general public schools (Ministry of Education, 2007a; *see also* Chapter 4). The local board of education for Greenleaf Elementary School requires schools to develop IEPs for children in special education classrooms but not for children receiving support in special support rooms. The priority for Japanese educators seems to be to provide special education services addressing the individual needs of children without labeling children with disabilities. In this context, Japanese educators and parents may consider an IEP a guideline and not a contract to provide individualized support for children.

There also is variation in the implementation of the new system across Japan. Each local board of education creates its own guidelines based on the framework determined by the Ministry of Education. Even within a school district, the availability and quality of programs for children with developmental disabilities may vary. Each school creates its own programs using available resources within the school and the community. Greenleaf Elementary School was fortunate to have community resources, such as volunteers and teaching assistants, as well as educators who had skills and knowledge to provide special education services within general education classrooms. The local board of education also distributed their own curriculum standards, including for special education, and conducted research on the implementation of new programs for children with disabilities in collaboration with several model schools. Greenleaf Elementary School participated in one such research program focusing on the use of volunteer teaching assistants in general and special education classrooms.

As we will discuss in subsequent chapters, however, educators and children at Greenleaf Elementary School experienced challenges in implementing new special education programs. For example, children with developmental disabilities used to be incorporated into peer groups "naturally" as full members. Although they struggled academically and interpersonally, their struggles and differences from others typically were accepted by others as they learned in the same classrooms and grew up together. Receiving individualized support outside of their classroom can lead to labeling and possible stigmatization. Because the Japanese formal special education for children with developmental disabilities is new, a child receiving support outside of the general education classroom may be the only one leaving the classroom. In such a case, the child cannot leave without drawing other children's attention. Once the child starts receiving support at resource rooms or special support rooms, other children immediately recognize that the child may have a problem and their curiosity can make the child "different."

Providing support outside of their classroom can also result in removing children from a central developmental context—their peer groups. Therefore, educators must balance traditional socialization and educational practices of rearing and educating children within peer groups and concerns about stigmatization with the benefit for children of receiving formal special education services. To achieve the goals of both socializing children into Japanese society and providing special education services, adults must help children to utilize services while remaining fully integrated into peer groups.

The following chapters describe how the formal, special education policies outlined in this chapter intersect with traditional Japanese educational practices in the everyday lives of children, their educators, and parents at Greenleaf Elementary School. How did educators understand and address the challenge of implementing formal, individualized special education within the context of a traditional Japanese education system that emphasizes academic and social development within peer groups? How are these practices understood and experienced by children and their parents? In other words, we consider the intersection of formal policies with traditional educational practices in the everyday lives of Japanese children with disabilities, their educators, and parents.

Notes

1. With Japan's declining birth rate, there simply are fewer children within the community and at school.
2. Such education was not widely available. It typically focused on vocational training, such as acupuncture and playing a musical instrument for individuals who were blind. Some private tutoring programs/classes called "*terakoya* (temple schools)" also taught writing to children with disabilities, including hearing impairments (Nakamura & Arakawa, 2003; Sugawara, 2011).
3. During this time, education of children with disabilities began to receive more attention, as the attendance rate of school-aged children, both boys and girls, reached 90% by approximately 1905 and 98% by 1912. In addition, new methods to teach children who were "blind and deaf" were introduced, which opened up more opportunities for them to receive a public education (Nakamura & Arakawa, 2003).
4. The Great Depression, which originated in the United States in 1929, also affected Japan's economy.
5. The Fundamental Law of Education describes the philosophy, mission, and general purposes of education at home and at school, as well as parents' obligation to allow their children to receive a public education (Ministry of Internal Affairs and Communication, 2006). It is a foundation of the "whole" child perspective of current public schools. The 2006 amendment to the Fundamental Law of Education added the phrase, "individuals who are generous, creative, and respect the principal of public good," and deleted the phrase referring to labor (Ministry of Internal Affairs and Communication, 2006).

6. Support for children with disabilities outside of schools is provided under the Child Welfare Act, which was passed and enacted in 1947. This law determines services for children and their families who need extra support due to children's disabilities, home environment, and other reasons. Services required under this law include financial support, in-home programs, early intervention programs for children with disabilities, and residential programs (Ministry of Internal Affairs Communication, 2008a).

7. These are the disability categories for children receiving support at special education classrooms at the time when the School Education Law was passed (Ministry of Education, 1981; National Archives of Japan, 1947). "Abnormal personality" and "mental retardation" corresponds to "emotional disorders" and "intellectual disabilities" under the current law.

8. As of 2011, there were 45,807 special education classrooms in elementary and junior high schools (elementary: 31,507, junior high: 14,300; Ministry of Education, 2012a).

9. Beginning in 2007, "blind" and "deaf" schools were integrated into special education schools along with schools for children with other disabilities (Ministry of Education, 2006d).

10. Local governments have been obligated to create "blind" and "deaf schools" since 1923.

11. For children with disabilities to be able to interact with age-appropriate typically developing children, the Ministry of Education began a new exchange program of children in special and general public schools beginning in 1979 at several model schools, which aimed at forming equal relationships between children with and without disabilities and raising awareness of disability (Nakamura & Arakawa, 2003).

    Currently, the exchange program for children in special education classrooms/schools is described in the National Curriculum Standards for both general and special education schools (Ministry of Education, 2008, 2009d), but Japanese education still "separates" general and special education and is not yet considered "inclusive education" (e.g, Ichiki, 2010).

12. How inclusive education is defined varies, however, across the world (e.g., see Hall, 2002 and Hunt, 2011 for interpretations in the United States).

13. Children may receive services at resource rooms in other schools when their schools do not offer needed services.

    "Developmental Disabilities" such as learning disabilities and ADHD were not yet listed as a disability category eligible for support at resource rooms until 2006 (Ministry of Education, 2006a, 2006b), resulting from the ambiguity of definitions and criteria for assessment (Ministry of Education, 2001a). At the practice level, however, they might receive the support under other categories, such as "emotional disorders."

14. In addition, 0.4% of children attended special education schools. Thus, a total of 1.7% of children received special education (in 2005).

15. This amendment was part of educational reforms to further promote education for *kokoro* (heart and mind) and improve children's ability to learn skills necessary to live creatively and responsibly in the increasingly changing Japanese society. The 2002 National Curriculum Standards specifically focused on children's abilities to apply learned skills to solve problems, personality development, and health. The reform included reduced academic content and school hours for children to spend time learning and retaining learned skills (Ministry of Education, 2002e). Yet there was a concern regarding the consequences of reducing academic content. The 2008 amendment of National Curriculum Standards reinstated some content once removed from the curriculum back in all grade levels (e.g., Ministry of Education, 2008). We are grateful to Hisako Ando for pointing out these issues to us.

16. The national government distributes one-third of personnel expenses (general and special education) to each local government (up until 2006, it was one-half) (Ministry of Education, 2006f). In 2011, it is estimated that 88% of the special education budget of the national government goes toward salaries (Ministry of Education, 2011a).

17. The number of educators is estimated based on the law that determines the maximum classroom size and teacher assignment for general and special education classrooms, which includes the number of teachers who assist in general education classrooms for team teaching and small group instruction, as well as resource room teachers (Ministry of Internal Affairs and Communication, 2011a).

18. Children with autism spectrum disorders had received support at "special education classrooms for children with emotional disorders." In 2009 these classrooms were renamed to "special education classrooms for children with autism and emotional disorders" (Ministry of Education, 2009a).

19. In 2011, the Basic Law for Persons with Disabilities was amended partially, and developmental disabilities were added under the category of mental disorders along with physical and intellectual disabilities (Cabinet Office, the Government of Japan, 2011). The Basic Law for Persons with Disabilities is a basis of any support provided by the national and local governments for individuals with disabilities, including financial support and other resources.

20. These two government offices are responsible for laws determining support for children with disabilities. The government office responsible for the School Education Law is the Ministry of Education. The Ministry of Health, Labour, and Welfare is responsible for the Child Welfare Act.

21. The law does not specify any "subcategory" of autism—for example, whether it co-occurs with delay in intellectual development, and so forth.

22. In the Ministry of Education's definition, high-functioning autism refers to autism that is not associated with delay in intellectual development.
23. For example, autism is a spectrum disorder. After the implementation of the new special education system, all children with autism spectrum disorders became eligible for special education, regardless of the label of its subcategory.
24. The law that determines the maximum classroom sizes and teacher assignment was amended, and the maximum class size for first graders was decreased to 35 from April 2011 (Ministry of Education, 2011b). In the 2012–2013 school year, the extra budget was passed to decrease the classroom size for second graders to 35, but any amendment to the law was not made.
25. The availability of resource rooms may depend on each local board of education. In some cities, one in every three general public schools has a resource room. In other cities, children from 10 different schools may receive services in the same resource room.
26. Japanese compulsory education (first to ninth grades) does not include high school education, and currently only a few general education high schools have special education classrooms.
27. *See also* footnote 8 in this chapter.
28. High school (3 years, equivalent to 10th to 12th grades in U.S. education system) is not compulsory in Japan.

4 CHILDREN'S DAILY LIVES AT GREENLEAF ELEMENTARY SCHOOL

"I'm Manabie. Spread out! Catch the ball of learning (*manabi*)."

Every year at the Greenleaf Festival, children present their year-long projects, such as making tofu or growing vegetable gardens, to their parents, friends, and people from the community. This year, student members of the Festival Committee created posters of the festival with a drawing of an owl in a cap (left), who eventually became known as Manabie (named after "*manabi*", learning) and used as the festival mascot. A mother who heard about this story secretly created and brought a stuffed Manabie (right, almost the same size as a small child) to the staff room and surprised teachers. One more Manabie was made by another mother, and two Manabies, sitting on regular size chairs, greeted guests on the day of the festival. Since then, Manabie has been displayed in the hallway as a school mascot with the festival motto; "Spread out! Catch the ball of learning." (from Misa's field note)

As the festival motto illustrates, learning in Japanese elementary schools is understood as a series of exchanges, a game of "catch" among children, parents, educators, and community members. These exchanges include collaborations to create an environment that facilitates positive interactions between children, their peers, and educators not only in classrooms but in a variety of contexts at school and in the community. In this chapter, we focus on the developmental contexts in which Japanese educational goals, practices, and policies (described in Chapters 1 and 3) are instantiated at Greenleaf Elementary School. We will continue this discussion across Chapters 5 through 7, where we will emphasize the experiences of educators, children, and parents within these contexts.

We begin by describing the general educational contexts in which children learn, develop, and are socialized through daily experiences at Greenleaf Elementary School. The emphasis of Japanese elementary education on positive social relationships, education for *kokoro,* and learning within collaborative peer groups (Chapter1), along with the relatively small size and other characteristics of Greenleaf Elementary, can result in strong, mutually supportive bonds between educators and children within and across grade levels including those in the Challenge and Rainbow Rooms. On the other hand, if children do not fit in groups, then their experiences in school can be highly problematic, as we will discuss in greater detail in Chapters 6 and 7.

In the second part of this chapter, we describe contexts of support for children with special needs at Greenleaf Elementary School. Educators' flexibility in providing support can create opportunities for adjusting assessments and interventions to meet the varying and changing needs of individual children and their parents over time, including their sensitivity to other children's and parents' responses to the support they are receiving (Chapter 5). On the other hand, as discussed in Chapter 3, relatively less clear policies and procedures can result in some children not receiving timely assessment and intervention.

The Context of Education at Greenleaf Elementary School

A Day at School

Children at Greenleaf Elementary School spend approximately 5 to 7 hours per day at school. Typically, they spend most of their time in their classrooms with teachers. Depending on the classroom teachers' specialization and children's grade level, several subjects, such as crafts, music, home economics, science, and physical education may be taught by other teachers. In addition, at Greenleaf Elementary School, Math is co-taught by two teachers, and children may be divided into small groups and taught in different rooms.

Children come to school every morning by 8:25 a.m. Most children walk to school but some commute to school using a local bus service.[1] Children who arrive early play and talk with friends in front of the student entrance until educators open the door at 8:10 a.m. In the entrance, there are rows of shoe shelves. Children have their own space to store their outdoor and indoor shoes. After changing their shoes, children go to their classrooms on the second, third, or fourth floors. When children get to their classrooms, they put notebooks, textbooks, a pen case, and other materials in their desks and their school bag in the assigned shelf at the back of the classroom. In addition to their school bags, children store other materials, such as a recorder for music class and a box containing paints and brushes, in their own spaces.

The formal school day begins with a morning meeting led by classroom monitors standing in front of the class, who are assigned on a rotational basis. During the morning meeting, the classroom teacher reminds children of the schedule and special events of the day, such as swimming class, and children report on their health or anything else they wish to share. For example, one girl reported to her third grade classmates on an injury to her arm, which was in a sling. The classroom teacher asked her if she could do cleaning. Some other children offered to exchange jobs with her so that she could participate in the daily cleaning without using her arm. She also shared with the class that she was happy when one of her classmates helped her to prepare for class. That classmate then shared that she helped because it looked hard for the child with a sling to take things out of her school bag and put them in her desk. After several more children reported on who helped whom before the morning meeting, the monitors closed the meeting, and the first period of the day began.

Each class period starts with the monitor's request to "Please be quiet!" The other children respond in chorus, for example, "We will start the first period of study, Japanese Language." When the classroom teacher announces the end of the class, all children again say, "We will finish the first period of study, Japanese Language." Some children go out for a restroom break and others chat with classmates until the next period starts. One class period lasts 45 minutes, and there are four periods during the morning and two periods after lunch. Depending on the day and grade level, children go home after fourth, fifth, or sixth period. There are 5-minute breaks between first and second periods and third and fourth periods, and two 20-minute recesses between second and third periods and after lunch. During recess, children are free to spend the time as they wish within the school building—for example, in their classrooms and libraries—or on the playground. They also may go to the Challenge Room to use the toys and other materials used by children in the Rainbow Room, the special education classroom. Children enjoy playing with these items (e.g., a large tricycle, a vaulting box, and gym mattresses).

After fourth period, children prepare for lunch. Staff members working at the school kitchen deliver lunch to each classroom in a wagon containing large containers of the main dish, side dish, milk, rice or bread, and utensils. A group of five to six children (rotating weekly) are in charge of serving lunch. They put on white caps, smocks, and masks. With teachers' and kitchen staff members' help, they carry the containers from the wagon in the hallway to a serving table in their classroom. Each child serves one item, such as chop sticks, soup, rice, salad, and the main dish. During this time, other children move their desks to make tables of four to six children. When their table is called, children form a line to receive their lunches and then return to their seats to wait until all children have been served. Once all children have been served, monitors of the day announce, "Please be quiet," and children say in chorus, "With many thanks, *Iatdaki-masu* (literal meaning is 'receiving')," and begin eating. Classroom teachers eat with the children. Generally, children want the teacher or visitor in their group, so the classroom teacher may rotate daily to different groups. After lunch, the classroom monitors announce that it is time to say, "*Gochisou-sama-deshita* (literal meaning is 'it was a delicious meal')[2]" and start putting dishes back in the containers on the serving table and then the wagon in the hallway. Lunchtime lasts 45 minutes, including serving, cleaning up, and brushing teeth.

The 15 minutes following lunch are spent cleaning. Children are assigned places to clean, such as their classroom, the hallway, a restroom, a school nurse's room, the entrance, and the playground. Usually, children clean with peers from their own classrooms, but once a week, they clean in groups of children from first through sixth grades. Each group is responsible for cleaning one classroom or other assigned places. On such occasions, older children teach younger children how to clean, and if younger children do not participate (e.g., they play with cleaning cloths and brooms), then older children give them directions.

The purpose of the daily cleaning time is not to clean the school perfectly but to establish in children a habit of cleaning. Classroom teachers may clean with the children, especially with younger children. Before long breaks, such as summer and winter breaks, children spend about an hour cleaning and moving furniture from their classrooms. With teachers' directions, children carry desks and chairs to the hallway and clean the floor, so that teachers and volunteer parents can wax it after school.

After cleaning time, children have a 20-minute recess. Following the afternoon classes, children put their textbooks, notebooks, and other materials in their school bags along with announcement letters to parents from the school or their classroom teachers and wait for a "going home" meeting. Again, the class monitors announce to their classmates that the meeting is starting. Typically, the meeting begins with announcements, comments, and reflections on the day from children followed by their classroom teacher's announcement for the next day. The meeting takes about 10 to 15 minutes, depending on how much the teacher and children have to report.

The morning and going home meetings are used not only to discuss the day's schedule but also to unite the classroom as a group. The school's goal during 1 month of our study was to "Find something good about your friends and yourself." Misa observed a fifth grade class discussion of how to accomplish this goal led by two children. The classroom teacher also made suggestions, but the decision to write down good things they observed on a piece of paper every day during the going home meeting was made by the children. Several days later when Misa observed a second grade classroom during a "going home meeting," the classroom teacher asked children if they had found something good about themselves.

The fifth and the sixth periods end at 2:25 p.m. and 3:10 p.m., respectively. First graders are dismissed after the cleaning time 2 to 3 days a week, and the rest of the days they have a class during fifth period. Most days, second graders are dismissed after fifth period. Third-sixth graders have a sixth period class 1 to 3 days a week.

Additionally, club activities (third–sixth grades) and committee meetings (fifth and sixth grades) are scheduled alternatively on Friday afternoons. At the beginning of the school year, children in third grade and above sign up for one of the club activities offered by educators, such as basketball, computer, Japanese drum, cooking, crafts, and science. Children can pick different club activities every year. For new third graders, a tour is arranged at the end of the previous school year, so that they can visit each club and decide which club they want to join next year. Activities are led by educators but may be chosen based on children's input.

Similarly, fifth and sixth graders sign up for one of the committees, such as recycling, health, and animals and work with teachers throughout the year. For example, each day children on the animal committee feed the rabbits and clean their cages out on the playground. During our study, the recycling committee decided to collect pull-tabs of soda cans and plastic bottle lids and send the proceeds to an agency that donates wheelchairs (pull-tabs) and vaccines (bottle lids) for children in other countries. In the middle of June, the committee members explained the purpose of their project to all students during the school meeting and placed boxes to collect pull-tabs and lids near the students' entrance.

Special Activities Throughout the School Year

Throughout the school year, children work together to prepare and report on various activities. Some of these activities require that children spend months planning and preparing within peer groups. These school-wide activities typically are exciting, joyful moments in children's lives at school, and they look forward to them eagerly.

The new school year starts with the entrance ceremony in April welcoming new first graders. Through participation in activities such as welcoming parties and field trips, children transition from preschool and adjust to their new lives as first graders. In June or July, swimming classes begin, a source of excitement and sometimes anxiety throughout the summer. Summer break begins at the end of July and lasts for approximately 5 weeks. Many children enjoy meeting their friends after the long break, but some children experience difficulties re-adjusting to school. The first semester ends in the middle of October[3]. After a few days break, the second semester begins. During the second semester, several school-wide activities are scheduled, including the Greenleaf Festival portrayed in the opening vignette.

Winter break begins in late December, and school resumes about a week after New Year's Day. The school year ends with the graduation ceremony in March to celebrate and bid farewell to sixth graders. In addition, all children attend ceremonies held at the beginning and end of each semester, which are held separately from the entrance and graduation ceremonies. After the second semester, children also have a spring break for about 10 days before the new school year begins in April.

Among the special activities that occur during the school year are a day trip, a sports festival, 2- to 3-day field trips for upper grades, a summer camp, a summer festival, open house/classroom, and presentations of projects children have worked on during the school year. These activities, including entrance and graduation ceremonies, are part of the "special educational activities" determined in the National Curriculum Standard developed by the Ministry of Education (2008). The intention is to facilitate children's development not only through formal classroom instruction but also through their various experiences throughout the school year.

The National Curriculum Standard was developed based on The Fundamental Law of Education and The School Education Law, which are the two basic laws regarding public education in Japan (Ministry of Education, 2008). According to the National Curriculum Standard for Elementary Schools, the purposes of these group activities are "to promote children's balanced development of mind and body as well as personality, to facilitate the voluntary and practical attitudes towards better lives and interpersonal relationships as group members, and to cultivate children's abilities to think about their own lives and to make the best use of self" (p. 112). Accordingly, children are encouraged not only to enjoy these activities but also to think about their own goals in participating in them and reflect on what they have learned.

A parent–teacher conference is scheduled each semester. Classroom teachers meet with parents of children individually after school. Once a year, during the first semester, classroom teachers also visit the homes of all children in their classrooms. In addition, there are "Open Classrooms" scheduled several times a year, where parents are free to observe classrooms during instruction. Typically, this open classroom is scheduled in the afternoon and is followed by a group, parents–teacher meeting after children go home. These are usually exciting events for children. They look forward to their teachers' home visits and to seeing their parents at school. As a child, Misa also looked forward to home visits and waited excitedly for her classroom teacher. When children see their own mothers and other parents they know at school before class, they run to parents to say hello. Even during lessons, some children look toward the back of the classroom and wave to their parents.

Greenleaf Elementary School's Unique Educational Environment

Children's days at school follow a similar schedule across schools, and every school has similar annual events, such as entrance and graduation ceremonies, field trips, and a sports festival. These activities also reflect the unique educational environments and characteristics of each school. Within the framework determined by the National Curriculum Standard and the local board of education, educational practices at each school are modified and adjusted to meet the unique expectations and characteristics of the community in which the school is located, including available community resources. At Greenleaf Elementary School, the principal's emphasis on special education and close relationships with the community create a supportive environment for children with disabilities.

Neighborhood

Greenleaf Elementary School is located in a traditional residential and agri-
cultural community. The area this school serves is divided into several areas
organized by neighborhood associations, and most families belong to the
organization of the area in which they live. The neighborhood associations
support the school in several ways, for example, by assisting in planning
and organizing a summer festival at the school ground. People living in the
neighborhood also support the school individually. They are frequently invited
as guest teachers to teach skills such as growing vegetables. The principal
described the community:

> This neighborhood is spacious and has enough room...so, it is called
> a special agricultural district. Within this ward [of the city], this school
> serves the widest area and has the second smallest number of children.
> So, there are families of farmers going back three or four generations,
> and this kind of area may not be common in this city. These fami-
> lies are like...living with great grandfather and great grandmother,
> and grandfather and grandmother. [Children are] watching what they
> [adults] do, such as farming, growing something or things like that.
> And also because they've been living with these older people who have
> seen many children different from one another and who have lived
> through various historical events, they are able to accept a wide range
> [of human characteristics]...[They know] there are many different
> types of people, or something good at this moment may not always be
> good in the future, or like that. [They are] very open-minded (kanyou).
> This is because [they] have experiences...There is a relatively wide
> range [of ways of thinking]. It is something like we are together, doing
> something together peacefully (nakayoku).

Before urbanization of cities in Japan, intergenerational interactions were
common in Japanese communities not only within families but also between
residents in the community. Recently, however, children have less opportunity to interact with other people in their community. The principal described
such a community.

> I think, in newly developed areas, they are all the same nuclear
> families [living in] their houses [which all look alike], and they are
> narrow-minded, like thinking that children have to study hard and
> efficiently, otherwise, there is no future for them...If living in a place
> where neighbors and parents are all like this, the way of looking at

[children] can be focused, and it is like a multiplier effect...It is true that the civilization goes to the extreme, and there are [parents who] have never talked to children living in the next door of the same condominium [or apartment complex].

However, within the community in which Greenleaf Elementary School is located:

There are many people including elders, and the way of looking at things is kind of "multi-layered."...And also, it's very open. We are in the same place in terms of raising children together, collaboratively...[this neighborhood] is like, when [adults are] working in the farm and [find children walking and say], "Are you coming home?" It's open. If it is open, things can be dangerous, but, it is surprising that there are very few suspicious persons. It looks like they can't come in. I think so.

Collaboration With the Community: Raising Children Together

One of the unique characteristics of Greenleaf Elementary School is that people from the community, including children's parents, frequently come to the school and work as volunteers. They read books in classrooms, teach children how to use computers, assist in the supervision of children on field trips, and help children grow vegetables in the school garden.[4] To raise the level of educational quality, the local board of education started a city-wide program, so that schools can try out new approaches in public education to better educate children in contemporary society. Each school participating in the program has specific themes, including utilization of community resources, English education, and science education. Considering a history of accepting volunteers from the community, a goal of Greenleaf Elementary School is to establish and strengthen an organization coordinating and utilizing resources in the community to teach children. As a result, in collaboration with a team of parents called "Team Greenleaf," educators began establishing a system to utilize parent volunteers who have teacher certifications or other specific skills and experiences during instructional periods[5].

In the brochure that the school distributed to children's families and residents in the community, Team Greenleaf was defined as a group operated by parents to create a learning environment for raising mentally and physically healthy children in collaboration with families, the school, and the community. The team has worked at the school on many occasions. In 2009, the team opened an office within the school building and established a system to provide efficient support for teachers. Parents and residents in the community who are willing to participate are invited to sign up for membership. Once teachers place requests to the team, team members and teachers discuss how to make them happen (e.g., how many parents teachers need on what day), and the team members who work at the office match and assign members from the list containing each member's interest, specialty, and availability.

During Misa's participant observations, several classrooms began inviting parents through Team Greenleaf to assist in Math and Japanese Language classes. For example, when teaching the concept of "weight" in Math, third grade teachers decided to use parent volunteers to help children weigh various items from pens and erasers to school bags and to choose an appropriate scale on which to weigh them. Children frequently got confused reading the scales correctly, writing "g" or "Kg," and understanding that weight can be added and subtracted. Children completed these activities in two weeks, working with the same five mothers four times a week.

To demonstrate collaboration between teachers and parents, the fifth lesson on weights was opened to parents and educators of other schools. Comments and reflections from teachers during a debriefing after their classroom observations included, "Children are able to get immediate attention when they need it, which minimizes children retaining incorrect information," "Children can learn a lot through these activities," "I couldn't see who was a teacher," and "It's impossible to have this much variety of activities if there is only one teacher." Parent volunteers also suggested that they were able to "raise" other parents who observed parents working with children who were not their own. Children seemed to enjoy working with mothers and called them when they needed help. One teacher stated, "Generally, children like working with adults who get surprised with them when they find something interesting together," and "Such children become adults who like school, where the good memories are, and come back to work together." The assistant principal closed the debriefing meeting by saying, "I don't say 'thank you' to Team Greenleaf, because we are partners in raising children."

Small School Size

The smaller size of Greenleaf Elementary School made it possible to create a "home-" or "family-" like environment. Most teachers know children's faces and their names. When talking about the struggles of certain children during the staff meeting, for example, teachers know who the children are immediately because they have seen and talked to them in the school building. Therefore, one educator described that the children's problems tend to be "our" problems, rather than "their" problems. One teacher even described classroom teachers as "mothers" for children at school. The school and their classrooms are "families," as well as the places to learn academic skills, and children are brothers and sisters.

The close relationships between teachers and children at Greenleaf Elementary School can be seen during the in-school broadcast. As children prepared for their presentations for the Greenleaf Festival, children who were the members of the festival organizing committee visited each classroom during recess with a video camera and a microphone. With teachers' assistance, these members interviewed children regarding what each classroom would present on the festival day and their progress. Each class had decided what to present at the beginning of the school year and prepared for about 8 months. For example, some classes were growing soy beans to make tofu, learning about the community by interviewing people living there, and creating their own movies. Children in the Rainbow Room opened a restaurant using vegetables they grew. During lunch time, children watched the "news show" based on the interviews on a TV monitor in their classrooms. These shows occurred three to four times a week for 2 weeks proceeding the festival day. Each day, two children from the festival committee pretended to be the "announcers" of the news show and presented interviews from two or three classrooms, so that each classroom was featured on the show three times. When Misa watched the show at the staff room, teachers recognized the children in the show immediately and commented about them. Children also enjoyed finding familiar faces in the "TV show" and looked forward to seeing themselves on the show after they had been interviewed.

Children also have many opportunities to work with children in other grades. Each child belongs to a group consisting of children from all grade levels. These groups participate in regularly scheduled activities in which children learn and work together, such as cleaning classrooms and preparing for a school field trip and a sports festival. Two or three times in a month, these groups eat lunch together rather than eating in their own classrooms. When working in these groups, older children take care of younger children; for example, they help first graders get in line to receive their lunches, plan and lead activities during recess, and teach and help younger children to clean their classrooms. For younger children, older children are their "big brothers and sisters" who help them at school. Even second graders recognize themselves as older brothers and sisters for first graders and enjoy introducing their school to first graders who are new to Greenleaf Elementary School. Through these activities, children get to know other children in different grades and learn interpersonal and other skills from one another.

Yet the small school size also can create challenges. For example, the number of teachers available to provide additional support to children at Greenleaf

Elementary School is limited in comparison to larger schools. One classroom teacher who had worked at a larger school noted that she could ask other teachers to listen to children recite multiplication tables, but at Greenleaf Elementary School, teachers were too busy. So, she asked parents to come in to her classroom during recess to listen to children. Even administrators occasionally teach in classrooms as needed.

Social, Emotional, and Moral Education

In addition to academic skills, education at Greenleaf Elementary School, like other schools in Japan, is intended to facilitate children's social, emotional, and moral development. The most recent National Curriculum Standard for Elementary Schools indicates that "moral education" must occur throughout the curriculum, including special activities (Ministry of Education, 2008). Specifically:

> Moral education has to be done in a way that facilitates children's relationships with peers and teachers in collaboration with families and the community through various activities, such as field trips with overnight stays that involve group activities, volunteering, and activities in contact with nature, so that morality within children can grow. (p. 13)

Classroom teachers play an important role in moral education including through their social and emotional support of children. Several teachers specifically discussed the need for a "social skills" program in school and some of them had actually implemented it in their classrooms. Further, the local board of education established social skills training programs. These programs involve activities facilitating self-awareness, interpersonal skills, and collaboration in groups. Social skills education may be provided in classrooms, or children may be pulled out from general education classrooms for individualized instruction, depending on their needs.

Regardless of the setting, teachers commonly suggested that social, emotional, and moral education[6] be provided in a way that children can learn naturally through their daily lives or everyday experiences at school. For example, teachers can give immediate feedback when a child misbehaves, use activities such as field trips to teach children how to behave in public, have a classroom assistant who can help children behave and listen to lessons without becoming distracted, and use actual events in which the child has participated as case scenarios during individual discussions. The following excerpt from Misa's field note describes how Aoki *sensei*, Kakeru's classroom teacher, Sakai *sensei*, and his parents worked together to teach him social skills.

In the Challenge Room, Sakai *sensei* read to Kakeru an account prepared by Aoki *sensei* describing an incident at lunchtime when he threw beans from his minestrone soup on the floor. Then she read questions prepared by Aoki *sensei*. The first question asked Kakeru what he will do next time there is food he doesn't like at lunch. His answer was, "Throw it!"... Sakai *sensei* read the next questions,

SAKAI SENSEI: Do you throw [food you don't like] at home?

KAKERU: No, because my daddy is scary.

SAKAI SENSEI: Only at school?

KAKERU: Yes.

SAKAI SENSEI: What do you think about other children? What do they think?

KAKERU: They don't care.

SAKAI SENSEI: Do you have rules for eating at home?

KAKERU: Don't use my hands to eat. I used hands to eat, but now I am using a fork and a spoon and chopsticks.

After Kakeru left, Sakai *sensei* wrote comments to his parents and Aoki *sensei* on a "communication notebook[7]" they were exchanging on a regular basis to share their observations of Kakeru (Excerpt from Misa's field note).

Kakeru's classroom teacher, Sakai *sensei,* and his parents collaborated to encourage Kakeru to reflect on his behavior and remember the rules. When Misa ate lunch with Kakeru and other children in the Rainbow Room the following school year, Aoki *sensei* reminded Kakeru, "Do you remember the rules we made last year? We still have them."

More broadly, the principal discussed during the teachers' meeting the importance of raising children through activities such as the Greenleaf Festival, where students presented what they had learned to other children and their parents. This is consistent with what is written in the National Curriculum Standard that children's learning occurs within and outside of classroom activities, including classroom discussions led by children and special activities (Ministry of Education, 2008).

Teachers also described moral education to facilitate children's self-awareness and acquisition of basic rules and social skills. For example, Misa observed Kawai *sensei* teaching moral education in her third grade classroom. She read the class a story of a boy who was expecting a visitor while his mother was not at home. He was told by his mother to stay at home and give a packet to the visitor, but while waiting, his friends came and asked him to play. While playing with his friends, the visitor arrived and waited for him to return. Kawai *sensei* facilitated a discussion of how the boy and the visitor felt, and what the boy could have done differently.

However, some teachers criticized moral education as superficial. One teacher suggested that children might be able to better understand if they talked about themselves, rather than people in stories. In general, teachers preferred to create opportunities for children to learn social skills in their daily lives. For example, Nagai *sensei* explained:

> Children have experiences since they are very little that people are thinking like this in this kind of situation, or people usually do this or that in this kind of situation, although they may not notice [that they are learning]. They see, "That's obvious" or "Not surprising!" ... There are children who don't see things that are "obvious." So, I keep trying to find the best time to teach children [these skills] and I know I definitely have to teach them, but actually I don't have time [to do so].

The principal also shared a discussion with other principals during a workshop:

> Social skills are not determined in the curriculum currently [in contrast to moral education], so, [we] have to use moral education, classroom activities, and Japanese Language. Even if a child who needs to learn more social skills is identified and pulled out to teach social skills, [we] have to pull the child out during Japanese Language.[8] This is what [we] have to think about [and make changes] to provide better support.

Educating Children in Groups

In the "home-like" educational environment of Greenleaf Elementary School, children are expected to learn social and academic skills naturally. Children's peer groups are viewed as an important educational context, and educators utilize peer relationships as a tool to teach academic and interpersonal skills. The principal stated, "Japanese education has valued [teaching children] in groups efficiently, while having a high degree of freedom ... to take account of children's individual needs. It's a balance..."

Peer Membership

Interactions with others, including peers and educators, are regarded as a central part of children's "school lives," and context for accomplishing academic, social, and moral goals. The National Curriculum Standard for Elementary Schools identifies academic skills, moral education, and physical education and health as the three basic components of elementary education (Ministry of Education, 2008)[9].

Given these educational goals, teachers tend to prioritize children's functioning in groups, especially when children are in general education classrooms. They expect children to learn interpersonal as well as academic skills through their daily interactions with peers. As one teacher explained:

In general education classrooms, because [we have to follow] the curriculum, [the instruction] should be like letting children think of various way to solve problems and complete tasks together with other children. For example, if there is a wall [in front of children], they will try anything they can think of [to go to the other side] from their own experiences, such as going up a ladder, using a rope, or making stairs. A teacher's responsibility is to facilitate discussion so children can come up with the best way. I think math instruction is very close to this.

One teacher described group dynamics as facilitating children's abilities to solve problems by themselves independently of the teacher. Another teacher provided an example:

Being in a general education classroom means [children are in] groups. Learning interpersonal skills through living in a group is, as you know, important, and when interacting [with someone], we need certain rules, so [we have to] let children learn [these rules] in general education classrooms. And actually children learn by doing so.

Of course, within their groups children also worked independently to some extent, and teachers did attend to individual children. One teacher described her relationships with children in general education classrooms, "It is more like I have thirty one-to-one relationships rather than one-to-thirty [as a group]. I also look at the whole class." Another teacher further elaborated on how he managed children's behaviors within his classroom as a group:

It was really hard when there were three children, who had different [strong] characteristics, in one classroom. They reacted to each other perfectly [laughing]...[description of each of these three children]. It wasn't like they drew back from each other and became quiet, but it was like a multiplier effect. They tattled on each other for every little thing, saying, "He is doing this" or like that, and also, you know, physically fighting, like pushing one another down or pinching. It got noisy, and I couldn't continue instruction. Therefore, I assigned them desks where they couldn't see each other, or placed them where they could only see the blackboard.

Group dynamics are also used in special education classrooms, where educators pay attention to children's individual needs more so than in general education classrooms. Several teachers discussed that even if children have disabilities, they should be educated in groups.

Children Who Do Not Fit in Groups

Although peer group membership has an important function in children's lives at school, it can be a burden for some children who have problems in relationships with other children. Teachers described some children as "children who are not able to learn in groups," or "children who do not fit in with 'group life.' " For children who are struggling with interpersonal skills, unsupervised periods, such as 20-minute recesses, can be especially challenging. Sano *sensei*, the school nurse, described children who were not involved in peer groups during recess.

> Some people don't like a school nurse's room like this and say, "What's this room?" and ask me, "Can children come in during recess without any notes from teachers?" Well, but, I say, "Isn't it fine, because it's during the recess?" You know, in classrooms during recess, there are kids who can't find a place to belong and they are suffering. So, it's ok that these kids come here and play, sit, listen to the music, or measure their height. Anyway, during that time, they have something to do...Only these kids who are here care about what other children think. Other children don't think something like sorry for not having friends to play with, but kids here are worrying that their peers may think, "I don't have friends and they think I am an unhappy kid." So, I want to make this room a place where children can spend time without feeling like that. There are books, games, and music. I think this is fine, too.

At Greenleaf Elementary School, several children, including two of our participant children, Yusuke and Dai, were frequently absent because of interpersonal problems with other children. The increasing number of such children has been recognized as a problem in Japan. In Riverside City, there are programs for children with attendance problems, including home visiting by a teacher. Several schools also have classrooms for children who have attendance problems, which are open to children with similar problems in other schools within the city. Many schools also make rooms, such as a counseling room, available for these children so that they can come to school and study, even if they do not go to their classrooms. In many cases, children have to stay at the rooms alone or with their parents and work on worksheets without receiving instruction from teachers. In contrast, educators at Greenleaf Elementary School arranged teaching assistants to work with Yusuke and Dai and provided them with the Challenge Room. These children studied at the Challenge Room, played during recess, and visited their own classrooms as needed with teaching assistants.

Contexts of Support for Children With Special Needs

It is generally the responsibility of classroom teachers to teach and provide support for children struggling in general education classrooms. When children continue to have difficulties in general education classrooms, they may be pulled out several hours a week for small group or individual instruction. Greenleaf Elementary School hired a part-time teacher, Sakai *sensei,* who was a former classroom teacher, to teach children individually or in small groups once a week at the Challenge Room, a special support room. If children need further assistance, then parents as well as educators begin to consider placing them in the Rainbow Room for individual, special education services. If the school cannot meet their needs, then children may receive special education part-time at resource rooms located in another local elementary school.

When talking to children, educators as well as parents referred to the special education classroom and the special support room by their room names, either the Rainbow or Challenge Rooms. Resource rooms also are named— for example, "Classroom for Speaking and Hearing" and "Support Room for *Manabi* (learning)." Parents may or may not know the official names of these rooms. For example, one parent asked Misa, what was a "special education classroom?" When Misa told her it was the Rainbow Room, she understood immediately.

Classroom-Based Support

Greenleaf Elementary School utilizes teaching assistants to help classroom teachers in general education classrooms, a practice not necessarily common in other Japanese schools. Teaching assistants are usually college students taking courses required to obtain teacher certifications, retired teachers, and other individuals the administrators consider having professional knowledge and experiences to work with children. In addition, the local board of education has a volunteer program for college students who want experience in working with children. After individual interviews, volunteer students are registered and sent to schools as teaching assistants. They receive about $10 per day for travel expenses.

Teaching assistants' responsibilities vary and might include working with certain children individually, answering students' questions during group or individual activities, and assisting teachers during instruction and classroom management. They come to school from 1 day to several days a week. Sano *sensei*, the special education coordinator, supervises teaching assistants and assigns them to classrooms that need assistance. On a whiteboard located on the back side of the staff room, there is a space where classroom teachers post weekly schedules of their classrooms. If they have a request for assistance, then they put notes indicating the day and class period they need teaching assistants. Unless teachers have posted a request, Sano *sensei* assigns teaching assistants to classrooms primarily during Math and Japanese Language classes.

Beginning in July 2010, Greenleaf Elementary School began a project in collaboration with the local board of education and several other schools to establish a system for utilizing teaching assistants. Volunteer teaching assistants who have completed training programs offered by the board of education are assigned to work with a certain classroom, so that they can work with the same classroom teacher and children in a consistent manner, rather than being assigned to classrooms randomly. They are paid about $30 a day to cover transportation cost and other expenses.

In addition, Greenleaf Elementary School hired part-time teachers to work in a first grade classroom, co-teaching with a classroom teacher on a daily basis. The classroom teacher oversaw the whole classroom, and the support teacher worked with individual children who needed assistance academically or with daily skills such as organization of personal materials and maintaining relationships with peers. Sakai *sensei*, who taught at the Challenge Room, also went to general education classrooms to assist classroom teachers when no children were scheduled to study with her.

Classroom teachers also may provide individual support in their classrooms, during recess, or after school. For example, teachers may work with children who are behind to complete assigned tasks during one of the 20-minute recesses. One teacher also reported studying after school with a child who needed one-on-one assistance.

Instruction at the Challenge Room

When children need assistance individually or in small groups, they are pulled out of their general education classrooms to study with Sakai *sensei*, who works 1 day a week. She primarily teaches Math and Japanese Language in the Challenge Room, a special support room. Children come to see Sakai *sensei* once or twice on the day she comes, depending on their needs and their classroom schedules.

Children are usually identified by classroom teachers, but parents also can make a request independently for their children to receive support at the Challenge Room. According to Sano *sensei,* the school used to require documentation from the local board of education, which arranges for formal assessments of children's academic and social functioning and evaluates their eligibility to receive special education services. Currently, the only requirement for this support at the Challenge Room is parental permission. The school keeps "assessment sheets" for each child receiving support at the Challenge Room, but it is the classroom teachers' responsibility to evaluate and inform parents of children's progress, usually in report cards.

Individualized Special Education Services

If children need more intensive support, then they study in special education classrooms. In Riverside City, three types of special education classrooms are available in general public schools: classrooms for children with intellectual disabilities, with autism-emotional disorders, and with visual impairments. Schools are "allowed" to create any of these classrooms if children with corresponding disabilities attend the schools. Children with autism-emotional disorders at Greenleaf Elementary School are taught by two teachers in the Rainbow Room. Children who study at the Rainbow Room also maintain their seats in their grade level-appropriate general education classrooms where they participate as much as possible.

Several schools in Riverside City also have resource rooms that provide part-time special education services for children attending nearby schools. Four types of resource rooms are available in this city, specifically, for children with visual impairments, hearing impairments, language disabilities, and emotional disorders. These children typically attend their own schools but periodically attend other schools with specialized resource rooms. In such cases, parents are required to take their children to the resource rooms in other schools and bring them back to their schools after the class. Similar to special education classrooms, children who study at the resource rooms also have individualized education programs. One of the participant children, Yusuke, goes to a resource room once a week for his speech problems.

Eligibility

To receive instruction in resource rooms and special education classrooms such as the Rainbow Room, children must obtain documentation from the local board of education suggesting that they need individualized support. Classroom teachers work with a special education coordinator to identify children who may need more intensive support and suggest to their parents that their children may need to be assessed at the local board of education. Parents are also able to initiate a communication with the board of education directly when they observe that their children are struggling. Before a child is placed in a special education classroom, parents meet with educators working with the child, such as general education classroom teachers, special education classroom teachers, administrators, and a special education coordinator. These individuals are informed of the reasons why the child should be placed in a special education classroom and how the child can benefit.

Once a child is placed in a special education classroom, the child officially transfers from the general education classroom, even if the child keeps his or her seat in the general education classroom. Before officially transferring to the Rainbow Room, children may study there until they, their parents, and educators determine that the special education classroom is the best fit. For example, Yusuke and Dai studied at the Rainbow Room for more than a semester before completing the paperwork to officially place them in special education. At Greenleaf Elementary School, once a child is transferred to the Rainbow Room, an individualized education program is created, primarily by classroom teachers and approved by parents.

When a child has a diagnosis that requires additional support before starting first grade, it is a parent's responsibility to communicate with the principal of a local school and/or a special education school and the local board of education regarding the child's placement. They discuss which school is the best fit for the child—either a general or a special education school—and whether the child will be placed in a special education classroom.

Discussion

Elementary education in Japan is broadly conceived to encompass academic, social, emotional, and moral development, and designed to occur in a range of academic and non-academic contexts. Non-academic contexts include daily activities such as lunch time, cleaning classrooms and recesses. They also include important annual events—notably, sports and school learning festivals—in which children are involved for extended periods: planning, preparing, participating in, and reflecting on what they have learned. These contexts and activities are viewed as central to children's socialization. Lunchtime, for example, is referred to by the Ministry of Education (2008) as *shoku-iku*, which is literally translated as "eat and raise." Children who serve meals learn personal responsibility for other children waiting for lunch, and children waiting learn and understand the demands of serving meals. Because children experience both roles, they learn to cooperate with one another, which facilitates stronger interpersonal relationships. In addition, children learn the proper way to eat at school, including rituals (*itadaki-masu* and *gochiso-sama deshita*) before and after eating, that also are performed at home on a daily basis (Mansfield, 2000; Tsuneyoshi, 1994). Children learn to apply what they already know from the informal setting of home to the official setting of school (Dyson, 2003). Lunchtime, as well as cleaning time, at a Japanese school is on the borderline between children's official and unofficial worlds, and teachers actively participate in teaching children skills for their "unofficial" world.

In this chapter, we have begun our discussion of how Japanese educational policies, beliefs, and practices are instantiated in the everyday activities at Greenleaf Elementary School. Here, the daily schedules, special activities, focus on collaboration, and emphasis on social, emotional, and moral education may facilitate acceptance of children's individual differences, including "disabilities." Educators as well as children establish close relationships, not only within the same grade level but also across grade levels. A home-like environment is created, with older children serving as big brothers and sisters of younger children, and teachers as the "mothers" of children at school. White (1987) and Walsh (2004) also noticed the roles of "older brothers and sisters" in Japanese schools and observed that these relationships provided children with a sense of family at school. Children in this educational environment have many opportunities to interact with their peers with disabilities, which can facilitate their awareness and acceptance of their peers with special needs.

The emphasis on learning within peer groups can result in strong, mutually supportive bonds between classmates. On the other hand, for some children, "being alone is what I like the most" (Hosaka, 2005, p. 294). At Greenleaf Elementary School, there were children who tended to be isolated from peers, and as we will discuss in Chapters 6 and 7, several children even developed a fear of school and interacting with their peers.

Educators responded to children's interpersonal challenges with flexibility. For example, Sano *sensei* opened her office during recess for children who did not fit in groups and who may have been in trouble interpersonally. In her office, children could play games, read a book, talk with others, or just have a place to be during recess. Recess is the most flexible period of the day. If children who have difficulties with peers can deal with free time during recess, then they may be able to handle the rest of the day, which involves structured activities. For these children, the school nurse's office works as an important resource.

Educators also responded flexibly and with sensitivity to the social implications of children's struggles—for example, those arising from their disabilities. As we will discuss in Chapter 7, educators made the Challenge Room available for Yusuke and Dai, who were struggling with peer relationships and with academic instruction in their general education classrooms. Only after the children and their parents had accepted the need for special education were they transferred to the Rainbow Room. From an outsider perspective, the initial placement of Dai and Yusuke in the Challenge Room, rather than the Rainbow Room, delayed their timely receipt of appropriate support for their disabilities. To understand the Japanese educators' flexibility in providing support, in Chapter 5 we examine parents' and educators' responses to children's disabilities and special education focusing on educators' support of parents.

Notes

1. Most schools across the city serve a certain area around the school, but several have opened their schools to children living outside of the schools' attendance boundary to introduce new teaching strategies. At Greenleaf Elementary School, up to 10 children from outside its attendance boundary within a 1-hour commute can enroll in each grade level. During our study, several families from outside of the Greenleaf Elementary attendance area chose to enroll their children because of the support provided for children with developmental disabilities.
2. *Itadaki-masu* and *Gochisou-sama-deshita* are ritual words Japanese people use before and after eating meals.
3. Each local board of education makes a decision whether to follow a two- or three-semester schedule. Greenleaf Elementary School follows a two-semester schedule.
4. To maintain children's confidentiality, people from the community who have personal relationships with children outside of school are not invited during instructional activities, such as Math and Japanese Language, in which children's varying levels of achievement and understanding are clear.
5. To invite Team Greenleaf to instructional periods, educators and team members worked together and created a protocol to protect children's personal information.

6. Educators may refer to "moral education," narrowly, as classroom instruction using a textbook for moral education containing stories for children to think about and discuss various moral issues.

7. In Japanese elementary schools, parents and teachers use "communication note-books" to share concerns and other information about a child. For example, if the child felt unwell the previous evening, a parent might write a note to teachers that he might not focus well during classes and would not be able to participate in a PE class.

8. She described the reasons social skills are taught in Japanese Language class. It is not typical to pull children out from general education classrooms to teach social skills. When children are pulled out, it usually is for Math or Japanese Language instruction. In addition, social skills programs developed by the local board of education are mainly for facilitating communication skills and interpersonal relationships. Therefore, Japanese Language that focuses on children's ability to speak and express themselves is a logical choice for social skills training.

9. Under these guidelines, the Riverside City board of education established goals in five areas of children's development: learning, respect, life/health, [contribution to] the public, and openness [to others]. Greenleaf Elementary School developed its own more specific goals. They aim for children to (1) grow up healthy mentally as well as physically; (2) meet with people, question, and learn; (3) interact, deepen, and try what they have learned; (4) acknowledge what is good in others and learn from one another; and (5) learn and participate in the community.

5 HOW EDUCATORS SUPPORT THE PARENTS OF CHILDREN WITH DEVELOPMENTAL DISABILITIES

Playground after school

Yusuke's mother reflected on the support she received from educators when her child refused to attend school. "Everyone, teachers here at this school helped us, and we became able to see Yusuke smile, naturally. Therefore, we were able to get through this... Because they helped us, I was able to switch... how I feel [about Yusuke's extended period of absence and disability]... I used to feel ashamed of [him] or tried to hide, but I don't have that kind of feelings any more... He is just a good child, normal, and making an effort, even harder than me. I'm proud of him... I really appreciate this school and Yusuke. I learned a lot from them.... Because Yusuke found his place [in the Challenge and Rainbow Rooms], I don't think any more that we should let him go back to his general education classroom. Like him, I have to find my own *Ibasho* [place to belong]. Yusuke already has begun to go forward, so I also have to do so."

As described in Chapter 3, the Japanese government recently implemented a formal system of individualized, special education for children with developmental disabilities. Children's support outside of general education classrooms, however, poses challenges to parents. Before children with developmental disabilities can receive these new "services," their parents must accept their needs for "special" support and then grant permission for that individualized support. Yusuke's mother was not the only one who struggled. She described Dai's mother: "Right now, [she] keeps many many things [to herself], and is fighting too much anxiety, because she doesn't know how to do. I feel that [when I see her] I'm looking at myself, the way I used to be." Many parents are reluctant to expose their children's differences to other people's "eyes" by involving them in support different from that received by their peers. For them, their children's "difference" can be a source of stigma. One outcome of parents' concerns about stigma may be that some children do not receive the support they need to succeed and enjoy their lives at school in a timely manner.

Despite the opportunities created by the new special education system, only a limited number of children are actually receiving services outside of their general education classrooms. In 2005, before the formal implementation of special education for children with developmental disabilities, 1.74% of Japanese children from first through ninth grades received special education services either at resource rooms, special education classrooms, or special education schools (Ministry of Education, 2006g). In 2011, 4 years after the implementation of the new system, this percentage increased to 2.7%. As expected, this increase in support occurred primarily in general public schools—specifically, in resource rooms (0.36%–0.6%) and special education classrooms (0.89%–1.5%) (Ministry of Education, 2012a). Nevertheless, the percentage of Japanese children receiving *any* type of special education remains substantially smaller than one would expect. Nationwide, in 2002, Japanese general education classroom teachers of first through ninth grades identified 6.3% of the children in their classes as exhibiting academic or behavioral difficulties suggestive of developmental disabilities[1] (Ministry of Education, 2002a). In the United States, 4.78% of children between the ages of 6 to 17 years received special education in 2008 under the category of specific learning disabilities[2] (Data Accountability Center, 2012), a subcategory of conditions considered by the Japanese educators to be "developmental disabilities."

There may be many reasons for the relatively small percentage of Japanese children receiving special education services, such as the yet limited availability of resources. Another reason may be adults' concerns with stigmatization. In our interviews and informal conversations, many educators and parents expressed hesitation about placing children whose disabilities are not apparent in special education classrooms, in part, because of their concerns about stigmatization. Educators discussed parents' preferences for their children to receive additional support in general education classrooms. Even parents who understood their children's disabilities expressed their struggles to accept their children's needs for additional support and granting permission for them to receive such support. At Greenleaf Elementary School, as of July 2009, there were about 20 children (approximately 10% of the student population) whom specialists at the local board of education had assessed and recommended receive additional support including special education services. Only a few of these children, however, were actually receiving formal, individualized support outside of their classrooms. Indeed, when Misa asked the principal to refer potential participants for this study, she was only able to identify four children in general education classrooms[3] whose parents had accepted their children's "difficulties" or "disabilities."

In this chapter we will focus on (1) the role of parents in supporting the school functioning of children with developmental disabilities; (2) the challenges parents experience in placing their children in special education, including any role of stigma; and (3) how educators support parents' acceptance of their children's developmental disabilities and need for special education services.

Parents' Role in Supporting the Education of Children With Developmental Disabilities

Parents' Attitudes and Involvement in School

At Greenleaf Elementary School, educators described themselves as partners with parents in "raising" children. Indeed, within the traditional residential and farming community, Greenleaf Elementary School is known as a "school of the community." As described in Chapter 4, parents and other community members routinely visit the school as guest teachers and in other volunteer roles.

Many educators clearly emphasized the importance of parents' attitudes toward their children's developmental disabilities and school, especially when children are young and emotionally close to them. The principal explained,

"If the parent–child relationship becomes difficult, it has a great impact on children, their lives and development...so this is what concerns me most." Sano *sensei* explained:

> As I'm telling you many times, in elementary schools, mothers and children are very close, so if a mother feels she doesn't like this person or this place, the child senses it quickly and thinks that they should do the same way, unconsciously though...

Several educators described how Dai's mother's reactions to his disability and school negatively impacted his adjustment to school. One teacher explained: "In this case, his mother's anxiety has affected [him] largely...Something that she tells him gives him the same anxiety she has at the same time." Misa's field notes described the struggles of Dai's mother in her relationships with his teachers. Her reactions—for example, that Misa report to her if she saw a teacher forcing Dai to do something he did not want to do—were perceived by teachers as emotional and defensive, which made communication between them difficult. As a result of the tension between his mother and teachers, Dai did not receive consistent support at home and school, and he struggled throughout his third grade year.

In contrast, several educators described parents who understood and accepted their children's special needs. These attitudes facilitated educators' and parents' abilities to work together to provide children with appropriate services. The principal, who had previously taught children in special education classrooms, explained:

> [Some parents] don't view [the disability] as a handicap, but think about how [their children can] function with their difficulties while living in society...They are very positive and enjoy life [with their children] and also come to school to work together.

Another teacher described her collaboration with parents.

> When parents have already accepted their children's disabilities, I will ask them what they want...I can learn the details of what the children are like ahead of time, so there is no problem dealing with [their disabilities] or misunderstandings, because I can accept the children, as they really are, and I know how to take care of [problems caused by their disabilities].

Kakeru's parents accepted his needs and were willing to talk with teachers about the additional support he needed. They even requested that he receive instruction part-time at the Rainbow Room and initiated a meeting with the principal. The assistant principal described:

> Kakeru's mother is looking at [her child's special needs] very flat [without any biases], and also encourages Kakeru and tells him that the Rainbow Room is a place for children who are very good at one thing, meaning a place for children who are excellent. But of course, there are individual differences and honestly, his mother is not typical, I think.

Kakeru's father recognized that he needed different types of support to learn than his typically developing peers. He explained:

> [Kakeru's way of learning] is not obvious [like other children who are developing typically]. How much experience [he needs to learn] is very [different from other children]... Children like him don't have a sort of intuition, and don't [learn certain things as we learn] automatically... It's really hard to learn these skills "manually." [Before teaching him], we try to analyze what we do automatically.

Unlike Kakeru's parents, some disagreed among themselves about their children's disabilities and needs. Several educators and parents emphasized the importance of family members working together to support the child. A classroom teacher shared her experience:

> Mothers [usually] have more chances to come to school, so this mother had noticed that her child didn't fit in groups, looked a little bit different from other kids. But the child's father and grandparents definitely didn't admit it, saying the child's father was just like that when he was little, but he grew up to be an adult, an excellent employee of a company. So, there is no problem. Like this, it's not unusual that there is a disagreement between parents.

Yusuke's mother described her family:

> His father didn't understand Yusuke's problems at school, because he hadn't seen what Yusuke was like all day long and also didn't want to admit that his child was like that, so what he said was things like,

"He looks normal," or, "Why disability?" So, we couldn't get along, and Yusuke had seen us arguing and said, "I wish I wasn't born," or a lot more, so I can't apologize to him enough.

Over the year this family was struggling, Yusuke's parents received support from educators at school. For example, a teacher described to his father how hard Yusuke and his mother had been working, and helped him to understand the needs of his child. His mother also described the support she received from educators:

> I really appreciate Sano *sensei*. I don't know how many times I screamed and cried in front of her. I didn't know what I should do. The other day, Sano *sensei* told me she was able to help me, or do something for me because I didn't give up and went to see her. I thought [what I did] wasn't wrong.

After his parents reconciled, Yusuke's attitude began to change.

> [Recently], we got to understand each other, and also he [her husband] is able to listen to me about Yusuke. Since then, we have seen Yusuke smiling naturally. Yeah, honestly, if there is something parents don't understand about each other, children will know, immediately.

Parents' Preferences for Their Children to Participate in General Education Classrooms

Teachers indicated that parents tend to prefer to place their children in general education classrooms, rather than special education classrooms, even after their children have been evaluated and specialists have suggested that they need additional support. Even parents who understood their children's disabilities expressed a desire for their children to "grow up" with typically developing children as long as possible. Some parents chose Greenleaf Elementary School because of its small size and practice of placing children with developmental disabilities in general education classrooms. Dai's mother explained that before her son started first grade, she visited another school near their home. The principal, however, told her that it would not be possible to place him in a general education classroom because of his disability and the large size of the school. The principal of Greenleaf Elementary School at the time was willing to create two small first grade classrooms and work with her to place Dai in a general education classroom[4]. Dai was able to keep up with his peers in the small first and second grade classrooms. Kakeru's mother also discussed the advantage of a small school during the interview.

> Schools, as you know, in Japan, or more exactly, near here, they tend to see children using IQ, especially in a large school. Larger schools tend to see that way. Even in special education classrooms, for example, it is common that special education classrooms in large schools have more students...so each child is one of many children. Then, they have two classrooms, two kinds, for "autism-emotional disorders" and "intellectual disabilities", and they say there is no problem, but there is no "*Ibasho* [a place where children feel a sense of belonging, safety and acceptance]" for children who don't fit in the categories perfectly and are on the borderline... If he was in that large school, to tell the truth, I thought it would hurt his pride [self-esteem/self-respect], and he would not be able to receive appropriate support, as teachers said. We were sure that he would not go to the [large] school everyday smiling. So, here, in this small school, we thought we'd give it a try for a year... We are still lucky there is this school, letting us do like this, within one hour walk from our place.

Stigma As a Challenge to Parents' Support of Children With Developmental Disabilities

Henken: *Discriminative Views in Society*

Some parents reacted to the stigma of disability by denying and hiding their children's problems. For example, Dai's mother accepted the medical diagnosis of his disability and understood that the "label" could help him to receive support. Yet she and educators viewed the support Dai needed differently. It took nearly a year for Dai's mother to accept that by third grade he required individual attention outside of his peer group. Even after he began studying at the Challenge Room, she preferred that he study in his general education classroom as much as possible because studying at the Challenge Room made him "different" from peers.

Teachers provided several related reasons why it may be difficult for parents to accept their children's needs for specialized services, including discrimination and *henken* (negatively biased views, prejudice, stigma) toward individuals with disabilities, concern with what other people may think (*seken-tei*), and because the children do not appear different from other children—for example, "They look just like normal." In other words, children who appear to be "normal" should not be labeled as "disabled," which has negative meanings in society.

Teachers and parents described *henken* toward individuals with disabilities in society. The assistant principal observed that we all have discriminatory thoughts, consciously or unconsciously. "No one can say, 'I don't have it.'" Likewise, Kakeru's father explained:

> I also have *henken*, honestly, so, for example, if other people have *henken*, there is nothing wrong [or unusual that they have such biased ideas], and this is a thing like in a society, growing up in the society. So if I meet with someone [who has a stigmatizing condition], I would have *henken*. So if someone has *henken* toward my son, I can't blame them...

Several teachers specifically described the impact of negative associations with disability on children's concepts of self, for example, "What parents are concerned about is that children would think about themselves negatively because they have disabilities." Kakeru's parents explained how they socialized their son to understand and respond to *henken*:

> FATHER: I can't run together with him [and protect my son] all the time...so, I want him to learn a sort of sense of self, like he has to keep fighting to live without being influenced by *henken* toward him in this society.
> MOTHER: I want to teach him [about how to deal with *henken*], and want him to be strong.

Henken also can result in parents' feelings of shame that their children are different from other children. When Yusuke refused to come to school in fourth grade, his mother struggled to accept that he was not a "normal" child any more. Once she accepted his disability, her way of thinking seemed to change:

> The most important thing I've learned from this is that instead of hiding, why my child is like this or why he is not "normal," I can say right now, "Look at my child!"...I am proud that [I can say that I am proud of my son], and so, I don't feel, "I'm ashamed," or feelings like that anymore.

Dai's mother also discussed the effects of *henken* on her family. She had accepted her son's medical diagnosis but still hoped that he would develop typically in school. He was able to study in general education classrooms in first and second grades, which made it especially difficult for her to admit that he needed additional support in third grade. She explained:

> I didn't think it was necessary to pull him out, because he's been doing well "normally".... *Henken* towards people with autism is still strong, like [people think they are] stupid.... If there is an incident, we often hear [the media] say something like "the darkness of *kokoro* [mental problems]." But it's not like that. If we look at it carefully, it's very clear [what the problem is], but people around that person haven't noticed it, and the secondary and tertiary disabilities are emphasized too much [because problems are misunderstood by others]. I think it's not that difficult to fix the "fundamental" problem [if we understand the real problem]...

Some educators described classroom teachers' values and attitudes, including *henken,* as impacting both parents and children. The principal explained, "It's a culture, so classroom teachers' and educators' way of thinking will influence children growing up [in their classrooms]." Another teacher discussed that *sennyu-kan* (subconscious influence, preconceived notions, or prejudice) expressed by classroom teachers affects what parents think about children who need additional support. This teacher explained:

> It varies, but one of the things is that it depends on the classroom teacher of the year, very much...If [a teacher] explains it [children's difficulties] clearly, it can be understood....last year, the parents in my classroom this year had developed a sense like, "My child is not accepted at all," "[My child is] very behind academically," "My child is the worst," or "The first and the second are this child and that child." I think this was because the [former] classroom teacher had this kind of attitude, otherwise, that many parents wouldn't look at [children] like that. This year, during the Japanese Language classes, many parents came to help, and they said, "[Children in my classroom] can greet us and talk to us properly," or "[They] can be lively [active] like this." So, if there is a chance, it is possible to wipe out the *sennyu-kan* parents have unconsciously...[Indeed], I heard from parents this year, for example, if it was a parent whose child was not able to read and write, she said, "This year, [my child] became able to do homework without being told."

Misa's field notes also described differences in children's attitudes during the second year of her participant observation with different teachers. Those children who had struggled during the previous year came to school happily most days.

Several educators identified a lack of understanding of children's struggles by some educators as a persistent issue in children's receipt of necessary support. For example, Sano *sensei* described one classroom teacher who believes that "equality" means giving all children the same amount of support, and so forth, regardless of their individual needs. In contrast, Sano *sensei* explained her understanding of special education:

> ...everyone has different [abilities], so, if this person needs one, one is enough. It's ok, but if another person needs three to function at the same level, give that person three. If there is a person who doesn't need any, it's ok not to give any, but keep eyes on this person. This is "equality" for me.

Accordingly, educating teachers about special education is one of the important roles for Sano *sensei* as a special education coordinator.

Other People's "Eyes"

Other parents also could be a source of stigma. Some parents were concerned about "other people's eyes." Sano *sensei* described such a mother, "It seems that she doesn't like to talk to me on the 1st floor [hallway], I mean, she looks away, so maybe she doesn't like [other people to find] her talking with me [because they will] find out that her child is different from others." Another teacher listening to this conversation commented, "Parents have a strong network in that class." Yusuke's mother also described her experience with parents of other children in Yusuke's fifth grade classroom:

> The other day, I went to the parents' conference and joined a group of parents of other fifth graders. I hadn't been [in such a place] for a long time. I had a feeling that there was a gap, and then I found that this was what made Yusuke unable to come to school, and I felt sorry that I hadn't noticed it until now. Anyway, there is a distance that makes me unable to enter [the classroom], even if I was willing to. I was very sorry, but I felt I wasn't able to smile and go in to the world of parents of children in the general education classroom. I was really anxious and thought I wanted to run away from there... What is this really? They [other parents] understood but didn't

understand actually. Even though I explain to them, their children are able to come to school everyday, and their children don't have disabilities, so no matter how much I explain to parents of other fifth graders, and even though they say they get it, they don't get it completely. I haven't noticed it until now. Because they were worried about us, I explained to them, seriously...I found the other day, I was explaining to the wrong persons.

These parents showed empathy toward Yusuke and his mother but did not actually understand how they felt. In contrast, she said that she felt easy when she was with parents of children in the Rainbow Room who had had similar experiences and who were able to easily understand one another.

Despite continuing struggles, several educators discussed *henken* toward special education as weakening over time. One teacher explained:

I feel there has been a lot more *henken* in the past. It was called "special classroom (*tokushu*: special; *gakkyu*: classroom)," and I remember there were more children with intellectual disabilities, and there was *henken* because they were in such classrooms. In terms of *henken*, now it is paid attention to very carefully, and children are taught clearly, so it is not automatically considered "special," rather, we tell children that they are studying at the place that is good for them and they are doing the same way as other children, so, in this sense, it is not like children who need "special" or "individual" support are viewed as "different," I think. If children were to keep saying things like that [and emphasize negative aspects of disabilities], then there would be something like a breeding ground for such an idea [*henken*].

Invisible Nature of Developmental Disabilities

Children with developmental disabilities do not appear obviously different from typically developing children. As one parent explained, they "look just like normal." Dai's mother described how difficult it was for her to understand Dai's struggle.

The most difficult thing [for me] to understand was that even though I was told that he was struggling, to me, he didn't appear to be struggling. It took a long time [to understand]. When he went to preschool,

[he] smiled and looked happy. [Specialists] said, "He is working very hard [just] to go to preschool," but I wondered if it was really [true]... Because his facial expression looked happy, it was really difficult to understand that what he looked like and how he actually felt were different.

Teachers also may misunderstand the struggles of children with developmental disabilities, and those misunderstandings may result in negative attributions. Sano *sensei,* the special education coordinator and school nurse, described her observations of children with developmental disabilities and their classroom teachers over 20 years:

I've seen many kids who were experiencing difficulties in "living," or kids who were not able to be understood by classroom teachers, or who were unable to fit in a "square" frame like other kids... [They] may look moody, sulky, grouchy, or disobedient, and as a result, [they are] misunderstood, but it isn't like that. When they look like that, they tend to have problems, and get stuck and can't do anything, but [other people] don't understand... People who become teachers are usually excellent persons, and have lived through without any major problems, so they just behave in a way they get accepted in society. That's why they don't understand why [children with problems] behave like that.

The ambiguities involved in interpreting the struggles of children with developmental disabilities can make it difficult for educators and parents to understand their struggles and determine their best interests. Sano *sensei's* observations also underscore the importance of providing continuing education and guidance to classroom teachers.

Educators' Support and Guidance for Parents of Children With Developmental Disabilities

Given the sensitive nature of disabilities in Japan, educators thoughtfully established their relationships with children's parents. They carefully supported parents through *mimamori,* and they watched over them with empathy/*omoiyari.* The focus of educators' interactions with parents of children with developmental disabilities was steadfastly on emotional support, communication, relationship building, and partnerships with parents. Educators did not attempt to force parents to accept that their children needed additional support. Rather, they provided parents with opportunities that helped them to understand their children's needs, for example, by establishing trusting relationships with them, listening to them, and encouraging them to observe their children at school.

Sano *sensei,* whose responsibility as a special education coordinator includes explaining to parents about the availability of support for their children, described how she would communicate with parents of a child struggling at school:

> I [usually] talk to the classroom teacher [of the child] first, and then ask the teacher to talk with parents and suggest that they may want to stop by my office... but if they decide not to come, I won't keep telling them or chasing or like that. Rather, I'm always trying to be friendly, with an "I care about you!" aura, if I see familiar faces [of parents] in the hallway.

To communicate effectively with parents, it is necessary to develop relationships with family members. One classroom teacher described how Sano *sensei*'s knowledge of family members facilitates communication with parents:

> Sano *sensei* knows everything, not only about the children themselves, but also the children's family environments. If we want to do "special education" at school, we have to get parents' permission...we have to go along with parents...we have to be able to interact [with parents] "naturally," when we find [that children need special education]. And Sano *sensei* knows everything, like that child's mother is such-and-such.

Educators also emphasized the importance of developing trusting relationships with parents. Sano *sensei* explained, "[It's important to] 'set the antenna high' for children and their parents, so I can find out what they are struggling with and make it easier for them to tell me anything." The principal explained further:

> If we lose trusting relationships [with parents], we can't do anything, so it is necessary to make trusting relationships and make connections with them...I mean, [we need] relationships [in which] parents are comfortable with speaking and [letting us know] what they want us to do [for them] as much as possible. Also there are times classroom teachers should make personal relationships with parents, beyond their relationship as classroom teachers.

Several educators discussed how they work with parents who have not recognized or accepted their children's struggles at school and need for additional help. They emphasized that until parents are ready to accept their children's disabilities, teachers have to be careful in bringing up the issue with them. The principal described how she tries to understand and support these parents:

> The most difficult thing is that it takes a very long time until they accept their children's disabilities. It must be hard...Well, I meet a mother whose face always looks unhappy, anxious, and worried, and she is like that even when she is with her child. So, I try to think, first of all, how I can [help] this mother to be able to smile when she is with her child, and then, I tell the mother how much progress her child has made and what amazed me...not about what the child can do or can't do, but about the child, how wonderful he or she is. In so doing, mothers get to understand a little by little. Still it takes a long time, sometimes 3 or 4 years.

Other educators also described how they dealt with parents who have not acknowledged their children's disabilities or "difficulties" by carefully initiating contact with them—for example, offering indirect support before moving to direct support. Educators also created opportunities for parents to observe their children at school and understand the children's struggles at school, and then offered them more intensive support and services for their children. One teacher explained:

> I think it tends to be that parents haven't noticed or don't want to notice. If this is the case, we want to be careful. There were many times I was not sure how to deal with [this situation]...If they see what their children are like at school, that will help them understand, I think.

Misa's field note described a similar strategy employed with the parents of two children. These two children were always at the center of arguments and were not able to remain in their seats when their classroom teacher was presenting a lesson. The classroom teacher consulted with the principal, and they decided to invite the parents to school to observe their children in the classroom. Later, the principal told Misa that the parents were surprised and had not known that their children were having difficulties until they actually saw their children in the classroom. She said that showing parents their children's classroom behaviors was the best way to make sure parents were on the same page as educators and they could start thinking with educators about how they could help their children.

Several educators also described that some parents may externalize their struggles. The principal provided an example of mothers who expressed feelings such as anger to educators:

> The hardest for children is not only that their mothers can't accept [their children's disabilities], but also that they become enraged because they can't admit that such things have happened to them. They take their anger out on us, directly. So, we don't make excuses, but just listen to them and say, "I think so," and take it seriously and think together about what is best and what makes the children happy, and try to understand each other.

For example, Dai's mother was very sensitive to any actions that might single out her son as "different" and lead to discrimination. Rather than placing Dai directly in the Rainbow Room, educators first placed him part-time in the Challenge Room, which was next door to the Rainbow Room. This placement was intended to accommodate Dai's mother's sensitivity and allow her time to adjust to the idea of having him study in a special education classroom. In the Challenge Room, Dai's mother had opportunities to interact with other parents of children with disabilities and observe Dai playing happily with children from the Rainbow Room. Educators guided Dai's mother by creating an environment in which she had access to experiences and information that helped her accept Dai's placement. The principal clearly described the importance of parents' readiness to accept children's needs for special education services:

> I hadn't heard from Dai's mother for a long time [although his mother had kept in contact with Sano *sensei* on a daily basis and the principal had talked with Sano *sensei*]. If there was no contact, I was going to call her to talk this week, but it was good I heard from her. I'd been thinking it's about time, but it doesn't work if it's too early. His mother also needed us. It shouldn't be like she had to come here because she got a call. I think it's best to talk with her when she thinks that it may be a better idea [to place Dai in a special education classroom] after she has observed her child for a long time in this support system.

Yusuke's mother, who struggled to handle Yusuke's extended periods of absence from school, acknowledged the support she received from educators. She described how Sano *sensei*, Yamashita *sensei* (a school psychologist), and

Yusuke's classroom teacher created an environment in which she could recognize that she needed help and ask for support.

> I talked with Yamashita *sensei*...at first I thought I didn't have anything to talk with a psychologist about. They knew what to do. Sano *sensei* told Yamashita *sensei* to help me. It started like that, and then she called me and arranged that I was able to make an appointment, naturally. Yamashita *sensei* told me recently, "You were under so much tension and there was no room to get in, but if we didn't do something, [not only] Yusuke, but you would have crashed/collapsed (*tsubureru*)." So, Sano *sensei* and Yusuke's classroom teacher, all of them made a route for me to go to see Yamashita *sensei*.

Teachers, especially those who had experience teaching children with disabilities, discussed the importance of involving parents in setting and meeting long-term goals for children based on their strengths and current level of functioning. With common long-term goals, educators and parents can respond to children's behaviors and struggles in a consistent manner and guide them to acquire the skills and attitudes expected of them as Japanese adults. To succeed, however, these goals must be accepted by children's parents. The following communications between Dai's mother and Sano *sensei*, described in Misa's field notes, illustrate how Sano *sensei* set long-term goals for Dai, guided his development, and guided his mother in handling Dai's struggles. In this excerpt, Sano *sensei* and Dai's mother communicated by text messages over several days, strategizing on how to respond to Dai's refusal to go to school. These communications prepared Dai's mother to handle his school refusal without becoming emotional. The day before he was absent, Sano *sensei* and Dai noticed that *edamame* (boiled green soybeans, one of the popular snacks in Japan during the summer), which Dai did not like, was on the next day's lunch menu. Sano *sensei* responded to Dai's question of whether he had to eat them, "Can you eat just one piece of bean? I will eat the rest of them." From Dai's reaction, Sano *sensei* and his mother expected that Dai would refuse to go to school the next morning. Sano *sensei* understood that Dai's refusal to go to school was stressful for his mother. She suggested to his mother that she not force him to come to school but, rather, take time with him so both of them could relax. Given the suggestions from Sano *sensei*, Dai's mother played with him as much as he wanted that night. In the morning, his mother texted Sano *sensei*:

> It looks like [Dai] wants to go to school, but [can't go]. I didn't ask, but he said, "Mom, do you know why I don't want to go [to school]? It's

because I have to eat one piece of *edamame*." I asked him, "So, if you don't have to eat that one piece, [what would you want]?" He replied, "I'd go." Then, I told him, "Ok, I will ask Sano *sensei*."

To this message, Sano *sensei* suggested, "If you keep asking him what he wants to do [about school] many times a day, you will have to worry all day. So, why don't you take it easy and have your time with Dai?" His mother then responded to Sano *sensei* that after she told Dai about the message from Sano *sensei*, he smiled happily but still did not say he would go to school. She texted Sano *sensei*, "He asked me if we still had time [before going to school]. Is he waiting for me to say, 'It's time [to go to school]?'" Sano *sensei* replied that it should be his mother who decides what to tell him because she was the person with him observing him directly. She should be able to decide while considering his actions and facial expressions. In her message, Sano *sensei* also told his mother, "At this moment, the hurdle, coming to school and enjoying meeting goals, seems to be too high for him." Later, his mother sent her a message:

> I also think so. It's easier for me to get his "permission" to go to school every morning, but what you told me is exactly right. Because I am always like this, there is no progress since the preschool, is there? Classroom teachers [in general education classrooms] see him only during the period of one year [they teach him], but I'm glad to have conversations with you, looking at his future goals.

Dai did not come to school on that day after all, but his mother commented, "I'd like to practice with Sano *sensei*" to give Dai as many successful experiences as possible to help him learn that "I can do" and become more confident.

Discussion

Since the Japanese government implemented new special education policies, children with developmental disabilities have become formally eligible to receive individualized special education services. To be effective, however, this new system must be accepted by parents who must give permission for their children to receive special education services. Currently, the number of children receiving these new services is lower than expected. One reason for the relatively low rate of utilization of services may be parents' reluctance for their children to receive "special" support[5]. In this chapter, we described how educators worked with and supported the parents of children with developmental disabilities.

Some parents of children with disabilities experienced "courtesy stigma," or stigma based on their association with an individual with a stigmatized condition (Goffman, 1963). Their sensitivity to "difference," "other people's eyes," and *henken* was an obstacle to their acceptance of their children's need for services, and their willingness to work with educators to provide such support. Providing children with special education services clearly identifies them as different from other children who are developing more typically and places them and their parents at risk for experiencing stigma. Receiving additional support, especially outside of their classrooms, can label children as "different." Given *henken*, parents may be reluctant to label children who appear to be "normal" as in need of special education. Many children with developmental disabilities are on the "border line," and they are able to keep up with other children in the early grades. As they get older, however, their differences from other children become apparent. Then, their parents may experience challenges in accepting their children's needs for more intensive support. Just as Japanese policy makers and educators had to balance the potential value of special education services against the risk of stigmatization, so, too, do parents.

Of course, sensitivity to stigma attached to special education may not be unique to Japanese parents and children. When Misa shared her observations of Greenleaf Elementary School, one U.S. special education teacher described her observation of parents' resistance to the services their children with learning disabilities received based on stigmatizing beliefs. She also noted, however, that in the United States, children may have a somewhat easier time leaving their general education classrooms to receive special education because support provided outside of their general education classrooms is fairly common for a variety of reasons, including to participate in gifted programs. Because formal special education for Japanese children with "developmental disabilities" is new, not many children are receiving support outside of their general education classrooms. Once the child starts receiving services outside of the classroom, it highlights the child's "difference."

Especially in a culture in which people are sensitive to other people's eyes and responses to what they do and say (e.g., Doi, 2001; Lebra, 1976), parents' concerns with stigmatization can make it difficult for them to accept their children's "difficulties" or disabilities and grant permission for them to receive additional support. Even parents who understand their children's disabilities may struggle with accepting their needs for additional support. They may worry about possible negative messages they and their children may receive implicitly or explicitly from other people. It took a year for Dai's and Yusuke's mother to accept that the Rainbow Room was the best place for their children.

Misa also noticed parents' sensitivity to disabilities through their reactions to her wheelchair in her everyday interactions with children and their parents. Younger children tended to approach Misa's wheelchair with less discriminatory ideas. Many of them wrote to Misa after her visit to their classrooms that they enjoyed hearing her stories and riding in a wheelchair. For example, one child described, "I learned the secrets of her wheelchair today." As they get older, more children wrote comments such as, "I'm sorry," although they appreciated the opportunity to learn about more positive views of disability. Unlike children, the majority of parents did not explicitly ask Misa about her wheelchair. Sano *sensei* shared with Misa that one mother was hesitant to ask Misa directly about sensitive issues such as her wheelchair. For such parents, special education services that highlight their children's "differences" from their peers can be problematic.

Knowing parents' concerns, teachers are careful about initiating conversations with parents regarding their children's potential need for additional help at school. Most educators described parents as partners in supporting children with developmental disabilities. Close collaboration between educators and parents is necessary for providing children with developmental disabilities with support in a consistent manner at home and school. To help parents to accept their children's special needs and work collaboratively with them, educators supported and guided parents through non-coercive practices. At Greenleaf Elementary School, educators' careful *mimamori* of parents created an environment where parents were able to collaborate with educators in decision making.

Educators' *omoiyari*, their kind understanding of parents' sensitivity to special education, led them to avoid direct confrontation with parents as much as possible. They chose to deal with parental resistance indirectly by developing relationships with them and through non-coercive practices. As we will describe in Chapter 6, educators employed similar strategies within their classrooms to support children with developmental disabilities—for example, through creating supportive classrooms and facilitating voluntary cooperation between children with disabilities and their peers.

Notes

1. Five years after the implementation of the new special education system, these numbers remained almost the same. In 2012, among 53,882 children from first through ninth grades across Japan (except three prefectures hit by the Great Eastern Japan Earthquake in 2011), 6.5% of children were identified by their classroom teachers as exhibiting academic or behavioral difficulties (4.5%, academic only; 3.6%, behavioral only; 1.6%, both academic and behavioral; Ministry of Education, 2012c).

2. 11.2% of U.S. children between the ages of 6 and 17 years received special education services in 2008.

3. One child was not invited to participate, because the child was absent most days while Misa was at Greenleaf Elementary School.

4. Placing Dai in a general education classroom was also beneficial for other children. Administrators were looking for more children to attend Greenleaf Elementary School to create two small first grade classrooms. At the time, the maximum classroom size determined by the law was 40 (Currently, 35 for first and second graders). If there were 41 first graders, then schools were able to create two small classrooms of 20 and 21.

5. Of course, there are other reasons, including the educational budget and availability of educators who have knowledge and experiences working children with disabilities.

6 HOW EDUCATORS SUPPORT CHILDREN WITH DEVELOPMENTAL DISABILITIES AND THEIR PEERS

First and sixth grade children working together in the library

It was Dai's first day at the Challenge Room. After working with a part-time teacher from first through third periods, Dai returned to his third grade general education classroom. As soon as his classmates saw him they immediately surrounded him, "Dai!" "Here comes Dai!" They took hold of his school bag and helped him to carry it to his desk. Kawai *sensei*, their classroom teacher, was concerned about other children's reactions to Dai's comings and goings and considered how to help children to welcome Dai back to the classroom more "naturally." A few days later, children began greeting Dai following his return from the Challenge Room using a ritual greeting word usually used at home, *okaeri-nasai* (welcome back). Dai did not understand what they meant and asked me, "Why *okaeri-nasai*?" I told him, "I think they want you to say, '*Tadaima* (I'm back).'" Greeting Dai by *okaeri-nasai* means these children recognize their classroom as their "home" at school and Dai as a member of their "family." Next time he returned to his classroom, he entered saying, "*Tadaima!*" and children said, "*Okaeri-nasai!*" Later, Dai told me that what he liked about his third grade classroom was their *okaeri-nasai*. (Excerpt from Misa's fieldnotes)

In this chapter, we will describe how special education is understood and practiced by educators at Greenleaf Elementary School, including strategies they
utilized in their general and special education classrooms, and how children
responded to such support. Currently, Japanese educators are required to
provide individualized instruction to children with developmental disabilities
while maintaining traditional educational practices emphasizing children's
peer group dynamics. Like Dai's teacher, many of the educators participating in our research met this challenge with creativity to socialize and support
children with developmental disabilities, as well as their typically developing peers. Just as they supported parents through *mimamori* and through
providing a context in which they could "naturally" support their children
(Chapter 5), so too they supported children through creating a "naturally"
accepting social ecology in their everyday activities at school. At Greenleaf
Elementary School, educators created a home-like classroom environment by
"staying close to children's *kokoro* (hearts/minds)," understanding children's
needs through *omoiyari* (empathy/sympathy), and "raising" all children to
respect diverse abilities and show kindness to others. Educators supported
the positive peer relationships of children with developmental disabilities by
involving peers in providing support for them and helping when peer groups
experienced problems. Yet some children with developmental disabilities
struggled in their peer groups. Educators attempted to guide these children to
develop self-confidence and self-esteem and to secure their voluntary cooperation in school activities.

Special Education in General Education Classrooms

Special Education As an Extension of the General Education System

Many educators explained that the current preference in Japan remains for
classroom teachers to provide special education services for children with
developmental disabilities in their general education classrooms, as much
as is possible and appropriate for children's needs. At Greenleaf Elementary
School, this support is provided as an extension of regular educational activities in general education classrooms. Even when children need instruction
in small groups or individually (e.g., at the Challenge Room), such support is
typically provided by part-time teachers, such as former or retired classroom
teachers, and classroom teachers in their planning time. Most of these teachers do not have a special education certificate[1]. Even teachers in the Rainbow
Room do not necessarily have special education certificates. Accordingly, it

remains the classroom teachers' primary responsibility to provide additional support for children with special needs in collaboration with other educators. The principal, who had previously taught children with disabilities, explained:

> [We] have to bring out the personality [or individuality: *kosei*] of each child efficiently in groups, so I think special education is something that classroom teachers have to do in their classrooms, in group instruction. And then, if [we can make] teachers' skills high enough, we don't have to pull children out [for small group or individual instruction]. I mean, we can do good enough without special education[2].

Educators discussed strategies they have employed to attend to children's diverse needs in their classrooms. In general, they described the importance of designing classroom activities and instruction so that all children can enjoy learning—for example, by using visual aids and gestures—without lowering the level of instruction. Classroom activities and instruction must be attractive to children who can complete tasks easily, the so called fast learners, as well as children who are struggling. Fast learners have to be challenged so that they do not become bored and inattentive. As one teacher described:

> There are children who get things quickly, and those who do not. So, for those who can finish quickly, just let them go ahead working by themselves, because they can do with less attention from teachers. So, I can take time for slow learners. I didn't think about letting children do [worksheets] at the same pace because there would be children who would have to wait for [slow learners to catch up] and these children may start talking or stop listening to me.

The assistant principal explained that there are commonalities in instructional strategies in special education and general education classrooms that can make learning accessible and enjoyable for all children:

> I know there is no such thing as "perfect" instruction [in general education classrooms], but if there was, I believe that it would contain elements of special education. The real perfect instruction should be satisfying and enjoyable for everyone. There may be individual differences, but the instruction has to give all children pleasure and make them want to participate. So, I am beginning to think that the elements, or the way of thinking about special education and the elements to develop such

instruction [that is enjoyable for every child], are nearly equal. For example, this child has understood this, so give the child suggestions doing this or that, or this child's level of understanding is average, so it's ok for now, or this child can be motivated more if I tell this. It's like taking care of each child by focusing on [the progress of] each child, isn't it? Support depending on individual needs like this [in general education classrooms] and special education to meet needs of each child [with a disability], are almost the same, I think. So if I want to make this school better, the only way we can do so is by raising the teachers' abilities to give instruction.

Other educators also explained that attention to "special education" benefits all children. A teacher who had been in several other schools described Greenleaf Elementary School:

If there are children who need additional help, not only classroom or special education classroom teachers, but the whole school, we all share the children's information, and raise these children together. That's the priority in this school, so, it's not whether or not [children have disabilities]. Of course, if [they] have disabilities, we'd take care of it. It's like we are going to make a system that whenever there is a need, we will take care of it, as far as I understand.

Accordingly, children may receive support within general education classrooms for a variety of reasons including disabilities, family problems, and language and communication difficulties[3].

Providing Support "Naturally" for All Children

For those children with developmental disabilities struggling in classrooms, educators preferred to provide them with individualized support "naturally" as part of their everyday routine activities. Aoki *sensei*, who had taught in both general and special education classrooms, described how she provided individual support, naturally and unobtrusively, in her general education classroom.

Some children with disabilities in general education classrooms have difficulties in copying what is written on the blackboard into their notebooks, and listening to teachers. What I am doing is to put a magnet sticker meaning "write" on the blackboard where to start writing and say, "Write." If I do like that, children can write. The shape of the sticker should be age appropriate, [I use different ones] for fourth graders and second graders. For example, I use a "pencil" for second graders. Other children can write whenever I say, "Write from here," and that's fine. It doesn't matter for other children if there is a sticker or not, but I have learned that for children with disabilities, they can write if something useful for them is there naturally [*futsu-ni*: normally, usually], without drawing too much attention [*sarigenaku*: casually, unobtrusively].

Aoki *sensei* continued, "If the additional support makes it easier for a child with a disability, almost all children in the same classroom can understand [benefit]." Such practices, which do not single out children with disabilities, provide them with more opportunities to maintain their membership within peer groups while receiving the necessary support. A teacher who recently began studying special education described his experience of implementing such practices:

I heard that children get very anxious if they don't know how things are going on, so, recently, I tell children [at the beginning of the class] something like, "We do this and this and this and then, do this next, and this is done, done." [In the first grade classroom, this teacher put the day's schedule on the top of the white board at the beginning of the class, and when each task was done, he crossed it off.] It seems that it makes it easier for children, I mean, children can easily see how much is left.

For fast learners:

I tell them such things at the beginning of the class, so, children stopped asking me "What are we gonna do today?" or like that.... For example, in first grade there is a large difference in how quickly children understand Math, so, before [I did this], children who had already done asked me, "What do we do next?" or "What should I do?" But now, without my direction, they come to turn in [a worksheet] and I tell them, "Then, go get that [extra worksheet]", so I have more time for children who need additional instruction.

Creating a Home-Like Environment

Children with disabilities, however, may require formal support beyond what is available within their general education classrooms. The support provided

to individual children can create extra interpersonal challenges for some children, especially when it is provided outside of their general education classrooms, such as at the Rainbow and Challenge rooms. Educators supported
these children emotionally and socially by creating a home-like environment
in their general education classrooms.

Staying Close to Children's kokoro (Hearts/Minds)

Several teachers identified one of the challenges of implementing the new
special education policies as helping children with developmental disabilities
to feel comfortable with receiving extra support. Such support was provided
with careful consideration of each individual child's feelings and responses.
When Misa asked how she should work with children as a teaching assistant
in general education classrooms, Sano *sensei* advised, "It depends, there may
be a child who likes to work with a teacher one-on-one, or there may be a
child who prefers that [a teaching assistant] sit behind [him or her], so it looks
like [the teaching assistant] is helping two or more children, alternatively."
Accordingly, when providing children with support, it is important for educators to learn and know each individual child and to adapt the ways they interact with each child. Ono *sensei* described her practice in her general education
classroom:

> I need to know about the children [in front of me]. I mean, every child
> has likes and dislikes. For example, [this child] doesn't like to be treated
> like this, or if I do this, this child looks happy, or that kind of thing.
> There are many times I find I should not have said this to this child. If
> I say so, the child will never hear me... Therefore, I'd like to learn more
> about how to give them directions in a way that children are willing to
> hear... When this child is excited, if I say, "Can you tell me [your] story?
> I want to hear!" I can see the child calms down immediately, and also
> if I say, "It's great!" and praise him, he looks very happy and is able to
> work more and show progress.

Sano *sensei* called this practice "looking at children's *kokoro*." Some children do
not express their thoughts, preferences, and desires explicitly. During everyday interactions with children, educators as well as parents tried to understand their thoughts, feelings, and, more broadly, *kokoro*, which is generally
viewed as central to children's development in Japanese elementary education. Misa's field note summarized Sano *sensei*'s description of one child and
how she "looked at" his *kokoro*.

We often say, "Stay close to children," but it is more like looking at children's *kokoro* (hearts/minds), rather than what teachers expect of [the children]. There was a child, who said, "I wanna run with others." Then we talked, "Let's practice together," and set the date to practice, but on that day, he said, "My legs hurt." Then after that, he said he'd like to participate in a program called "Road Run," and again, on the day to practice, he said, "My ankle hurts." Now, there is a "Kids Marathon" in March. He was going to practice with Kikuchi *sensei,* but again, he said that his legs hurt. When we asked him, he said he was really looking forward to it, but we wondered if that was what he really thought. His body was honest, and showed what he really thought…like too anxious or might be struggling between what he really wanted and what he wanted to be, so, I'd like to find and look at what children really think. (Excerpt from Misa's field note)

Dai's mother also shared how the advice the principal had given her helped her to see Dai's *kokoro* at home. When Dai began having problems at school, he did not mention it at home, but his mother noticed a change in his attitude:

The principal said Dai would never talk to us if we kept asking him . [what's wrong], so, she told me, "It may take a while, but he will tell you from himself, if you stay close to him and how he feels." I did as she told me, and then soon after that he told me [what he thought before I asked him]. Since then, he has been able to tell us when he is struggling.

The principal and experienced teachers also clarified that considering each child's individual needs and accommodating them are different than allowing them to disobey rules other children have to follow—for example, remaining in their seats and classrooms during instruction. As much as possible, educators expected children with developmental disabilities to stay within the framework of basic school rules and expectations.

Practicing omoiyari

Educators commonly practiced *omoiyari* (empathy/sympathy) to attend to the feelings of children experiencing difficulties. Some classroom teachers also acted as "interpreters" between children with developmental disabilities and their peers. For example, educators handled children's transitions to and from the Challenge Room and the Rainbow Room with care. A number of teachers expressed concern that children receiving support outside of the classroom would be perceived as "special" among their peers and that this perception might make them feel uncomfortable in their general education classrooms. The principal cautioned that if children required individualized support outside of their general education classrooms, then it had to be done in a way that children could leave their classrooms without feeling out of place (*iwa-kan*), or inferior to others (*retto-kan*).

Reflecting on these concerns, teachers facilitated "natural" transitions through the metaphor of classroom as "home," a place where members come and go but still belong. Similar to Dai's teacher, Kawai *sensei*, several teachers implemented the ritual greeting typically used daily in family homes to make it easier for children to come and go from their general education classrooms. Kawai *sensei* explained during the individual interview:

> I thought how Dai wanted to be treated when he came back to the classroom, so I explained to children like that. I told them it would be great if we could make our classroom...like where we say "*itte-rasshai*" (Come back here) [when he leaves] and he says "*tadaima*" (I'm back) [when he comes].

By instructing Dai's classmates to greet him using a ritual, Kawai *sensei* served as an interpreter of Dai's feelings and created an accepting atmosphere in her classroom. Several teachers described similar strategies they used to create an atmosphere in which children experiencing difficulties are accepted and feel comfortable and safe in their classrooms. For example, one teacher described that she would explain to other children how a child with special needs was feeling and the meanings of the child's behavior when he or she was struggling. Ono *sensei* emphasized that it was important to attend to children's feelings carefully. She described one child, Yusuke, who had become anxious about attending school and was studying in the Challenge Room. To make it easier for him to return to his classroom, she explained to his classmates how Yusuke felt about entering the classroom and described what he was doing in the Challenge Room. She hoped this would help children to accept Yusuke when he returned to the classroom.

Raising Children in Peer Groups

Most classroom teachers characterized interactions with children with disabilities as learning opportunities for entire peer groups. Just as it is important for children with disabilities to learn from their peers, so, too, is it important for their peers to learn from them. An important goal was to socialize all children so that they accept those with disabilities voluntarily, spontaneously, and naturally. Teachers generally expected children to learn to deal with problems and help one another within their peer groups. Aoki *sensei* described:

> The child [with a disability] can get along with other children in a general education classroom, if [a classroom teacher] provides additional support. And it's going to have a positive impact on the child. I also want to work with them in a way that other children can learn something positive by getting to know [children with disabilities].

The following excerpt describes peers' reactions that illustrate how children learn about and accept the additional needs of children experiencing difficulties through their daily activities. Misa was a teaching assistant in a first grade general education classroom during Math. She worked with a child who was struggling with addition and subtraction.

> When we were working on the worksheet, another child asked [the child who was struggling], "Are you still doing that?" So, I told him that the child wanted to take time to think. Later, another child came and asked the same question. This time, a girl who was sitting at the same table [and had overheard my earlier explanation] told that child, "She wants to take time to think." (Excerpt from Misa's field note)

The small size of Greenleaf Elementary School also facilitated such learning opportunities. As one teacher explained:

> This school has an at-home [atmosphere] and relationships between grade levels are closer than other schools... This means children in the special education classroom also have more chances to interact with other children. In a large school like a school size of 700 children, we have to make an effort so children can work together. They don't even know children in other classrooms and other grades, so they know about children in special education classrooms even less... So, there is less opportunity to learn why [they are in special education classrooms], or learn from one another. But, in this school [Greenleaf Elementary], these children [with disabilities] are elsewhere in each child's life. Yes, this is very good, I think. Even if we find children having biased ideas, we are able to deal with them, teach them immediately...

Teachers provided opportunities for children to learn from and support one another, but creating a supportive atmosphere in classrooms also depended on how children respond to such opportunities. Maekawa *sensei*, Dai's second grade classroom teacher, described his class from the previous year as a group of children who were less competitive than children in the other second grade classroom. In his classroom, Dai received support from peers when he needed it. Although the children had conflicts with Dai, Maekawa *sensei* believed that they learned and overcame many difficulties. Soon after the two classrooms were combined in third grade, however, Dai began struggling in his general education classroom. Not only was the classroom larger, but the atmosphere among the children had changed and was not always supportive. Accordingly, Maekawa *sensei* and other teachers indicated that they had to devote more attention to facilitating positive relationships between children with developmental disabilities and their classmates.

"Raising" Other Children

One strategy educators used to facilitate positive peer relationships involved "raising" and educating typically developing children to recognize and understand the special needs of children with developmental disabilities. Some teachers also involved other children in a support system for a child experiencing difficulties. Educators were careful, however, to educate other children about their peers' special needs without labeling and in a way in which children could understand and empathize. For example, Nagai *sensei* explained the behavior problems of a child with ADHD to his peers using the metaphor, a "cup of tolerance" (*see* Chapter 1). Children's response, "His cup has overflowed," suggested that this metaphor was meaningful to them.

This practice of "raising other children" is based on the belief that children have the ability to understand their peers' problems and provide support for them when they are struggling. For example, a classroom teacher asked his fourth graders to write about children with disabilities after Misa had visited their classroom and shared her experiences of being in a wheelchair. Children also had heard about the rules Ototake's peers created so that he could participate in their activities and play from his power wheelchair[4] (*see* Chapter 1). The teacher's writing prompts and children's responses include:

TEACHER: If your friend has a disability, what do you do?
CHILD RESPONSES: Play together. Create play we can do together.
   Talk to him, enjoy, and eat lunch together.
   Take notes for her. Help her when she has a problem.

> I won't say, "He can't do," but treat him as one of us.
>
> I will give them a task they can do when we clean the classroom.
>
> I will help her when she needs help.
>
> TEACHER: If you have a disability, what would it be like at school?
>
> CHILD RESPONSES: I want my friends to be with me, help me, and play with me.
>
> I want to do by myself whatever I can.
>
> I want to be treated just like others.
>
> I don't want to be laughed at, like "You have a disability."

The practice of raising other children is not limited to children with disabilities. Ono *sensei* also used this strategy to help peers to accept children who had interpersonal problems. She described a fifth grade child who was frequently involved in conflicts with other children and who, despite her repeated efforts, did not change his behaviors. Therefore, "I had to educate other children [to deal with this]. So, I described the child's strengths to other children as well as to him," and "praised him more when he did well [because he is always the one who is disciplined], so he can be in the group of children smoothly." Several other teachers described that peers' reactions to behaviors and problems caused by children with disabilities is influenced by their classroom teachers' attitudes. If teachers focus on the strengths of children with developmental disabilities, rather than simply addressing their difficulties, then other children's attitudes toward them become more positive.

Raising peers of children with disabilities also involves providing them with emotional support to facilitate their understanding and acceptance of children with disabilities and the support they are receiving, which may be perceived as "special." Aoki *sensei* described the benefit of educating children with disabilities within peer groups and how she balanced the needs of children with disabilities and their peers.

> I know children who have diagnoses are working harder, twice as hard as other children, but I also know how difficult it is to let other children know about this... Children who listen to [what I tell the child with a disability] also want to be accepted [by me]. You know, there were times when I felt it was difficult to keep the balance... I'm trying to sense/gather what children feel. When I find from their faces and other things that this child also wants to get attention [while I work with a child who needs additional support], I will try to think how I can follow up, such as playing with the child during recess, or something like that. If the child can play with me, he or she may feel better. But the

best way is to tell something to children. They all want their teachers' attention... I'm trying to do so, but there are times when I can't discern children's voices and feel it is very difficult.

By facilitating other children's awareness and acceptance of the needs of children with developmental disabilities, educators created a context in which children with special needs were integrated into the lives of other children, so they could learn from one another. Kawai *sensei* stressed, "If [typically developing] children do something together with these children [with special needs] since they are young, I think bias or that kind of thing will be eliminated a little by little." When they are older, they might recall their friends with disabilities and be less inclined to discriminate against those with disabilities.

Teachers also reported on the flexibility of some (but not all) children in responding to and accepting the uneven competencies and tendencies of children with developmental disabilities. For example, Kawai *sensei* described children's ability to adjust to Dai's changing behavior in the Challenge Room. Dai was very quiet in his classroom but began expressing himself forcefully and articulately in the Challenge Room. Kawai *sensei* was initially concerned that this change in behavior might confuse the other children. A third grade classmate of Dai's, Jun, visited him at the Challenge Room. He was initially surprised when Dai gave him directions, but quickly adjusted:

When Jun came to the Challenge Room to play, Dai and I [Misa] were still cleaning the room after lunch...[Jun helped Dai clean a large table.] While wiping the table, Dai gave Jun directions, such as "Not here, yet!" Jun then said, "Dai is strong, here." I asked him, "Is he different in your classroom?" Jun said, "Different."...After cleaning, they went to play together [as if nothing unusual had happened]. (Excerpt from Misa's field note)

Such everyday interactions with children with diverse abilities can provide typically developing children with opportunities to learn how to interact with peers with diverse abilities and responses.

Several teachers identified typically developing children who interacted well with children with special needs and who voluntarily provided them with support as needed. For example, Sekine *sensei* observed that some of her students had known the children with disabilities in her classroom since preschool. They knew how to deal with those children's difficulties and to help them. Another teacher appreciated a child's willingness to help her peer, who tended to cause problems. Knowing that they had been classmates since pre-school, their teacher assigned her a desk next to his. She helped him to complete assigned tasks and prompted him to follow their classroom teacher's instruction. Aoki *sensei* stressed, however, that it is also important to guide children carefully so that one child does not take too much responsibility and become overwhelmed and as many children as possible are able to provide support.

Working within peer groups to support one another and solve problems, however, can be very challenging for children, as illustrated by the following excerpt from Misa's field note:

> When I worked with a group of children preparing for a presentation, some of the group members started arguing and one of them cried. While 2-3 children tried to comfort the crying child, two other children joined the argument, and one of them cried after another child threatened to kick him. Some group members went to talk to these children, and others went to find their classroom teacher, who was in another room. The teacher asked the children one by one what happened and how they felt, and let them tell her what they should have done. After that, she told the group members to keep working on the project, asked one of the group members to lead the group, and then she left the room. The child [who was in charge] assigned tasks in a way that everyone agreed, and things went on as if nothing had happened. (Excerpt from Misa's field note)

Educators viewed such short-term inconveniences and stresses of peer groups as far outweighed by the long term benefits. As one teacher stated,

> When there is a child with a disability in a classroom, the classroom becomes kind to other people....I don't let children interact in a way that would prevent the child from being independent. They [peers] are able to learn what the child can do. Well, I [told peers] to let the child do by himself whatever he can do, and other children help [him] only with what he can't do.

Peer Struggles and Secondary Disabilities

In a supportive classroom environment, children are expected to learn and respect the strengths of their peers through their daily interactions. Yet peer group membership can be a burden for some children, especially those with interpersonal problems or learning disabilities that cause them to lag behind their peers. Further, peers' reactions are not always positive.

Several teachers expressed concerns about children with developmental disabilities who had problems with peers in their classrooms, especially those who exhibited verbal and physical aggression, and behaviors that might appear unusual to other children. One of these teachers described:

> It depends on what [difficulties/disabilities] a child has. If the child just can't organize properly, it may not be a big problem, but if a child has something emotionally,...they tend to have interpersonal problems. They are very sensitive to what they are told by others and easily hurt, but they give their friends relentless words. So, other children don't know the child is such a child [with a disability]. Therefore, they look at the child as an "equal" friend, and the child becomes a "nasty kid." Both of them don't understand [about the disability], and they keep attacking each other to protect themselves.

Ono *sensei* described that once children decide, "This child is like this," the child may be avoided by peers and become socially isolated. In such a case, it is difficult to re-establish more positive and supportive peer relationships and to "teach them [peers] to think and look at [the child] differently."

When children with disabilities do not exhibit problematic social behaviors, they still may internalize their problems. Two of the children Misa worked with as a teaching assistant, Yusuke and Dai, internalized their fears of being teased or left out of other children's play and isolated themselves from their peer groups. Adults did not recognize their struggles until they began refusing to go to school. At the beginning of this research, Yusuke and Dai refused to remain in their classrooms and studied most days full time in the Challenge Room with a part-time teacher and teaching assistants. A teacher who taught Math in Dai's third grade classroom reflected that he had thought Dai was doing well in the classroom and did not notice his struggles. Kawai *sensei*, Dai's classroom teacher also remarked:

> I'm confused to find that he looks very active and lively in the Rainbow Room. But I thought he was doing well [in my classroom]. It made me realize that he had been bearing (*gaman*), and once I learned that he was forced to manage [in the general education classroom], I can't say [he should come back to my classroom]. That's what I feel right now.

Of course, some children who were not diagnosed with specific disabilities nonetheless had interpersonal difficulties. For example, when Misa observed a study group meeting where teachers discussed various issues including classroom management and teaching strategies, a classroom teacher shared the results of social skills assessments of all children in her classroom and how she understood the dynamics of their interpersonal relationships. The teachers discussed how she could support children who tended to be left out by other children. During the discussion, Sano *sensei* (the school nurse) shared her observations that some children who tended to be left out by their peers in this classroom were the children who usually came to her office at recess. Indeed, whenever Misa stopped by her office during recess, she saw children, frequently more than 10, from various grade levels chatting, reading books, and playing cards and other games.

Guiding Individual Children With Developmental Disabilities

Facilitating Children's Self-Esteem and Self-Confidence

Educators reported that for those children who are struggling academically and interpersonally, additional support can strengthen their self-esteem and self-confidence. Several educators believed that the self-confidence, self-awareness, and self-esteem of children with developmental disabilities were enhanced through learning in general education classrooms with their peers. Tanaka *sensei* stressed that if children have disabilities, it is especially important to identify their strengths and create opportunities in which their strengths are accepted by others and they can accept themselves as, "I'm great!" Nagai *sensei* described that in general education classrooms, "children are able to learn how to interact with friends and may learn how other children think, more than when they are [taught] individually." Sano *sensei* also emphasized the importance of being with peers. For example, "slow learners" who study with "fast learners" can learn how fun it is to understand and complete tasks and become inspired.

When children with developmental disabilities have special skills of which they are proud and that are socially valued, their interactions with peers become more positive. Maekawa *sensei* shared his observation of Dai, who was in his classroom during the previous year:

It makes a difference whether what a child is confident about is valued [by peers]. Last year, Dai was called, "Mr. Fish," by the other children who admired his knowledge of fish. He also told them stories of fish during lunch.

Teachers viewed it as part of their responsibilities to identify children's strengths and create opportunities in which children can use their strengths to become more confident in peer groups. As one teacher explained:

> ...each child [with a disability] has different needs, so it is a danger to use the same rules [as other children in general education classrooms], but they still have something in common they can do [with other children]...It is like creating a place where children can accept the strengths of other children and get suggestions from one another. If they have that kind of interaction, they can guide themselves in the right direction [to raise] each other.

Kakeru also had particular strengths that served as a source of confidence and pride and might have provided protection from stigma in his general education classroom. His special knowledge of bugs provided him with some status among his peers, who referred to him as "Dr. Bugs," and motivated him to study and interact with peers in his general education classroom. His classroom teacher also publicly recognized his strengths. The following field note describes a conversation between Kakeru and a boy from another second grade classroom shortly after they returned from a field trip to a nearby park.

> A boy [from another second grade classroom] came in with his classroom teacher. The boy said to the class, "Excuse me, sorry for coming during class. I have a question for Kakeru. Can you teach me the name of the crab you found the other day?" Kakeru said the name of the crab immediately and with confidence. The child said, "Thank you." Kakeru replied, "You are welcome."...Kakeru's classroom teacher remarked, "You know very well!" (Excerpt from Misa's field note)

Both children and teachers respected Kakeru's knowledge, and teachers used it to motivate him—for example, by allowing the boy from another classroom to ask questions during the class period. Although Kakeru required frequent prompts and reminders to follow directions, his classroom teacher understood that he was working harder than other children. In response to her support, he said to his parents, "I want to study hard with Aoki *sensei*."

In general, educators created opportunities for children with developmental disabilities to be involved in their age-appropriate peer groups as much as possible, in part because such inclusion was motivating. For example, Misa's field notes described how a fourth grade child responded to individual support in her general education classroom.

> When I visited the classroom, she was struggling to follow the teacher's explanation, and a girl sitting next to her taught her how to solve the math problems. When I visited the classroom the next time, she was sitting with her friends [Math was taught in a small group instruction classroom, and children picked their seats as they came from their classroom]. Later, she was told by the teacher to sit apart from them and study with me. The following day, she sat by herself apart from other girls without being told to by the teacher, and smiled at me and waited for me to come. While working on math problems, she explained to me that she would have a meeting for the Greenleaf Festival [coming in a few weeks] during recess, so, she had to go back to the classroom early, together with other classmates. On that day, she finished all questions assigned by the teacher in order to make the meeting. Even though she was behind the other children, she proudly showed what she had done to the teacher. (Excerpt from Misa's field notes)

As a result of observing and hearing about the positive responses of children with developmental disabilities to individualized support, several teachers described changes in their own thinking about the desirability of providing such support for children outside of general education classrooms. They gained respect for children's needs for more intensive support. Hashimoto *sensei* reflected:

> When I heard [that Dai's mother had called and said] things like, "He doesn't want to go to school, today," I realized that it might not necessarily be good [for him] to be in a general education classroom and *gaman* (endure, bear)... There is a fifth grade girl who used to be in a general education classroom all the time. After she started going to the Challenge Room, she is beginning to enjoy and have interests in studying. Also, I heard that a second grade boy is studying with a teacher one-on-one, and doing better. When I heard these stories, I thought it was good for them to work [with teachers outside of general education classrooms]. Someone may ask, "Why are they going to [the Challenge Room]?"... I used to think they should not be pulled out or felt sorry [that they had to be], but now, after I heard that they were enjoying [the support], I think it must be good for

them. Perhaps, it's really hard if they can't ask questions and there is no way for them to understand, but if they are pulled out [from their classrooms] and there is one teacher for one or two children, they must be able to have more experiences like, "I see!" and it's very good for them.

Educators also reported that academic support in general education classrooms or the Challenge or Rainbow Rooms helped children with developmental disabilities to improve their self-confidence and motivated them both academically and interpersonally. Nagai *sensei* described a child in her classroom who had been studying at the Challenge Room once a week for several months, "She says, 'It's fun', because she can understand, and be praised." She further articulated:

When it's getting difficult, is there anything harder than listening to something [we] can't understand? And then, they are told to do and if they don't, [the teacher is going to say], "It's homework." There is no way. Instead, it must be fun [for a child if a teacher] lowers the level so she can understand and start from where [she] understands, though it's only once a week. Of course, [we know] the differences from other children, but [the child can] learn at her own pace, like, "Look, look! I did this." ... [we say,] "Good job!" Yeah, it's like this.

Nagai *sensei* also stated, "Even chatting with a teacher might be ok if the child can calm down and go back to [his or her] classroom happily." Another teacher shared how she worked with a boy struggling emotionally:

There may be a child who is behind only in Math and should be pulled out. On the other hand, there is a child who is emotionally unstable, and you know, [we can] calm down if we are in the place where it is quiet and there are only a small number of people, don't you think so? [Similarly,] if the child can spend at least one hour a day in such a place, it makes a difference, for example, there is one in my class. He calms down immediately if there is one-on-one time with [a teacher] even once a day. ... I thought he could benefit from pull out services once a day, but we talked about why he had to be pulled out [considering his academic performance]. So then we decided it might be better to meet with him after school. I'm working with him after school[5], studying together, and it works for him, calming down and being happier...

Guiding Children Toward Voluntary Cooperation

In addition to supporting academic skills, educators viewed teaching social skills as their responsibility. To teach children social and interpersonal skills, educators frequently turned their needs and misbehaviors into learning opportunities. Their goal was to secure children's voluntary cooperation, so that they would "spontaneously" learn and behave in socially appropriate ways. For example, rather than giving explicit directions and responding immediately to problems, they often practiced *mimamori*. They watched over children carefully, gave them choices, acted as role models, made suggestions, and observed how children responded. They often waited for children to solve their own problems.

Sano *sensei* shared an example of how she used a real experience to guide Yusuke toward appropriate behavior, rather than simply directing him to follow rules. Yusuke had become fearful of school, and his goal at that time was to come to school regularly. Most elementary school-aged children travel to school independently or with peers. Yusuke, however, came to school with his mother 1 or 2 hours late. Yusuke and several other children were put in charge of making an announcement to all children from first through sixth grades during the morning meeting of the school. To make the announcement, Yusuke had to arrive at school early. His mother could not bring him early because she had to take his younger sister to preschool. Sano *sensei* suggested several options to Yusuke: allow her, his classroom teacher, or another teacher to pick him up at home; come to school by himself; ask his mother to come with him to school very early before going to preschool; or ask his father to take a day off and come with him. Yusuke asked Sano *sensei* to pick him up and then did a nice job during the morning meeting. By giving Yusuke choices, Sano *sensei* created a situation in which he had to make his own decision, and consider the most acceptable solution.

Guiding children toward voluntary cooperation was a widely used strategy by other teachers as well. For example, when Dai ran away from the Challenge Room, educators who saw him hiding in the hallway did not force him to go back but watched over him (*mimamori*), allowing him the opportunity to solve the problem by himself. After a few minutes, he returned to the Challenge Room, smiling.

Guiding children toward voluntary cooperation, however, can be challenging because educators could not always anticipate a child's response. For example, Sano *sensei* gave Dai and Yusuke a choice of where to eat their lunches: the Challenge Room, their general education classrooms, or some "other place" they preferred. Dai picked "other place." Sano *sensei* had not expected that Dai or Yusuke would pick some "other place" and later confided to Misa that she should not have offered it as a choice.

SANO *SENSEI*: Do you have to go to the "other place"?

DAI: No.

SANO *SENSEI*: How about the Challenge Room?

DAI: I don't like [to eat at the Challenge Room].

SANO *SENSEI*: If you want to eat somewhere else, you have to get permission [from other teachers who are in charge of the rooms and the principal], so, I'm suggesting, you really don't like to eat at the Challenge Room? Where would you like to eat?

DAI: Where no one is there.

[Sano *sensei* explained to him what he had to do if he wanted to eat in another room, and wrote the instructions on the blackboard.]

DAI: Then, I won't [eat lunch; began crying].

SANO *SENSEI*: Well, I will be back later, so think about where you'd like to eat by then. (Excerpt from Misa's field notes)

Sano *sensei* provided advice and alternatives and then allowed Dai to experience the consequence of his actions—in this case, crying and refusing to eat. Dai eventually decided to eat at a small group instruction room and, with a teaching assistant's help, successfully followed Sano *sensei*'s earlier instructions for gaining permission to do so.

Several teachers also worked collaboratively to guide Dai toward choosing to participate in a summer camp at school. The camp was a week-long program involving study time, swimming class, and other activities such as Japanese drums, basketball, crafts, cooking, and science. While Yusuke and other children talked excitedly about the camp, Dai asserted, "I won't because [the camp has] a swimming class." Tanaka *sensei* explained that he did not have to swim, but he insisted that he would not participate. The following excerpt is from Misa's field notes describing educators' response to Dai in the several weeks preceding the summer camp.

When I talked about the camp with Sano *sensei*, she said, "After talking [with other children and teachers], he may change his mind, a little by little." I asked Dai about the camp again, but his response was, "No." During the following weeks, we talked about the camp several times but I decided not to ask him if he would participate. On the last day before the summer camp, I heard Tanaka *sensei* excitedly talking with Dai's mother about Dai's decision to come to the camp. Later, I asked

Tanaka *sensei* what made him change his mind. She said, "Because he has found his *Ibasho* [a place where he feels comfortable and accepted] here [in the Challenge Room and the Rainbow Room]." (Excerpt from Misa's field notes)

Sano *sensei* observed Dai's progress in her comments on Misa's daily teaching assistant's log:

Even though he shuts down when he is told to "correct" [his behavior], he has learned from it, and the next time [when he is in the similar situation], he can deal with [the situation] smoothly without shutting down. It seems that he has noticed that shutting down [to resist adults' directions is not appropriate] and is struggling. When he finds or [someone] teaches him a better way, and if he actually experiences [that it works], he learns from it perfectly, and is able to handle the situation [next time]. I feel that if we interact with him carefully [in this way] he can learn social skills, and he will be able to have a decent life.

In the next excerpt, Sano *sensei*, who knew that Yusuke needed to be more assertive, used a more direct strategy to encourage him to communicate with the principal. Yusuke found that he had to go to the principal's office to obtain her permission to eat in the Challenge Room, but he was hesitant to go. Yusuke viewed the principal as a person in authority and knew that he had to follow her directions and "behave himself" in front of her. With Sano *sensei's* encouragement, Yusuke was able to talk to the principal:

After 4th period, when Yusuke and the other children [in the Rainbow Room] were about to go to their general education classrooms to eat lunch, he told me [Misa], "I told Akiyama *sensei* [the principal] I will eat lunch in the fifth grade [classroom today], but I couldn't say I wanted to eat at the Challenge Room." I asked him, "Do you want to go ask her if you can change [the place to eat]?" He said, "I'll go," so, I went to the 1st floor [where the principal's office is located] with him. In the elevator, he looked very nervous. I asked him, "Do you want to see Sano *sensei* [instead of the principal]?" He said "Yes!" and we went to the school nurse's office. Yusuke said to her, "I told Akiyama *sensei* that I would eat at the fifth grade [classroom], but I changed my mind. I want to eat at the Challenge Room." Sano *sensei* said, "Well, can you tell Akiyama *sensei*? Do you want to practice with me?" ... [After leaving Sano *sensei's* office, Yusuke found that the principal had a visitor] and explained to the assistant principal that he wanted to talk to Akiyama *sensei*. She noticed Yusuke and came to talk to him. Yusuke repeated what he told Sano *sensei*. The principal [who knew that Yusuke usually enjoyed eating lunch with Dai] suggested to him that he eat at the Rainbow Room with Dai and Tanaka *sensei*. (Excerpt from Misa's field notes)

Yusuke happily accepted this suggestion and ate lunch with Dai, Tanaka *sensei*, and Misa at the Rainbow Room. Through these conversations, Sano *sensei* and the principal encouraged Yusuke to speak up about his needs and experience the success of doing so. Just as educators guided parents toward any support they might need to manage their own feelings of stress and make decisions for their children (*see* Chapter 5), they allowed children to make choices, rather than forcing children to follow their directions.

Variation in Classroom Teachers' Skills and Knowledge

Of course, there is variation in classroom teachers' skills and knowledge about special education. Most classroom teachers at Greenleaf Elementary School understood the new requirement of providing special education services for children with developmental disabilities, but not all had the skill or experience to carry it out. The principal described her own attempts to educate herself and suggestions for other teachers:

> Most classroom teachers do not know what children [with disabilities] need because they don't have [a special education] certificate. I am also one who doesn't have the certificate. While working with [children in a special education classroom] for three years, I wondered what I could do, and then, I went to workshops after school. I had to pay because it was not offered by the [local] board of education. I also bought books. It was not that cheap, but I wanted to learn to be a professional, as much as possible. There were in-school workshops or study groups at the board of education, but I learned by myself. What I found during that time was that if I had skills and knowledge, I'd be able to help children who were struggling. So, now, I'd like as many staff members as possible to learn this kind of stuff.

Many teachers who had experience teaching children in special education classrooms described that their attitudes toward children with disabilities changed as they learned how to teach and interact with them. They viewed their experiences also as useful when teaching children in general education classrooms—for example, their ability and sensitivity in identifying the needs of individual children and providing them with additional support while overseeing the whole class. One teacher clearly indicated that teachers should have some experience with children with disabilities while they are in college. This teacher continued that experiences with children with disabilities could widen their "values" and allow teachers to be better able to understand children's perspectives, rather than insisting children meet teachers' expectations. Similarly, another teacher described:

> Differences between teachers are still significant...There are teachers who are not able to adjust to children's own pace, and this is the fact [unfortunately], so, I can't say anything about this, but for these teachers, even though they love children [who have difficulties in their classrooms], children are suffering. I think both of them are suffering, but if they [teachers] know what to do, specifically, they may be able to handle [the situation better]. If the only thing teachers can do is to tell children, "Do it," and then feel that, "I'm telling them [as much as I can]," but children don't do, can't do. It's very [stressful] for children, too, because teachers keep telling a lot, but nothing changes, so it's stressful [for both of them].

The principal also described that teachers' lack of knowledge and skills may contribute to their negative attitudes toward children with disabilities:

> A little more thought as to how to [support children with disabilities], and we can maintain dignity as humans. But when we don't know, or haven't been able to figure out what to do and how to support...It's also our responsibility, but it's not easy, so the first thing teachers do may be to attack and regard it as if that's not their responsibility, to make themselves feel better.

Teachers who have less experience and knowledge about special education also expressed anxiety in working with children with disabilities who have interpersonal problems with other children. For example, one teacher expressed anxiety because she did not know what to do:

> Honestly, I know I have to learn more. Well, it's like I'm worried about it. It's like learning together with [children] at the same time, so I feel somehow, you know, I don't know what the best is for these children,

and feel sorry for them. It shouldn't be like this, but the only thing I can do is to understand them, or accept them [as they are].

Support Sources for Inexperienced Teachers

For educators to gain skills and knowledge, several resources were available, including workshops regularly organized by the local board of education. In addition, teachers who have experience and knowledge about teaching children with disabilities, such as the principal, Sano *sensei*, and Aoki *sensei*, served as resources for other teachers. For example, when Dai's general education classroom teacher was struggling with handling his transition to special education, she appreciated the support she received from the principal, "[She] told me she would explain to [other children], so, I'm relieved now." She also described Sano *sensei*, "[She] knows everything [about children and what each child needs]." Another general education classroom teacher stated:

> There have been times, many times, when I wasn't sure how I should deal with [a child]. I usually consult with an "authority" within the school. In the schools [I have taught], there were at least one [who knew very well about special education], so I asked them like, "Today, [a child] behaved like this and did that, so what could I do for [the child]?" Because I am with the child for a year, I think it's my responsibility to ask for suggestions if I don't know what I can do, even if I have to ask every day, for example, how a child felt when the child behaved in a certain way and what I could do. This works much better than whatever I can think of that might work, and also children can stay calm.

This teacher shared a successful example:

> I had a child who wanted to stick to a time [schedule]. He can't bear it if we went on a minute over or less, if I give them the specific time [to work on tasks]. I didn't know that, so I just told them like, "Ok, let's finish by…" and the child told me, "One minute over!" So, I was told that if I gave them the specific time, I should tell the child to stop working, even though other children kept working. It makes the child feel better. Since then, whatever happened, I let him finish the tasks at the time I had informed [the class] of, or do whatever I said I would.

Discussion

Japanese educators understood children's disabilities as among many human "differences" that have implications for interpersonal relationships. Their descriptions of how they support children with developmental disabilities, as well as participant observations, revealed a blending of traditional Japanese socialization and education practices with new, formal special education services. These practices addressed the dilemma of how to implement new formal special education services without stigmatizing children or restricting their opportunities for the social, moral, and intellectual development within peer groups necessary for full adult functioning in Japanese society.

Ideally, educating children within their peer groups allows both those children experiencing difficulties with social or academic skills and their peers to learn through their interactions. Children with developmental disabilities learn how to make and maintain friendships. When they have difficulties in understanding academic content, they can learn the joy of understanding and completing tasks by working together with their peers. At the same time, their peers learn about and respect individual differences. In their daily interactions, typically developing children are encouraged to think from the viewpoint of children with disabilities—for example, through teachers' interpretations of the children's behaviors that cause conflicts within classrooms, which strengthens children's empathy and sensitivity to others' feelings and needs (*omoiyari*). They also learn appropriate ways to help individuals experiencing difficulties. By exposing typically developing children to peers who have developmental disabilities, educators hope to reduce discrimination when children are older.

Within Japanese classrooms, relationships between peers are critical. Maret (2008) found that those Japanese children who were struggling academically, but who had supportive relationships with their peers, tended to stabilize in their general education classrooms. At Greenleaf Elementary School, teachers attempted to create general education classrooms where children with disabilities felt comfortable and were able to participate—for example, by creating a home-like environment including the involvement of their typically developing peers in supporting them. In general, children's classrooms are intended to be places they can create their *Ibasho,* just like their homes where they feel safe, comfortable, and accepted, rather than only a place to learn academic skills. When children received support at the Challenge Room or the Rainbow Room, their general education classroom teachers continued to support their relationships with peers in general education classrooms. These practices facilitated *Ibasho* creation and education for *kokoro* for all children.

Teachers intentionally created environments and opportunities for children to interact with others—for example, by asking peers to create a classroom like "home" as Dai's classroom teacher did. In short, children with special needs receive socialization into Japanese culture, as do their typically developing peers who benefit through increased empathy (*omoiyari*) and education for *kokoro*.

Rituals to welcome children back from the Challenge Room were observed in several classrooms, especially for younger children. They also illustrate the close relationships of children with their peers and educators. For example, children understood their classroom teacher's explanation that welcoming Dai made it easier for him to come back to their classroom. Dai, who was confused at first began enjoying and participating in the greeting ritual. At the same time, welcoming children back to their classrooms could lead to labeling them as different. When Misa shared this story with a U.S. teacher, she expressed concerns about singling the children out. The U.S. teacher's interpretation underscores the problems inherent in attempting to transfer directly and literally practices from one culture to another. Her interpretation may have arisen from a lack of understanding of the implicit meanings attached to the Japanese greeting words. Japanese children know that the greeting ritual is used at home when someone is leaving or coming back home. A person who leaves home says, "*Itte-kimasu*," and the person who stays at home says, "*Itte-rasshai*." When the person comes home and says, "*Tadaima*," the person who is at home greets the person by saying, "*Okaeri-nasai*." There are no English words that have the same meanings. A close translation of *okaeri-nasai* may be "welcome back" or "welcome home," but parents do not use these English greeting words everyday to greet their children when they come back from school. The feeling of, "I'm a member of this family/group" may be stronger in these Japanese greeting words than the corresponding English words.

Just as educators preferred non-coercive practices when interacting with children in peer groups, so, too, were these practices preferred when providing children with individualized support. Based on careful observation of each child's needs, educators adjusted their instruction and support in a way that the child could easily understand and follow. Sano *sensei*, for example, routinely created a zone of proximal development for children: a gap between what they could accomplish independently and that which they could accomplish with support from others with more experience (Vygotsky, 1978; Wertsch, 2008). For example, Yusuke was given a chance to practice before talking with the principal. Sano *sensei* encouraged him to overcome the challenge by lowering the "hurdle," but not eliminating it, and by providing support. She intentionally created a gap between his current level of performance and expectations for him. Her goal was not only to increase Yusuke's competence but also to enable him to experience the joy of overcoming challenges and completing difficult tasks, which can motivate children and help them become more confident.

Social interactions involving emotional experiences can facilitate the establishment of close relationships between children, peers, educators, and parents. Cave (2007) suggested that these sort of emotional experiences tie children together as a group. Further, Quinn and Strauss (1997) argued that emotional experiences involved in classroom instruction can help children internalize what they are taught. For example, as a consequence of his initial choice to eat lunch at the "other place," Dai found that he was in a more emotionally difficult situation. Other researchers who have examined Japanese preschools have identified similar practices. In these studies, teachers waited for the appropriate time to intervene and even created an opportunity for children to learn by letting them misbehave and engage with problematic situations (Peak, 1991; Tobin et al., 2009). For example, a teacher waited to intervene until a child who had been misbehaving, pulling another child's hair, came to an emotional "boiling over" and cried (Tobin et al., 2009). Peak also observed, "When Japanese children cry after inappropriate behavior at preschool, it is rarely due to having been punished or scolded by the teacher. Instead, crying results from having been forced to experience the consequences of an incident that the child instigated himself" (p. 156). Tobin and his colleagues (1989) discussed that U.S. educators interpreted this practice as Japanese teachers ignoring children's misbehaviors, including physical fights, which required immediate attention in U.S. schools. To find the right time to intervene, Japanese teachers practice *mimamori*. This thoughtful and intentional strategy of watching over children with compassion as protective figures can put children in a more challenging situation emotionally than when they are punished for their mischievous behaviors. Lewis (1995) characterized the Japanese disciplinary focus as on children's internal motivation, rather than tangible rewards and punishment. The goal is for children to become responsible members of the school community (*see also* Benjamin, 1997; Sato, 2004).

In an educational environment that stresses peer group membership, Japanese children who do not fit into peer groups may find their classrooms and school a source of stress. Japanese children with developmental disabilities may have an especially hard time adjusting, more so than children in a culture where individuality is valued. This stress can impact children's functioning through a loss of self-esteem and motivation to learn. Once they are recognized as "different" and isolated from their peers, as Ono *sensei* indicated, it may not be easy for these children to get re-integrated into their peer groups. As the new special education services for children with developmental disabilities in general education classrooms is fully implemented and educators' awareness, knowledge, and skills increase, they may be able to identify children who begin to develop problems early when they can benefit from less intensive and restrictive support. Yet not all classroom teachers are trained to teach children with disabilities or to recognize their special needs. When teachers find that children are experiencing difficulties, their problems may already be serious—for example, refusing to come to school as in the cases of Yusuke and Dai. In the next chapter, we will describe how children experienced and navigated the newly implemented special education.

Notes

1. In addition to a regular teaching certificate, classroom teachers in special education schools are required to hold a special education certificate (Ministry of Internal Affairs and Communication, 2008c). Achieving special education certification entails the completion of specific courses related to teachers' specialization, such as hearing and visual impairments, intellectual disabilities, and physical disabilities, in addition to teaching experiences, including as a student-teacher. Educators in general public schools can teach children with disabilities without special education certification. As of 2011, only 32.8% of special education classroom teachers in elementary schools held a special education certificate (Ministry of Education, 2012a).
2. She, however, noted that if specialized programs and technologies are available to teach children with disabilities, then they can benefit from such programs.
3. Japan is generally known as ethnically homogeneous, but recently the number of immigrants, (e.g., from other Asian countries and Brazil) are increasing. These children may experience language and communication difficulties.
4. He also participated in activities without using his wheelchair, as suggested by his classroom teacher, which further facilitated other children's voluntary cooperation to create rules for Ototake.
5. This teacher did this during her regular working hours after children are dismissed. Classroom teachers' working hours are from 8 a.m. to 4:45 p.m. After children are dismissed, around 3:30 p.m. on typical days, teachers spend their time preparing for instruction, staff meetings, and other activities, such as participating in study groups and workshops. Not many teachers go home at 4:45 p.m. Many of them work "voluntarily" until 7 p.m. or later.

7 CHILDREN'S AND PARENTS' EXPERIENCES OF DISABILITY AS THEY TRANSITION INTO SPECIAL EDUCATION

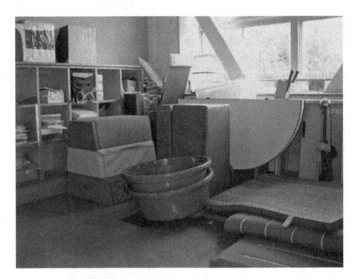

Challenge Room (Play Area)

Children in the Challenge and Rainbow Rooms looked forward to recess, a time when they played with the many attractive toys in the Challenge Room. Several children from general education classrooms also enjoyed playing in the Challenge Room and "checking on" their classmates who were transitioning into special education. In Dai's third grade general education classroom, as soon as class was over, several children suggested, "Let's go to the Challenge Room!" Children from Yusuke's classroom also stopped by the Challenge Room to talk to Yusuke and join the play. When children arrived early, they waited in the hallway for Yusuke and Dai to finish their worksheets. If Yusuke and Dai were still cleaning after lunch, some children helped them clean. In their general education classrooms, Yusuke and Dai were quiet and cautious when interacting with other children. In the Challenge Room, however, they were lively and active, creating play together, and even acting as leaders of the group play (Excerpt from Misa's field notes).

As we have seen in previous chapters, educators carefully attended to parents' and children's feelings and their emotional readiness in providing special education services. Children's experience of the new system of special education also was influenced by the responses of their peers. As the opening vignette illustrates, some of children's general education classmates sought them out during recess and joined them in enjoying the toys at the Challenge Room. During Misa's observation, three participant children transitioned from receiving their instruction in their general education classrooms with some support in the Challenge Room to receiving most of their instruction in the Rainbow Room with some continuing participation in their general education classrooms as appropriate. All three children generally enjoyed the support they received at the Challenge and Rainbow Rooms but also expressed anxiety during their transition, including struggles in maintaining peer relationships. They expressed a general recognition that they were different in some ways from their peers in general education classrooms. Dai and Kakeru did not express additional curiosity about the nature of those differences, or the implications of studying at the Challenge and Rainbow Rooms. Yusuke, on the other hand, was quite concerned and began to openly question his ability to learn and eventually initiated a conversation with his mother, who spoke with him about his disabilities and their implications for his future.

This chapter describes children's perspectives on their disabilities or "difficulties" and how they experienced the new, formal system of special education and their transitions to the Rainbow Room. To a lesser extent, it also illustrates the challenges and responses of their parents. Dai's case illustrates the role of educators in helping children and their parents transition to the new system of special education. Educators created an environment in which Dai could fully benefit from support outside of his general education classroom and guided his mother to accept his needs for special education. Kakeru's case illustrates the importance of parental understanding of their children's disabilities and provision of developmentally appropriate support in collaboration with educators. Kakeru's parents actively collaborated with his teachers. They also created a protected environment at home from which he could face the challenges of learning new skills, both academically and interpersonally, at school. Yusuke, who is older than the other two children, articulated his own understanding of his difficulties. His case illustrates his struggles and the process through which he learned to cope with hardships and understand his "difficulties."

Dai (3rd grade–4th grade)

Dai's "hiding place"

Dai was 8 years old at the beginning of the study. He had a diagnosis of high-functioning autism. His parents recognized and were concerned about his struggles beginning in preschool, but Dai continued to participate with his peers in general education classrooms through second grade without major problems. When Dai received appropriate support and adults dealt with his behaviors in a consistent manner, he functioned well at school. Dai appeared happy and took the initiative to expand his activities on tasks in which he was interested, such as drawing fish, but when adults pushed him to work on new or difficult materials, he gave up quickly and withdrew.

By third grade, Dai was clearly struggling with peer relationships and increasing academic demands. He had done well in his second grade classroom, which had less than 20 students. In addition, Dai's second grade classroom teacher, Maekawa *sensei,* was known as one of the "experts" in special education[1] at Greenleaf Elementary School and understood his needs for additional support. At the beginning of third grade, Dai's general education classroom size increased to 37 children. In addition, it was the first time the teacher of third grade had taught a "child like Dai." Dai soon began having difficulties—for example, refusing to go to school in the morning. He also developed a fear of being left out of other children's play during recess.

Despite his struggles in third grade, however, Dai's mother was concerned that any involvement by Dai in special education services would lead to stigmatization, including by peers. In light of his mother's hesitation, educators suggested that Dai study part-time in the Challenge Room rather than immediately referring him to the Rainbow Room. Even after Dai began studying in the Rainbow Room, educators waited to complete the necessary paperwork until his mother was ready to officially place Dai in special education. This transition created opportunities for his mother to observe children in the Challenge and Rainbow Rooms, interact with their parents, and carefully consider the best placement for Dai. During his third grade year, Dai continued to struggle with conflicting desires and expectations: his own desires, his mother's expectations for how he should receive support at school, and teachers' expectations for him to be more independent.

Transition to the Challenge Room

Misa's observations of Dai began in mid-June, 2009 on his first day studying at the Challenge Room with a part-time teacher, Sakai *sensei*. Sano *sensei* carefully monitored his reactions to being pulled out from his general education classroom. At the end of third period, Sakai *sensei* and Dai discussed whether he would continue to study with her during fourth period or return to his third grade classroom. During the break, Sano *sensei*, who heard this conversation, suggested that Dai return to his classroom. She explained to him that he should participate in the classroom discussion about an upcoming field trip. Sano *sensei* was concerned that Dai would become too attached to Sakai *sensei* and decide to stay at home on days when she was not at school and he had to study full-time in his general education classroom. On the way back to his classroom, Dai pretended to be a "tour guide" and took a hand towel from his pocket and waved it like a flag, so Sakai *sensei*, Sano *sensei*, and Misa followed him. Still, he looked nervous and told them that other children might be surprised if he arrived during the middle of the day.

As Sano *sensei* had anticipated, Dai quickly came to prefer the Challenge Room to his third grade classroom. During his first week, Dai studied in both his classroom and the Challenge Room. On the days Sakai *sensei* did not come to school, teaching assistants, including Misa, worked with Dai and Yusuke[2] in the Challenge Room. During the next week, Dai began to refuse to go to his classroom, choosing to study at the Challenge Room almost all day long.

Dai's rather abrupt transition to the Challenge Room created confusion and curiosity among his third grade classmates. At his mother's request, teachers did not initially explain to the other children why Dai was going to the Challenge Room. They became confused and wondered what Dai was doing at the Challenge Room. For example, one child speculated in front of Dai, "[He is going to the Challenge Room] because he is behind," and another child asked him with whom he was studying at the Challenge Room. Dai also noticed that other children asked their classroom teacher about his absences from their general education classroom. He looked nervous when he overheard his teacher explaining his work at the Challenge Room to other children. Through this discourse on "missing Dai," Dai and his peers began to openly recognize his "difference." They also began to understand that studying in the general education classroom with other children could overwhelm Dai. Some children were concerned about Dai, and when they saw Misa in their classroom or the hallway, they asked her if he was at school and doing ok. Dai also noticed that his attendance at the Challenge Room made him "different" from other children. By the third week, Dai only went back to his classroom when he had a question for his teacher, Kawai *sensei,* or to get his lunch, which he brought back to the Challenge Room to eat.

Still, Dai seemed to think about his peers while he was in the Challenge Room and asked Sakai *sensei* and teaching assistants, "What do you think they [other children in his classroom] are doing?" and asked them to come to the classroom with him. Yet these visits frequently resulted in Dai getting extra attention from his classmates, which made him uncomfortable, so he began to avoid such situations. One day, on the way to his classroom, he told Misa that he preferred to go to the classroom during recess or 5-minute breaks, or if the class had already started to "*ton ton* [an onomatopoeic word indicating knocking on a door]." Gradually, however, he became anxious about going back to his classroom and hid behind Misa when they approached the classroom door. As he began to find his *Ibasho* at the Challenge Room, he spent more time there. After a while, he began to recognize himself as a child of the Challenge Room.

Nevertheless, Dai was always welcomed in his general education classroom. When his third grade classroom held an Apricot Party before the summer break, Dai, who had not participated in the weeks-long preparation, decided the day before to attend the party. Children had planned and prepared to make apricot treats in small groups. Not only was Dai allowed to come to the party, but he was able to join one of the groups in making treats. Children welcomed Dai by using a ritual greeting word, *okaeri-nasai* (welcome back), to which Dai responded with the ritual response, "*Tadaima* (I'm back)." This greeting ritual had been initiated by their classroom teacher to create an accepting atmosphere in her classroom in which Dai felt more comfortable coming and going (*see* Chapter 6). By using these ritual words, usually used at home on a daily basis, children implicitly sent a message to Dai that he was a member of their "family" at school. Dai also expressed appreciation of the ritual when we talked about his classroom during the individual interview.

Coping With "Difficulties"

Although Dai's parents and teachers had not discussed his diagnosed "disability" with him, he did know that he was struggling with "difficulties" different from those experienced by other children. His second grade classroom teacher, Maekawa *sensei,* who had experience teaching children with autism spectrum disorder, found that teaching Dai was challenging. He described Dai's struggles in his peer relationships.

> I think it is stressful for him in many ways...To explain it straightforwardly, he was sensitive to the fact that he was not able to do things [like other children], so I found it was very difficult to work with him...I anticipated that the most difficult thing for him in third grade would be the classroom size which would be doubled...even though he was good at observing [other people], gathering information, and imitating others. So, in this respect, it may work better for him if he is with friends...but sometimes children's minds were not there [and they had conflicts with him]. If we consider his [development] for an extended period of time, he can't avoid it [and needs to find some way to interact with his peers].

Some of the strategies Dai used to cope with conflicts with others were to avoid potentially difficult situations, for example, he avoided going back to his classroom and refused to engage in unfamiliar activities. Misa and other teaching assistants observed that he gave up easily and tried to switch tasks when activities, academic or otherwise, including playing with other children, were difficult. Frequently, he quit or got confused when he made a mistake and did not like his mistakes to be openly corrected. If adults pushed him to correct his mistakes, he would say "No" and withdraw. Sano *sensei* described such a situation to Misa. Children usually eat lunch in their classrooms, but each day several children eat lunch at Sano *sensei*'s school nurse's office, including children in charge of announcing the day's lunch menu. Dai sometimes joined them when teaching assistants were not available to stay with him in the Challenge Room. On one such day, he refused to follow Sano *sensei*'s directions. She explained:

> Before eating lunch, we washed our hands, but Dai touched a table in my office. I told him, "Children who are sick also come here, so this room may be full of germs. You touched the table, go wash your hands again. [It's not only for you, but] other children also have to." He then said, he didn't like to be corrected, and if his mother did the same thing at home, he would go to his room, shut the door, and put a note on the door saying, "Don't come in." Instead of washing his hands, he said, "I won't eat lunch" and went to the other side of the room while we were eating. He faced the other side of the room, but it was not like he didn't mind at all. He sometimes looked at us [eating], but didn't come to us. We talked about our experiences of being disciplined. Other children, they were fifth and sixth graders, described similar experiences, and we discussed that when parents correct their children, it means that they care for them . . . We did not ignore Dai, so if he asked questions, we answered. He looked at us, but didn't come. After a while, he asked me, "Is it too late to eat lunch?" I told him it was not too late. He said, "I'm gonna go to the bathroom and wash my hands." After he came back to my office, he finally started eating. (Excerpts from Misa's field notes)

Sano *sensei*'s response to Dai's refusal to wash his hands before eating lunch is one example of how educators created opportunities for him to experience "success" and motivated him to learn social skills using his real life conflicts. Sano *sensei* explained, "He may not understand what he is told right now, but he will be able to understand later." The conflict with Sano *sensei* actually motivated Dai to follow the rule of washing hands before eating. Several weeks later, when Misa ate lunch with Dai at the Challenge Room, he asked, "Did you touch anywhere? Let's go wash our hands." Following Sano *sensei*'s suggestions, when Dai refused her directions, Misa let him do as he chose, although she noticed that the outcome of this choice might be uncomfortable for him. Sano *sensei* and teaching assistants intentionally allowed him to refuse to follow adults' directions so that he would experience the conflicts that emerged from his decisions and "naturally" learn the value of following the school rules.

Maekawa *sensei* described his goals for Dai.

...instead of saying "No" automatically, like an allergic reaction, I'd like him to be able to go along with [these challenges], even though he doesn't like [to do so] or finds it difficult. Otherwise, he will be stressed out. I also think I want him to be able to [cope with difficulties] through interactions with other children. So, I think this year, he must be struggling. I think he should have a feeling like he wants to [study and play] with [other children]. He should have a feeling that he wants to make an effort. I don't think he doesn't want [to make an effort] any more, but probably, his feeling, his willingness to do his best, is heading somewhere else. Then, it makes it more difficult for him. I don't know what it is like right now [because he is not in my class this year], but unless we set somewhat lower goals for him, so he feels he can do it, and those goals are met on a daily basis, his life at school may become more difficult.

After he moved to the Challenge Room, the initial goal that teachers set for Dai was to adjust to his new environment and to establish relationships with the people there, e.g., teaching assistants including Misa. As Dai met this goal, he began to enjoy the "freedom" of being in the Challenge Room. He started refusing tasks and requesting to go to the library and other rooms while other children were studying in their classrooms. Sano *sensei* and the principal discussed that he should learn that the rules of his general education classroom still applied in the Challenge Room—for example, following adults' directions.

Despite educators' acceptance and support, Dai still needed a place to isolate himself from others, and occasionally ran away from the Challenge Room. When he was asked to let adults know where he was going before leaving, Dai protested, "Then, I can't hide." Dai and Misa then agreed to make a hiding place in the Challenge Room. The hiding place, a space enclosed by partitions, provided a safe place for him to calm down and ready himself for interacting with others. Dai's tolerance for interactions with peers increased as he was allowed to self-regulate contact with them.

[After recess, Dai was cleaning the Challenge Room with Yusuke and children from the Rainbow Room.] Dai pulled the tricycle over to the cabinet, but he put it where the other children were going to place a vaulting box. I told him, "The tricycle is in the way of the vaulting box, why don't you put it there?" but he refused, "I won't." When I asked him again, he was not smiling any more. I decided to let him do as he wanted. As I had anticipated, the vaulting box hit the tricycle. When the tricycle fell toward him, he withdrew and said, "I will go there," and pointed to the hiding place. As soon as I said, "Ok," he walked to the hiding place and stayed alone. After five minutes or so...Dai said, "I'm ok now," and came out from the hiding place. (Excerpt from Misa's field note)

Struggles of Dai's Mother

Dai's mother also struggled with his transition from the third grade general education classroom to the Challenge Room and subsequently to the Rainbow Room. She did not want other children and parents to know about his problems. She understood that Dai needed more support than was available in his general education classroom but was not able to accept that Dai could not remain in the classroom. She shared her experiences:

It was really hard from the beginning [to take care of him]. First and second grades were the exceptions. It was the only time I thought things went well...like a dream. Right now, I feel like it's turned back, again. During these two years, he had developed [as other children did], and I thought he was going to develop [without any problem], so I was shocked. It was too much, yes.

It was clear to educators who knew him well that Dai appeared happier in the Challenge Room. During his first few days at the Challenge Room, Dai was very quiet and read books alone at recess, but over the next week, he gradually joined and played with the small group of children there. In addition to Yusuke, Dai had a chance to play with three other children from the Rainbow Room, which was located next to the Challenge Room. Children from general education classrooms also came to play with the equipment in the Challenge Room, such as cushions, gym mattresses, blocks, balls, a tricycle, and other materials. Yet Dai's mother was less pleased with this transition to the Challenge Room. Misa's field note described Sano *sensei's* observation:

What Dai thinks and what his mother thinks are a bit different. There was a choice to place Dai in the Rainbow Room [directly from his general education classroom], but we decided to start with the Challenge

Room [for Dai's mother, not for him]. His mother wants him to study in the general education classroom, but Dai has already accepted the Challenge Room and likes it better. After he started studying in the Challenge Room, he looks good, so [I think] what his mother thinks may have changed recently. It might be a detour for him, but we decided [to place him in the Challenge Room, not the Rainbow Room] for his mother. (Excerpt from Misa's field note)

In short, Dai was placed in the Challenge Room as a transition until his mother accepted that he needed support at the Rainbow Room. In the Challenge Room, he was able to study with teaching assistants, which was better than not coming to school. Yet studying with different teaching assistants each day was not optimal for his long term progress, which was also his mother's concern. Sano *sensei* clearly stated:

We have to consider children's outcome on a long term basis, even after they graduate from here. We just can't make a decision day by day to make children happy.... To tell the truth, other children already know he is different because he is in the Challenge Room. I think the transition to the Rainbow Room may be easier than the transition to the Challenge Room [for his mother]. (Excerpt from Misa's field note)

"A Child of the Rainbow Room"

Two weeks before the summer break, during a meeting with the principal, Dai's mother agreed to place him in the Rainbow Room. The next morning, however, educators noticed that she had not fully accepted this transition when she expressed shock at finding Dai's desk in the Rainbow Room. Educators explained to her that the desk in the Rainbow Room was to welcome Dai, and that he still had a desk in his third grade classroom. Although Dai had begun studying at the Rainbow Room, educators delayed completion of the paperwork to officially place Dai in special education until the end of the school year to accommodate his mother's emotional readiness. Dai, however, preferred the Rainbow and Challenge Rooms to his third grade classroom.

After he began studying at the Rainbow Room, Dai described his thoughts about school. He described the Challenge Room as a "different" place where "there are many text books [for Sakai *sensei* to teach children from various grade levels], toys but not much, a computer, and many things [that he has not seen in his third grade classroom]." For Dai, studying at the Challenge Room was "easy," partly because to keep him motivated to learn the teachers selected worksheets and other materials that involved content he had already mastered in first and second grades. During this period, providing an environment Dai was able to enjoy and improving his school attendance, not teaching new academic skills, were the priorities. Dai responded to Misa's question about which classroom he liked the best:

DAI: Sure, the best is the Rainbow Room and the second is the Challenge Room.
MISA: Ok, then why do you think the Rainbow Room is the best?
DAI: Because, you know, there are lots of toys. There are many things I wanna do. It looks like fun [to play with] them.
MISA: In the Rainbow Room?
DAI: Yes, and the teachers are kind.

Dai then described his third grade general education classroom, "[After] two second grade classrooms became one [third grade] classroom, and it got difficult studying... because there are 37 children. So I think it's noisy." He continued, "Sometimes I don't have friends [to play with during recess]... but here [in the Challenge and Rainbow Rooms], there are toys and other things, so it's ok. I can play by myself."

In short, interpersonal problems and the increasing academic demands overwhelmed Dai and made it hard for him to go back to his third grade classroom. In the Challenge and Rainbow Rooms, he enjoyed studying at his own pace, free from the pressure to maintain interpersonal relationships with other children.

At this point in time, Dai spent most of the day at either the Challenge Room or the Rainbow Room. He began considering himself as a member of the Rainbow Room. In the following conversation with a second grader, Dai described himself as a child of the Rainbow Room but expressed confusion because he also was a member of the third grade general education classroom. When Dai and Misa went to the library, they stopped by the third grade classroom. The classroom was empty and only children's school bags were on their desks. A second grade boy saw Dai in the hallway and asked:

BOY: Dai! Dai! Where are all the third graders?
DAI: I don't know, too.
BOY: You don't know? You are in third grade, right?
DAI: Because I'm in the Rainbow Room.
BOY: Aren't you in "Fight" [the name of the third grade classroom]?

(Dai appeared confused. Later, he and Misa went to see the classroom again but were unable to find the other third graders.) (Excerpt from Misa's field note)

Dai also was confused about whether he was allowed to participate in activities in his third grade classroom. Dai's mother, who attended as one of the volunteer parents helping children cook and clean at the Apricot Party (described earlier), shared what Dai had asked her:

[Dai] said last week he didn't want to come [to the Apricot Party]...the class will have a farewell party for a child who is transferring to another school, but Dai hadn't heard [from them] to come to the party. [Yesterday], he asked me, "Why?" so I said, "Because you weren't in [the classroom when they discussed it]." Instead of [the farewell party], I asked him if he wanted to come to the Apricot Party. He asked me, "Do [you think] I can go?" I said, "Sure" and, "Do you want me to call Kawai *sensei*?" and I called her. Then, she told us [not only to come to the party], but that he could join the group [and make his apricot treat]. (Excerpt from Misa's field note)

Kawai *sensei* reflected on the conversation with Dai's mother: "It looks that Dai thought he was not allowed to come. After I heard this from his mother, I thought, I should have told him directly, 'Come to [the party]'."

After the children ate the apricot treats and cleaned the dishes, children talked about their afternoon classes. It was the first time Misa saw Dai talking with other children about the Rainbow Room.

One of the children asked Kawai *sensei* what they would do in 5th period. When Kawai *sensei* answered that a Japanese Language quiz was waiting, children said "Really??" Dai, who was listening to this conversation, smiled and said happily to them, "I'll do craft. I made a calendar [of September for after the summer break], so I'll go find plants [to put on the calendar] that look like *susuki* [Japanese pampas grass, usually found during the fall]. Doesn't this sound nice?" (Excerpt from Misa's field note)

These excerpts illustrate that Dai wanted to remain connected with children in his third grade classroom, but at the same time recognized himself as a child in the Rainbow Room.

Six Months Later: Dai's Struggles

Following the summer break, Dai began struggling because of conflicts between his mother and Tanaka *sensei*, one of the two Rainbow Room teachers. His mother had initially trusted and relied on Tanaka *sensei* but had lost trust in her over several months. She complained about Tanaka *sensei* to the principal and even directly to the local board of education. By January, Dai's attendance became an issue. Before the summer break, he was absent or came to school late with his mother once or twice a week. However, by January, he was absent 2 to 3 days a week. Even when he came to school, he was always accompanied by his mother and arrived 1 to 2 hours late.

Tanaka *sensei* had high expectations for Dai. For example, during this school year, all children in the Rainbow Room went to their general education classrooms to eat lunch, and Tanaka *sensei* expected Dai to do so as well. Yet eating lunch in the general education classroom was increasingly stressful for Dai, a concern of his mother even before Dai moved to the Rainbow Room. When Misa met Dai in January, he was given choices regarding where he would eat every day, but it overwhelmed him. Dai knew that Tanaka *sensei* wanted him to eat in the general education classroom. Therefore, the "choice" given every day by Tanaka *sensei* created an atmosphere in which he felt compelled to eat in the general education classroom. Dai's mother reported that deciding where to eat lunch created extra stress at home and pressure for her and Dai to avoid school every morning.

The principal, who heard about the lunchtime problem, talked with Dai and his mother. She explained that it was OK to not eat lunch in the third grade classroom, if it made it easier for him to come to school. However, the next day, Tanaka *sensei* again asked Dai where he wanted to eat. Dai's initial response was to eat at the general education classroom. Yet when Tanaka *sensei* told him that he could choose wherever he liked, he could not answer. After a silence, Tanaka *sensei* told him to decide by the end of fourth period. He then asked Misa:

DAI: Where will you eat today?

MISA: I haven't decided yet.

DAI: Here [with me]?

MISA: With you? Ok, then which room [the Challenge Room or the Rainbow Room]?

DAI: There [the Challenge Room.] (I saw Tanaka *sensei* who was nodding, and we let him go to the Challenge Room.) (Excerpt from Misa's field note)

Despite the principal's intervention, Tanaka *sensei* continued to ask Dai where he wanted to eat lunch. This ongoing conflict disrupted her relationship with Dai and his mother.

Tanaka *sensei* described to Misa the situation with Dai and his mother, after Misa had left the school. Tanaka *sensei* had seriously thought about Dai and was genuinely concerned about his lack of independence. In addition, she was frustrated with Dai's lack of progress, including in his relationships with other children in his third grade classroom and in preparing for the upcoming achievement test. In general, she felt frustrated with how difficult it was to work with Dai.

Tanaka *sensei* also was confused by what she viewed as his mothers' overly sensitive reactions. She felt that whatever she did, his mother would react defensively—for example, complaining about her to the principal and the board of education. His mother also canceled, at the last minute, Dai's participation in school-wide activities[3] and a meeting to make an official decision to place Dai in the Rainbow Room. Tanaka *sensei* had worked with Dai's mother to prepare and arrange for someone to take care of Dai at home so that she could attend the meeting. All these thoughts and conflicts created tensions between Dai, Tanaka *sensei*, his mother, and other educators and, consequently, put Dai in a more difficult environment, where he received conflicting messages from his teacher and mother. Too often, what he was told at school was changed when he went home, or vice versa.

Note that although Tanaka *sensei* was an experienced teacher, she was not a special education teacher. Dai's behaviors and reactions were not unusual for a child with autism spectrum disorder. Nevertheless, as Maekawa *sensei* described, these behaviors were challenging especially for educators who do not have specialized knowledge and skills. Administrators and Sano *sensei* worked closely with Tanaka *sensei* to help her handle the conflicts and re-establish relationships with Dai and his mother. To provide children with a more structured and supportive learning environment, administrators assigned Aoki *sensei*, who held a special education certificate, to the Rainbow Room the following school year. Tanaka *sensei* and another Rainbow Room teacher returned to teaching in a general education classroom.

Fourth Grade in the Rainbow Room

Dai officially transferred to the Rainbow Room in fourth grade. According to the new Rainbow Room teacher, Aoki *sensei*, his transition at the beginning of the school year in April was difficult. Yet when Misa visited the school in June, every time she saw Dai in the hallway or his classroom, he was smiling and working happily as a member of a group of seven children in the Rainbow Room. During the 5 weeks Misa was there, Dai came to school almost every day. He arrived at school in the morning and attended the morning meeting every day in the Rainbow Room. He also enjoyed participating in other activities with the children there and went home with a child living near his home. This school year, all children, not only Dai, were able to choose where to eat lunch, and Dai enjoyed eating with other children in the Rainbow Room. During the third and fourth periods of the morning, children in the Rainbow Room went to their general education classrooms depending on the subjects being taught. When Misa visited the Rainbow Room, Dai stayed there while all other children went to their general education classrooms. He enjoyed his time at the Rainbow Room with two teachers. He worked on worksheets by himself, as the teachers prepared for the rest of the day. Dai had less time to interact with children in his general education classroom than other children of the Rainbow Room but enjoyed visiting his classroom during cleaning time and playing outside with other children during recess.

Misa saw Dai's mother once at school, but she was not there to observe him. She was working at the library as a volunteer. She appeared happier and calmer than when Misa had seen her several months earlier. When Dai has a teacher who creates an environment where he has less stress, he functions better which also positively affects his mother.

Yusuke (Fifth Grade–Sixth Grade)

At the beginning of the study, Yusuke was 10 years old. He had a learning disability affecting his ability to decode written text and calculate as well as speech

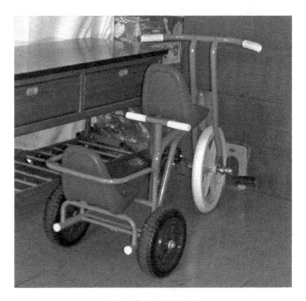

Yusuke's "Train"

problems. He was aware that he could not read and write at the level of other fifth graders, which negatively impacted his self-esteem. Yusuke was very sensitive and attentive to other people's feelings. He tried to accommodate others as much as possible by setting his desires and emotions aside, but this frequently made it difficult for him to express his own struggles and needs.

Aside from his speech problems, Yusuke was considered a typically developing child until fourth grade. At this time, Yusuke refused to come to school because several children from other grades made fun of his stuttering. He also told his mother that he could not understand the instruction. He described himself as "hopeless," and even proclaimed, "I wish I wasn't born." Educators suggested that Yusuke study in the Rainbow Room, where he could interact with a small group of children. Yusuke, however, refused. During the remainder of his fourth grade year, he studied at the school nurse's office, a counseling room, or the principal's office. At the beginning of fifth grade, the principal made the Challenge Room available for Yusuke. Until he was joined by Dai, Yusuke studied in the Challenge Room by himself with Sakai *sensei* or teaching assistants. Here, he found his *Ibasho,* a place where he felt comfort and belonging. Toward the middle of fifth grade, Yusuke began to study in the Rainbow Room and officially transferred there in sixth grade.

Misa observed Yusuke's progress over 1 year in the Challenge and Rainbow Rooms. In fifth grade, as his parents came to understand his disability and needs for special education and to work collaboratively with educators, Yusuke began to enjoy playing with other children and to understand and learn how to cope with his difficulties in the Challenge and Rainbow Rooms. In sixth grade, he gained confidence and enjoyed his "life" at school with children in the Rainbow Room and his general education classroom.

Transition to the Challenge Room

To encourage Yusuke's school attendance, in fifth grade he was allowed to study at the Challenge Room everyday with teaching assistants rather than once a week with Sakai *sensei* like other children. In addition, and at Yusuke's request, his mother came to school with him every day. They usually arrived at school late, between 9 a.m. and 10 a.m. His mother stayed at the Challenge Room with him until lunchtime. She came back to school to pick him up after picking up his younger sister from preschool. She explained,

> In April, when [the school] created this room, he said, "I'll go to school if you come with me." Since then, I'm coming here every day...but

I couldn't accept it and felt, "How long do I have to do this?" or "Why am I here at school?"

Still, there were days when Yusuke could not come to school at all. Sakai *sensei* described Yusuke:

> Well, [I was shocked] when I saw him the first time. He kept telling me he was hopeless. It looked like [he had] no confidence… He looks better right now, but at the beginning of the year, he looked low and didn't come to school. He didn't come to school if his mother was not with him. He reported that other fifth graders studied in their classroom, but he was here [the Challenge Room], so he was not [as good as other children]. Children of his age already have established a sort of self-esteem [or self-respect], so, he [compared himself with other children and] struggled: why couldn't he do this or that? He also told me he wanted to be an adult soon. What he meant by he wanted to grow up was a little different, I thought, from other children. I mean, he likes trains, so, he wants to work at the O station [train station near his home]. Anyway, it's because the school is a place he can't really enjoy, I think. But it seems that [what the school means for him] has changed a bit [after being in the Challenge Room for three months].

When Misa met Yusuke in June, his attitude toward his fifth grade general education classroom had improved slightly. He went to eat lunch in his classroom occasionally and participated in meetings in his classroom to plan and prepare for an overnight field trip scheduled in July. Yusuke also practiced with other fifth graders for several weeks for the sports festival, held at the beginning of June. Sano *sensei* described that Yusuke looked better after that experience.

Still, going to his fifth grade classroom made Yusuke nervous. He frequently asked one of the teaching assistants to come with him. Ono *sensei*, his fifth grade general education classroom teacher, discussed how he benefited from being in the Challenge Room.

> He couldn't come in to the [general education] classroom. When [we] think of what we can do for him, now, there is a room for him, the Challenge Room, and always teachers [teaching assistants] are there, that really helps. For example, there are several [teaching assistants] in the Challenge Room, and when he and other children eat lunch, they

[children] can ask like, "Can you come with me?" and they [teaching assistants] come to classrooms with the children. Things like that, for these children, if [there is someone coming with them], you know, they can feel easy about [going to their classrooms]. But, we didn't have that kind of [support] last year, so he might have thought that he had to go to the classroom or might be able to give it a try, but couldn't make it…that made it more difficult to come to school, I think.

Eventually, with the teaching assistants' help, Yusuke began to try going back to his classroom—for example, during lunchtime and other periods, including Music, Social Studies, and to prepare for the field trip.

Understanding "Difficulties"

Although Yusuke did not understand his learning disability at the beginning of fifth grade, he was aware that he had speech problems. Yusuke's response to Dai and Misa in the following excerpt illustrates Yusuke's perceptions of teasing.

In the elevator, Dai stood on one leg while holding up the other behind him. He hopped and told us,

> DAI: Look look!
> MISA: What are you doing?
> DAI: I'm pretending. I'm a person who can't use a leg[4].
> MISA: Well…pretending [like this] may not be ok.
> DAI: I can see what happens if that person can't use a leg.
> MISA: That's right, you can see what these people are like, but it's not good to imitate just for fun.
> YUSUKE: Imitating isn't good…someone did to me [imitating the way he speaks]. (Excerpt from Misa's field note)

Yusuke also recognized that children in the Rainbow Room all have some sort of disability. For example, after he played with children from the Rainbow Room, which was located next to the Challenge Room, he shut down a computer one of these children used during recess, saying, "Because Akira [a fifth grade boy in the Rainbow Room] is a child with a disability [I am taking care to do what he didn't], but he knows [about certain things] very well." Yusuke once refused to study at the Rainbow Room in fourth grade, but after spending some time together with the three children from the Rainbow Room, his attitude gradually changed. His mother described:

Yes, recently, the presence of Akira becomes very important for Yusuke. How to describe... they are helping each other, well, probably, he is helping Yusuke... it was very good for him to be able to get along with these children. He becomes able to admit that he has a language disability, stuttering, and it's the same as these children who have autism. He used to hide "stuttering" but he came to admit that only the names of disabilities were different, and they were all the same, "disabilities." I guess, he thought he got picked on because "I have a disability." While watching children [in the Rainbow Room] and receiving energy from them, he must have learned very naturally through experiencing the same things together from them that even though [they have disabilities], they can come to school and have fun. Therefore, he is able to say without hesitation to Akira that he has a language disability and stutters a lot.... Yusuke also knows they have disabilities, too, so he tells them about his disability, honestly, like, "It's my way to speak. That's why I'm going to Parkside Elementary School [a nearby school with a resource room for children with language disabilities]," he became able to say like this honestly. So, I really appreciate that [the school] created this [Challenge] room [next to the Rainbow Room].

Although Yusuke accepted his language disability, he continued to feel uncomfortable about his academic struggles. For example, in the Challenge Room, Yusuke acted as a big brother to Dai helping him to interact and play with other children. When it came time to work on worksheets, however, Dai sometimes was ahead of him and would comment, "I've done the same one." This made it hard for Yusuke to come to school, even to the Challenge Room. Sano *sensei*, who heard about Yusuke's discomfort from him and his mother, suggested to the teaching assistants that Yusuke and Dai sit apart when they study together at the Challenge Room, so they would not interrupt each other. Yusuke's mother described how his learning disability was related to his struggles in school:

Children in the Rainbow Room have some sort of diagnosis, such as autism. Yusuke also has [disabilities]. [I took him] to the hospital, but [a doctor] didn't give him a diagnosis [of learning disability]. Yusuke goes to the "Classroom for Speaking and Hearing," [a resource room in Parkside Elementary School], but that's it. He has to "live" in his general education classroom during the rest of the time. He was told at the hospital that he had a bit of a learning disability and a bit of ADHD, and also stuttering, but [the doctor said he] couldn't give him a diagnosis of learning disability because he had only part of it.....If we can give him a diagnosis, like "You have a learning disability" and give him the name of the disability, things may go very smoothly. He may think, "I am like this, so I'll learn something [I am good at]," but when [we are] told, [that the doctor] can't give him a diagnosis because it's just a part of it, he has to hang in there in the general education classroom. But actually, if he goes to his fifth grade classroom, he can't follow instruction, can't write, can hardly understand anything. This can make him anxious, and this was one of the reasons he couldn't go to the classroom.

After being in the Challenge Room with Yusuke for several months, his mother noticed the change in his attitude at school and home. Before he stopped going to school in fourth grade, she described that he was overly active after he got home although he was very quiet at school. She observed that he might have thought that he had to endure [*gaman*], even if he had problems at school. In the Challenge Room, she continued, "He walked and ran around [as he wanted, even during the time he was supposed to study], but he was not as hyperactive as he used to be at home."

Finding Ibasho *in the Challenge Room*

As Yusuke began to accept his "difficulties," he also began to think more positively, recreate his relationships with other children, and rethink his future. As Yusuke established new relationships with children from the Rainbow Room, he began to enjoy playing with them and regained his self-confidence. When Yusuke was asked about studying in the Rainbow Room several months into his fifth grade year, he happily agreed and looked forward to studying and playing there with other children.

During this process of reconnecting with school, he found his "place," his *Ibasho*, where he felt comfort and belonging. Yusuke created his own "world of play" in the Challenge Room and the "world of study" where he confronted hardships. Although he had begun to enjoy his life at school, he still had problems academically and interpersonally, especially when he went to his general education classroom. In the world of play, however, he was a "train driver," which was his dream. This play became a source of motivation for him to work hard, and he began to find new friends. As Yusuke pretended to be a train driver using a large tricycle, other children joined the play. They recognized the tricycle as a train, and created "stations" in the Challenge Room using desks and gym mattresses. During the play, Yusuke functioned as a leader, for example, he created rules for passengers and gave other children directions as a "train driver." This imaginary world functioned as a safe place for Yusuke, which protected him from stress at school. He actually used the phrase "world [of study]" to express his readiness to begin studying. In the following excerpt, recess had ended and the other children had gone back to their classrooms, but Yusuke was still in the play area of the Challenge Room continuing to pretend.

> [Misa said] "One more minute!" and counted down. When I said, "30 seconds," Yusuke said, "I'm going to the world of Japanese Language." ... He said, "I need to prepare," and briefly lay on a gym mattress and then went to his desk. (Excerpt from Misa's field note)

Yusuke's pretend play and the tricycle allowed him to calm down when he was frustrated and connect with peers. Yet his dream also was a source of anxiety because it reminded him of challenges he has to face because of his "difficulties." Toward the end of fifth grade, his mother explained to him that it might take longer for him than other people to become a "train driver" because of his disability. Still, he kept going back to the tricycle. The tricycle seemed to connect the real and imaginary worlds for him. By going back and forth between the worlds of study and play, he gradually re-established relationships with his peers both at the Rainbow Room and his general education classroom.

Transition to the Rainbow Room

Yusuke and Dai began studying together in the Rainbow Room before the summer break and their official transfer there. Unlike Dai's mother, Yusuke's mother responded very positively to the Rainbow Room. On the first day at the Rainbow Room, Yusuke ran to school by himself at 8:05 a.m. and waited with the other children for a teacher to unlock the door of the student entrance. His mother who usually came to school with him arrived at the Rainbow Room during the second period. She reported, "I told him, 'Don't come to school any more for Akiyama *sensei* [the principal, but come to school for yourself].'" A few days later, she described:

> MOTHER: He is a child who starts running without thinking and can't continue, so I'm still anxious that he may feel overwhelmed, but now, at least in these couple of days, he is enjoying, so, I think it's good enough.
> MISA: He was very excited yesterday.
> MOTHER: Yeah, [he said,] "I'm going," "I wanna run with them," and "I wanna do the morning meeting." [Running in the gym was part of the

morning meeting for children in the Rainbow Room.] Because he was here [in the Challenge Room] alone, he might have felt lonely sometimes, I think.

Yusuke actually described that the Rainbow Room was the place he liked the best because the same teachers were there, and he was able to be with other children and enjoy running, exercising, and studying together. He described the Challenge Room as similar to the Rainbow Room—for example, studying difficult subjects—but quieter. In contrast, the general education classroom was noisy and made him nervous.

Acceptance of Learning "Difficulties"

Six months after transferring to the Rainbow Room, Yusuke did not require teaching assistants' support when he went to his fifth grade general education classroom. He went to the classroom with Akira, another fifth grade boy in the Rainbow Room. He also did not require his mother to come to school with him each morning. Rather, he walked to school with friends. His mother still came to school on a daily basis in the middle of the day, and he looked forward to it, but he was independent and smiled more often than when Misa saw him in summer.

Still, when problems occurred in school and he felt sad, it was hard for Yusuke to come back to school the next day. In such cases, he was absent or came to school late with his mother. His classroom teacher at the Rainbow Room accommodated him—for example, by helping him to go home in a good mood as much as possible. For example,

> Yusuke was looking forward to band practice for a music recital for children in special education that was scheduled for the following month. He waited for a teacher to get a key to the music room during the morning recess, but found out that they had to go elsewhere [to prepare for another school-wide activity]... Furthermore, children did not have recess after lunch that day. Still, Yusuke kept asking teachers if they could practice. His teachers decided to take some time after school for him, and all of the children went to the music room to practice, even though some of them wanted to go home. Later, Tanaka *sensei* said, "If we didn't do that, he won't come to school tomorrow" (Excerpt from Misa's field note).

In fifth grade, Yusuke also began questioning his ability to learn and becoming increasingly frustrated. One day, he did not come to school. The following field note excerpt describes Sano *sensei*'s explanation to Misa of his absence from school:

> He was absent yesterday because he asked his mother about his difficulties. Sano *sensei* talked with his mother...and heard that he had asked, "Is there something wrong in my head? You know about it, Mom." His mother could not answer, and talked with a teacher at Parkside Elementary School [where he goes to a resource room for children with hearing and speech problems once a week]. The teacher told his mother that it might be too early to tell him about that, but his mother was concerned because he kept saying, "I am working very hard, but I can't do. I don't get it.... I'm hopeless."... He can't accept [that there is something] he can't do well because there are things he can understand easily, but when he looks at what he is not good at, it's like this [gesture showing uneven ability]. (Excerpt from Misa's field note)

A few days later, Yusuke asked his mother the same question again. His mother had continued to read and think about how to respond to Yusuke. She came to the conclusion that withholding information he had asked for would be harmful. She also felt that it was too soon to name the "disability" for him. She kept him home from school to talk with him. Later, she described to Misa how she explained Yusuke's disability to him. Misa summarized in a field note:

> She had kept the results of the tests [from the doctor]. She showed it to him and explained that his ability to listen and learn was 10 out of 10, but his ability to read, memorize and write what he looked at was 3 out of 10. What other people can memorize in two hours, for him, it may take 6 hours. Therefore, if he tries to keep up with other people, he will be overwhelmed. She said it seemed that he wanted that kind of explanation. He also has a dream to be a train driver, but it may take 4-6 years, if it takes 2-4 years for other people.... [She also told him that] he has to be able to ask someone for what he needs, and if he knows what he can and can't do, he will be able to ask for help...She did not think he would understand if she told him about his learning disability, so she did not tell him the "name" of his disability yet. (Excerpt from Misa's field note)

Yusuke seemed more contented after discussing his "difficulties" with his mother. Although school was a challenging place for him, Yusuke's perception of school gradually changed as he began spending time with Dai and other children in the Rainbow Room. Just as Dai had found his place, Yusuke found his place, his *Ibasho*, at the Challenge and Rainbow Rooms.

Sixth Grade in the Rainbow Room

When Misa met Yusuke about 4 months later, he was in the sixth grade. Sixth graders have special roles as big brothers and sisters (*see also* Chapter 4). One of their roles is to take care of younger children in their small groups consisting of children from all grade levels—for example, while eating lunch, cleaning rooms, and during field trips. On such occasions, sixth graders go to the first grade classroom to pick up the first graders in their groups and take care of them. Yusuke also took this "leader" role. Misa saw him several times in the first grade classroom taking care of them as a "big brother."

From April, the beginning of the new school year, Yusuke officially transferred to the Rainbow Room. He had been tested by specialists at the local board of education, and they suggested that he could benefit from special education.

> The principal made it clear that he was in the Rainbow Room not because of his attendance issue, but because he needed assistance in learning. However, he is on the borderline and his IQ is higher than other children in the Rainbow Room. If his academic performance is improved as a result of being in the Rainbow Room, he may not be eligible to receive special education next year, in junior high school, even if he continues to have interpersonal difficulties in general education classrooms. (Excerpt from Misa's field note)

In the sixth grade, Yusuke worked more independently and enjoyed studying, playing, and interacting with other children, especially with children in the Rainbow Room. He went to his sixth grade general education classroom by himself, and further, he was able to report to the classroom teacher when Akira, another sixth grader in the Rainbow Room, decided not to come. One day, Misa visited the home economics room when all sixth graders were cooking "breakfast." Yusuke worked collaboratively with children from his general education classroom, laughed and talked with them. Nonetheless, his face looked more relaxed when he was in the Rainbow Room.

Yusuke continued to walk to school every day with friends. At the end of January in fifth grade, his mother began working at the school kitchen. During Yusuke's sixth grade year, she occasionally visited the Rainbow Room but did not stay for long, leaving after talking with teachers and seeing that Yusuke was studying.

Although Dai continued to approach Misa to talk whenever he saw her, Yusuke did not rely on her anymore and enjoyed being with other children. He tended not to express his anxiety verbally, but his teachers in the Rainbow Room took this into consideration when organizing activities and provided support as needed. For example, Yusuke had a problem with night terrors, which concerned his mother. When the Rainbow Room children had an overnight fieldtrip, the classroom teacher talked with his mother about his night terrors before making a final decision regarding the bedroom arrangements on the field trip days.

In the safe environment of the Challenge and Rainbow Rooms, Yusuke felt comfort and belonging and was able to push his limits in acquiring new academic and social skills. During his sixth grade year, he even served as a leader of the "Japanese drum club" for third through sixth graders. During the summer festival in mid-July, members of the Japanese drum club played the drums in front of the other children, their parents, and visitors from the community. As a leader, Yusuke had to make an introductory speech. His classroom teacher, who knew that he was nervous, went to see him before their performance. He delivered the speech successfully and appeared confident during the performance.

Kakeru (Second Grade–Third Grade)

At the beginning of our study, Kakeru was 7 years old. He had high-functioning autism with some other behaviors, including hyperactivity and impulsivity. His

Children's work hanging in hallway outside the "We all are friends" (second grade) classroom

mother was a former preschool teacher, and his father worked with individuals with disabilities. They understood Kakeru's struggles and actively worked with educators from the time he was in preschool. Kakeru enjoyed his parents' visit to his school and would excitedly complete his tasks during their stay. He studied with his typically developing peers in his general education classroom through second grade with the support provided by his classroom teacher, Aoki *sensei,* who also held a special education certificate[5]. Kakeru was energetic and enjoyed talking and playing with friends in his classroom but frequently did not listen to others or consider their thoughts and feelings. Although some of his behaviors, such as talking at inappropriate times, were distracting, some of his responses also functioned as icebreakers and encouraged the active participation of other children. For example, when his classroom teacher introduced his mother, who came to help with checking children's worksheets, Kakeru excitedly cautioned his classmates, "My mom gives you 'X's if your writing is messy!" Although Kakeru was behind academically in his general education classroom, his special knowledge of bugs motivated him to study and maintain relationships with peers and educators. The following observation illustrates Kakeru's pride in his expertise. During a 5-minute break after a field trip to a nearby park, children discussed a crayfish they captured:

> A child said, "It's a female."...I asked, "How do you know?" He explained that the claws of [females and males] are different. Kakeru came back to the classroom [and heard our conversation.] He then picked up the plastic cage and examined the "bug" carefully, providing a comprehensive explanation of the sexual differentiation of crayfish. (Excerpt from Misa's field note)

Aoki *sensei* also allowed a child from another second grade classroom to ask Kakeru about bugs during a class period and publicly praised his knowledge (*see* Chapter 6). Even Dai, who was a third grader, respected Kakeru's expertise.

Despite these successes, Kakeru noticed his struggles within his general education classroom. Over the course of the year, he began to find his *Ibasho* in the Challenge and Rainbow Rooms and established his identity as a child of the Rainbow Room.

Preschool and First Grade

During Misa's interview with Kakeru's parents, they described his developmental history, their understanding of his disability, and how they used this understanding to carefully prepare and teach Kakeru in a developmentally appropriate manner. Prior to his second birthday, Kakeru's parents began to notice some unusual behaviors—for example, he did not make eye contact with them. Although he passed the regular developmental check-up at age 2 years, his parents consulted with specialists, and when he was 3 years old they realized that he had some sort of disability. In preschool, he struggled to get along with other children. Yet according to his mother, Kakeru viewed himself as a full member of his classroom and felt as competent as other children. To help him, Kakeru's parents created a safe and protected environment at home so that he was able to make an effort at school.

> We started from accepting him, so he can trust our family...letting him know that [when] there are things he feels bad [about outside], when he has a problem, his family can help him. If he feels safe [at home], that can be a foundation for him...We are sending a message to him, "We're here for you." That's our starting point.

Yet raising a child with a disability is challenging. Like other parents, Kakeru's parents occasionally became frustrated.

> FATHER: There are many things I want to teach him. I can't count how many things I want to tell him, a lot of things, but, you know, [we have to] wait, right?
>
> MOTHER: [Waiting for] his development and [appropriate] time to [tell and teach].
>
> F: Exactly.
>
> M: [We are waiting] for it.
>
> F: I think parents of other children say the same thing. They also have to wait until [children are ready], but,
>
> M: [for him], much longer than other [children] and...
>
> F: Much more than others. [We know] that, but...
>
> M: [There are times we feel] It's annoying.
>
> F: Yeah, it's hard, but [we] have to be patient.
>
> M: I feel I want to teach [him] more, a little bit more, so he can take it. But [if I give him too much], he can't take all of it straightway....While watching over his development, [we tell and teach him] in a way that is best at the time.

Kakeru's parents considered that first grade was a time for him to learn that school is a place where he can have fun. They appreciated that his first grade teacher gave him the first impression of school, that "It's not a bad place," and helped his transition from preschool[6]. Although they were not serious, Kakeru frequently had problems. He was nervous about doing new activities and had difficulties making friends. When these problems accumulated, he refused to go to school. His parents listened to him and helped him to solve each individual problem.

As a second grader, however, he began to realize that the difficult situations he faced were not typical of other children.

Receiving Support in the Second Grade General Education Classroom

Unlike Dai and Yusuke, Kakeru was in his general education classroom full-time when Misa visited Greenleaf Elementary School during the summer of 2009. Kakeru was fortunate in second grade to have a classroom teacher, Aoki *sensei*, who had studied special education in college. His disability was recognized by Aoki *sensei* as well as his parents. Kakeru received the necessary support from Aoki *sensei* on a daily basis in his classroom, including support to stay focused, keep on task, and learn social skills. In addition to the support Kakeru was receiving in the classroom, his parents appreciated that whenever Aoki *sensei* noticed incidents that could make him feel down, she let them know, so that they were able to follow up at home. In response to the consistent support he received at home and at school, Kakeru said to his parents, "I like the second grade. It's fun." His mother continued:

> There have been many things [he struggled with] in terms of relationships with friends during first grade, but other children have developed as well. I think [other children think] like he does something strange, but he is not that bad. Also, he believes that he knows about bugs better than any other child...He insists that he wants to study hard. When he has something he isn't good at, he says he wants to study with Aoki *sensei*...He already has things he doesn't like at school, but still, he holds [positive] feelings. I think it's because he is coming through the right track.

Kakeru also enjoyed active play with other children at recess. Whenever Misa went to Kakeru's classroom before recess, he was one of the first children to find a ball and run with others to the playground. If she arrived late, he was already somewhere playing. One day, Kakeru complained to Misa that the recess was cancelled because they had just come back from a field trip to a park. He appeared disappointed but then happily showed other children and Misa the crawfish he had caught at the park.

During the first semester of second grade, Kakeru's parents initiated a meeting with the principal concerning the test results sent from the local board of education. The test report did not clearly label his disability[7] but did suggest that he could benefit from special education services. Kakeru's parents requested of the principal that he be allowed to study part-time in the Rainbow Room.

At this point in time, Kakeru might have known that he was "different" from other children, but he enjoyed studying with them and Aoki *sensei* in his second grade classroom. Although Kakeru required frequent prompts and reminders to follow directions, Aoki *sensei* understood that Kakeru was working harder than other children and provided assistance to him as needed. For example, when Aoki *sensei* instructed the class to have a textbook ready on their desks and open to a particular page to read aloud, Kakeru continued working on something else. Before instructing the children to start reading, Aoki *sensei* took Kakeru's textbook out from his desk, opened it to the proper page, and indicated by her finger where he should begin reading. Accordingly, Aoki *sensei* always assigned Kakeru a desk in the front row so she could give him immediate assistance.

Transition to the Challenge Room

Kakeru's parents understood that he might have to transfer to a special education classroom as he got older, but they were very careful about telling Kakeru about his own disability. His father explained that he had not shared Kakeru's "disability" with many people because Kakeru did not yet understand his own struggles. His mother agreed and said, "He has not noticed about himself." His father further elaborated:

> I will tell him myself [about his disability, rather than having him hear about it from others], and then he will notice [his "disability"]. He can start [to learn about himself, including difficulties he has to handle] when he understands, "I am that kind of person [with a disability]", but he is not ready yet [to learn about himself]. He's still warming up. So, [what is important] at this moment is how much [we] can prepare for him, such as [creating] an environment [in which he is accepted].

His parents described that each year they had considered whether they should talk about Kakeru's disability with the parents of his classmates, who might have found some of his behaviors odd. They had decided against doing so because they did not want to risk Kakeru hearing about his disability from someone else. They felt strongly that it was best for Kakeru to hear about his disability from his own parents at the right time, and he was not yet ready.

When Kakeru came back to school after the summer break, however, he became frustrated with the increasing demands of schoolwork. He noticed that he had been working with "300%" of his energy and ability to keep up with his peers. Kakeru was better able to keep up "for Aoki *sensei*" because he liked her and wanted her praise. He also noticed that he might behave inappropriately when he found something fun and became excited. He began to pay attention to other children's reactions to his behavior. Once he noticed others' reactions, he found that he was no longer able to keep working as hard or enjoying recess. School was no longer so enjoyable. It was becoming difficult and exhausting.

As Kakeru began to recognize his differences from his friends, his parents thought that it was the time to talk with him about his "difficulties." To help Kakeru re-engage and enjoy school, his parents gave him the option of studying at the Rainbow Room. They explained to him that there was a place at school where he would be able to study in his own way, with less homework and longer recesses. It was time for Kakeru to openly recognize and accept himself as "different."

Around the same time, Aoki *sensei* talked with Kakeru and his classmates about *kokoro* during moral education class. *Kokoro* refers to mind, heart, attitude, value system, and humanity. Education for *kokoro* is emphasized in Japan as an important component that facilitates children's personality development (Okamoto, 2006; *see also* Chapter 1). Kakeru's parents also had been talking with him about *kokoro* at home to help him to cope with feelings when he had problems and to understand himself, both strengths and weaknesses. As Kakeru listened to his parents and teachers, he began to think that it was not bad to do things differently from others, such as studying at a different place. Kakeru and his parents decided that he would transfer to the Rainbow Room beginning April, the start of the next school year. His mother stated that the transfer came earlier than they anticipated, but that it was a good chance for Kakeru to learn about his "difficulties."

After they had made the decision to allow Kakeru to transfer to the Rainbow Room, his parents asked Kakeru's teacher to create an opportunity for him to discuss his transition with other second graders. With his teacher's support, Kakeru's "transition" was discussed with his peers and accepted by the other children. Kakeru himself also looked forward to studying at the Rainbow Room. Indeed, his mother observed that he seemed to be feeling better after this classroom meeting. During the rest of his second grade year, Kakeru occasionally worked on different tasks from other children in his second grade classroom and also studied with Sakai *sensei* at the Challenge Room once a week, which he also openly discussed with his classmates.

Struggles to Maintain Ibasho

When Misa visited Greenleaf Elementary School in January 2010, she noticed that Kakeru's attitude had changed somewhat. During her weekly work with Kakeru in the Challenge Room, Misa noticed his mood changes. For example, following the practice for a collaborative reading project during which children from each second grade general education class read to one another, Kakeru commented, "Too bad...I couldn't read well." On that day in the Challenge Room, Kakeru was not able to concentrate on tasks Sakai *sensei* gave him, frequently asked for restroom breaks, and made excuses to delay working, such as, "I have to go get my scissors in my classroom." On other days, he made comments such as, "I can't do this," or, "I don't want to do this. Can I play there [the other side of the Challenge Room where children usually play with various toys and tools]?" Yet when he felt good, he was eager to work on his tasks. He also volunteered to teach a first grader addition and subtraction.

In his general education classroom, Kakeru not only enjoyed being with other children but also enjoyed some latitude in his behavior relative to peers. When Misa visited his classroom as a guest teacher to share her experiences in a wheelchair, Kakeru was one of the first children to ask questions, but after that it was hard for him to sit still and listen to other children. He went to the back of the classroom and lay down on the floor until he was comfortable with rejoining the group. During this time, other children and the teacher noticed his behavior but did not force him to sit with them. Such behaviors, however, made Kakeru feel, "I'm not a child [who belongs] here."

During this time, according to his mother, he was not in a good mood, in part because of the impending special activities, including the Greenleaf Festival and the end of the school year exams. He felt strongly, "I can't do [anything]" at school and was not happy to come to school each morning. He was willing to do the same things as other children, but these activities also could overwhelm him. He was not yet used to doing things differently from other children in his classroom and felt, "I wanna be with them and do the same things." Although Kakeru's "transition" to the Challenge Room was accepted by his peers and Kakeru enjoyed the accommodations, Kakeru was still struggling to keep his place, his *Ibasho,* in his second grade general education classroom.

Kakeru's mother considered studying at the Challenge Room once a week as a "refreshing time" for him. On the day he studied at the Challenge Room, she found he was excited even after he returned home. There were only a few children in the Challenge Room, so he did not have to worry about making mistakes and also he could find people who wanted to listen to his stories [about bugs and other things]. His mother hoped that through his positive experiences at school, including in the Challenge Room, he would regain confidence. The following excerpt from Misa's field note describes Kakeru's behavior in the Challenge Room:

> When Kakeru finished a worksheet, he asked, "5 minutes break?" but Sakai *sensei* said, "1 minute!" Then, I said, "How about 2 minutes?" and he was allowed to play while Sakai *sensei* checked his answers and wrote comments...[I went to the play area with him. He was in a big round container rotating like a spinning top] and said, "There are many people here [in the Challenge and Rainbow Rooms] who know about trains well." I said, "You too know well about bugs, don't you? It's great you all have something you are good at." However, he did not say anything, and the break was over. (Excerpt from Misa's field note)

As his mother described, Kakeru had lost motivation and confidence. His understanding of children in the Challenge and Rainbow Rooms was that they all had something they were good at—for example, trains. Misa reminded him that he knew a lot about bugs, but he did not respond. It seemed that he was not certain he could be "qualified" to be in the Rainbow Room.

Third Grade in the Rainbow Room

As was planned, Kakeru transferred to the Rainbow Room in April. He periodically returned to his third grade general education classroom (e.g., during Social Studies and Science). He recognized the Rainbow Room as where he belonged and made the ritual parting, "*itte-kimasu* (I'm coming back)," when he left the Rainbow Room to go to his general education classroom, rather than vice versa.

When he visited the third grade classroom, he still enjoyed talking with other children, especially if it was about bugs, games, or other special interests. During daily activities at school, however, he spent more time with children in the Rainbow Room. For example, during recess, he usually went out to the playground with children in the Rainbow Room, rather than other third graders. Kakeru acted as a member of the seven children from the Rainbow Room. He had conflicts with them occasionally, but these seven children looked like a group of "Rainbow" children always learning together.

Discussion

Children's Struggles and Adjustment

This chapter, which focuses on the experiences of children, deepens our understanding of Japanese parents', educators', and policy makers' responses to children's disabilities, including sensitivity to the risk of stigmatization posed by children's differences. By categorizing together as "developmental disabilities" challenges as diverse as those experienced by children with Autism Spectrum Disorders, speech problems, learning disabilities, and ADHD, the Japanese practices draw our attention to a crucial similarity of children facing these challenges; they are in some way "different" from their peers.

Just as the new special education system created challenges for educators and parents, so too did children experience struggles in re-adjusting their relationships with classmates and accepting that they needed support different from other children. Dai, Yusuke, and Kakeru all transitioned from their general education classrooms into the Challenge and the Rainbow Rooms over two school years. They enjoyed studying there, but studying outside of their general education classrooms made them feel that they no longer belonged to their general education classrooms. As discourse on "missing Dai" in his classroom facilitated his transition to the Challenge Room, children navigated their "differences" by re-establishing their relationships with peers. Through their everyday interactions with peers and educators, these three children established their identity as "children of the Rainbow Room" (*see also* Holland, Lachicotte, Skinner & Cain, 1998; Wertsch, 1991). Although other children had noticed Dai's, Yusuke's, and Kakeru's struggles in learning social and academic skills, their transition to the Challenge and Rainbow Rooms underscored their "differences." In comparison to U.S. elementary schools, relatively few children receive instruction outside of their classrooms in Japan. When children leave their classrooms, their peers in their general education classrooms become curious and begin to explicitly indicate the differences, which may affect how children with developmental disabilities understand themselves. In this process, Dai and Kakeru had to adjust their relationships with peers in their general education classrooms and struggled with balancing their identities as members of their general education classrooms and as children of the Rainbow and Challenge rooms. When Misa first met Yusuke, he had already isolated himself from his peers but was working hard to re-establish relationships with peers in his general education classroom.

Children with disabilities also initiated relationships with other children with disabilities. For example, Yusuke learned about disability from children in the Rainbow Room. Interactions with children with similar struggles may have affected his understanding of his own "disability." Indeed, playing and studying together with other children in the Rainbow Room served as a source of support for the three children during this transition.

After Dai, Yusuke, and Kakeru transferred to the Rainbow Room, their difference was also recognized by children in other grade levels, as well as in their general education classrooms. For example, a second grade boy was curious about why Dai did not know where other third graders were. Dai responded that he was a child of the Rainbow Room [special education classroom]. This is only one example, but such interactions happened at other times at school. Before long, most children in the school had learned which children studied in the Challenge and Rainbow Rooms, and their educational placements became "normal."

Finding Their Ibasho

During their transitions into the Challenge and Rainbow Rooms, adults carefully considered children's developmental and individual readiness when interacting with them around disability issues. Dai, Yusuke, and Kakeru recognized that they were "different" from other children, especially after they began receiving individualized support in their classrooms or the Challenge Room but not necessarily that they had "disabilities." Dai's mother was not willing to disclose his diagnosis to him. Although they discussed his "difficulties" with him, Kakeru's parents also thought that he was not ready to understand his disability. Yusuke, who was older than the other two children, began questioning his ability to learn, and it became a source of frustration for him. He was given an opportunity to hear about his "difficulties" in reading and writing, which motivated him to learn and focus on his strengths rather than his struggles. Yet his mother believed that it was too early to let him know the "name" of his disability.

Nevertheless, these three children experienced the transition differently. Whereas Kakeru chose to disclose to other children his plans to move to the Rainbow Room, Yusuke and Dai chose to isolate themselves from their peers. Peers may perceive children's difficulties differently depending on whether challenges are described openly or kept secret (Ochs et al., 2001). Dai's mother's sensitivity to "being different" made his difference an open secret, which created tension in talking about his difference. Indeed, his classroom teacher was concerned about other children's response to seeing Dai in the Challenge Room, where he appeared more lively than when he was in the general education classroom (*see* Chapter 5). In contrast, Kakeru's transition was talked about "naturally" as part of children's everyday experiences. Even during activities in his general education classroom, Kakeru shared with peers without any hesitation what he had heard and seen at the Challenge Room.

Educators' flexibility also allowed them to attend to children's individual needs and thereby helped them to find their places, their *Ibasho*, at school. They created contexts in which children with disabilities could find ways to cope with hardships. Yusuke initially isolated himself in the Challenge Room, where he created his own world of play. This play motivated him to work hard and eventually helped him to find new friends and re-create peer relationships. Through his interactions with children from the Rainbow Room, located next door to the Challenge Room, he gradually began to accept his disability and think about himself more positively. Dai, who preferred a more quiet and orderly environment, chose to stay in the Challenge Room and the Rainbow Room to isolate himself from peers. This allowed him to spend as much time as he needed to be ready to interact with other children.

Unlike the other two children, Kakeru received individualized support within his general education classroom. His peers valued his special knowledge of bugs, a source of pride for Kakeru, which motivated him to study and interact with peers at school. Further, his classroom teacher used his knowledge to create a classroom in which Kakeru was accepted as a full member. His parents also created a protected environment at home and carefully prepared for talking with him about his disability considering his level of development. These protected environments at home and school helped Kakeru to find his *Ibasho* in his general education classroom, and his decision to move to the Rainbow Room was openly accepted by his peers.

Notes

1. Maekawa *sensei* did not have a special education certificate but had participated in continuing education opportunities and incorporated various strategies from special education to teach children with developmental disabilities in general and special education classrooms.
2. Yusuke had been studying in the Challenge Room full-time with Sakai *sensei* and other teaching assistants.

3. Before Dai moved to the Rainbow Room, his mother was concerned about his participation in school-wide activities as a member of the Rainbow Room—not as a member of his general education classroom.

4. This incident took place a few days after another teaching assistant pretended to be a person who was blind and let Dai guide him to the staff room. In this excerpt, he then tried out what it would be like to be a person "who can't use a leg."

5. Her major in college was special education. She was assigned to teach children in general education classrooms to allow her to experience teaching typically developing children and to learn to better work with children with diverse needs.

6. In Japan, many children attend preschool/kindergarten, but it is not mandatory. Transition to first grade is challenging for some children, even if they do not have disabilities. They have to adjust to a new school building, new teachers and peers, and a more structured learning environment.

7. The purpose of this test was not to provide a "diagnosis" but to determine eligibility to receive special education.

8 IMPLICATIONS: A CROSS-CULTURAL CONVERSATION

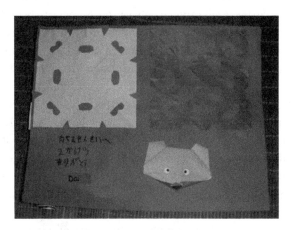

"Thank you" note to Misa from Dai

When Misa returned from her first visit to Greenleaf Elementary School in 2009, she was worried that educators in the United States might not understand her observations in Japan. Educators' flexibility and creativity in supporting children like Dai, Yusuke, and Kakeru as well as their parents seemed very different from what she had observed in U.S. schools. Indeed, to Wendy's American eyes, it seemed unfair that not all Japanese children who needed support consistently received quality support in a timely manner. In the United States, the special education system is legally based and focused on individual rights. Formal policies help to ensure that all children with disabilities receive prompt and appropriate services from specialists. To Misa's Japanese eyes, these U.S. practices looked fascinating but somewhat rigid and overwhelming to teachers. In some cases, these U.S. practices seemed to make it difficult for teachers to form trusting relationships with parents, children, and other educators. Through our discussions, we (Misa and Wendy) came to better appreciate how educational policies and practices with children with disabilities in both Japan and the United States were embedded within cultural and historical contexts. In Japan, these cultural ways include non-coercive support through "*mimamori*," an emphasis on peer groups in education and sensitivity to other people's "eyes." In the United States, these cultural ways focus on individual rights, access, and fairness. We began to wonder what social workers and educators in the United States might learn from Japanese educators, and what Japanese social workers and educators might learn from U.S. professionals.

Although our research is not comparative by design or evaluative in purpose, we did examine Japanese educational policies, goals, and practices through the lenses of both U.S. and Japanese cultures. Our dual cultural lens allowed us to interpret and understand the experiences of Japanese children with "developmental disabilities," their parents, and educators from cultural insider and outsider perspectives while reflecting on U.S. special education policies and practices. Of course, the macro contexts of Japanese and U.S. education are distinct. We noticed marked differences in the policy tools available to educators and in cultural preferences for responding to children with developmental disabilities and their parents. In addition, the United States is a much larger and more heterogeneous society in which ethnic minority children are over-represented in special education (Artiles, Kozleski, Trent, Osher, & Ortiz, 2010) and under-represented in other programs such as for the "gifted (Ford, Moore, & Scott, 2011)," which complicate the issue of stigma. In addition, many U.S. teachers are constrained by significant pressure to demonstrate their children's learning through standardized achievement testing (Genishi & Dyson, 2009). Japanese schools are not required to demonstrate Annual Yearly Progress (AYP), required by the U.S. No Child Left Behind Act, nor are test scores used to evaluate and give consequences to individual schools. Over the past several years, however, Japanese teachers have felt some pressure to demonstrate children's achievement through standardized tests. Many local boards of education have even implemented their own standardized achievement tests. In addition, the Ministry of Education began implementation of national achievement tests for sixth and ninth graders in 2007[1] (Ministry of Education, 2012c). Further, the most recent National Curriculum Standards have introduced requirements for educators to include more content into their curriculums[2] (Ministry of Education, 2008). It remains to be seen how these changes in Japan will impact educators' abilities to flexibly and creatively respond to the needs of individual children with developmental disabilities.

Despite significant variation in the macro contexts of education in Japan and the United States, we also noticed a variety of apparent similarities in educational beliefs and practices. Excellent Japanese and U.S. elementary school teachers nurture their relationships with children and parents, respond to children's individual needs, and support peer group relationships. Japanese and U.S. professionals, parents, and children all face the issue of the stigmatization of children who are "different" from their peers. For example, educators in the United States and Japan may be challenged to socialize peers who bring unkind attitudes and behaviors into the classroom, such as bullying, teasing, or otherwise "making fun" of children who are struggling.

Our "conversation" between cultural understandings of the meaning of children's struggles and how we support children with disabilities underscored a number of issues of relevance both to the United States and Japan, including the cultural context of policy and practice and a sociocultural developmental model of disability. Through reflection on the strengths and challenges in Japanese and U.S. systems, educators, social workers, and policy makers in both countries can learn from one another how to balance flexibility in the provision of sensitive and creative educational practices that minimize children's risk of stigmatization with clear procedural guidelines that assure the delivery of adequate services in a timely manner to all children.

The Cultural Context of Policy and Practice: Flexibility, Family Engagement, and Relationships

Japanese educational policies and practices for children with developmental disabilities are non-coercive and somewhat flexible for schools, parents, and children. Educational policies suggest that schools provide services, but the implementation of the policies largely relies on the availability of resources and budget of each local government and school. If schools do not have the resources, then limited services may be provided for children with disabilities. For example, in Riverside City, where Greenleaf Elementary School is located, not all schools have resource rooms. If children need special education part-time in resource rooms, then they have to go to other schools where such support is available, just like Yusuke went to a Classroom for Speaking and Hearing at "Parkside Elementary School". To receive such support, however, children have to miss several hours of school time traveling back and forth, and parents are responsible for providing transportation. Further, each local board of education has slightly different criteria to determine children's placement. In Riverside City, educators generally respect parents' preferences in determining where their children with disabilities receive support and patiently work with them to provide the most appropriate services. At Greenleaf Elementary School, as we have seen in previous chapters, educators suggest to parents that their children might benefit from services and provide opportunities for parents to understand the benefits of those services, but they do not overtly pressure parents to accept services for their children. Similarly, children are not overtly pressured to accept services outside of their peer groups. They, too, are provided with opportunities to express their preferences and try out services before committing to them.

Japanese educational policies and practices for children with developmental disabilities reflect, in part, a sensitivity to stigma. The issue of stigma is a widespread challenge for children with disabilities, parents, and educators across the world. With the increasing attention on children with developmental disabilities, many Japanese parents have read and heard about "developmental disabilities." Parents of our three participant children also had knowledge of their children's disabilities including medical diagnoses. Yet they were more concerned with understanding and responding to their children's disabilities as they impacted their relationships with other children than with the neurological bases and medical labels of those disabilities. In other words, their concern was with the social and academic implications of children's differences from other children, not the labels of their disabilities. Japanese adults located children's disabilities not primarily in physical characteristics but in their relationships with others, such as their peers, educators, and other parents.

In response to parents' concerns, Japanese educators displayed flexibility, sensitivity, and creativity in their educational practices with children with disabilities and their families. Their practices attempted to minimize stigmatization through a focus on the whole child, including the unique needs and strengths of individual children, development of trusting and collaborative relationships with children and their parents, and developmentally effective communication and intervention strategies. Through the use of metaphor, ritual, and play, Japanese educators created a context in which children, those with developmental disabilities, and their peers could learn through their everyday interactions to respond with *omoiyari* (sensitivity/empathy) to others who have a wide range of characteristics.

These Japanese ways provide models of family engagement, flexible responses to children's sometimes rapidly changing needs, and stigma-sensitive professional practices: important issues for U.S. school social workers, special education service providers, and others who work with individuals with disabilities and their families. Indeed, U.S. practices based on the IDEA have been criticized for not treating parents as equal, fully involved members in making decisions for their children (e.g., Blue-Banning, Summers, Frankland, Nelson, & Beegle, 2004; Summers et al., 2007). Some scholars also have described U.S. parents' resistance to labeling their children as "disabled" and criticized special education policies and practices as exposing children to stigmatization (e.g., Ho, 2004; Kendall & DeMoulin, 1993). Further, U.S. practices focusing on Individualized Education Programs (IEPs) formulated during IEP meetings have been criticized as overly rigid (IDEA Reauthorization, 2005).

United States educators and parents have indicated that too many bureaucratic procedures made necessary by the IDEA, including requirements to participate in various meetings, can create barriers to practice (e.g., Blue-Banning et al., 2004). Individualized Education Program procedures, including specific timelines and paperwork demands, ensure the timely receipt of special education services but can be a source of stress and barrier in establishing collaborative relationships with families, responding flexibly to individual children's changing needs, and minimizing their risk of stigmatization. Heavy paperwork demands on teachers also can drive excellent special education teachers from the field (IDEA Reauthorization, 2005).

On the other hand, the Japanese system sacrifices promptness and uniform quality in service provision more common in the U.S. rights-based system of special education. The flexibility that allowed Japanese educators to respond creatively to the needs of individual children also creates barriers to educational practice. In the absence of more specific educational policies and funding, not all children with developmental disabilities receive timely, quality support. Indeed, several educators explicitly described a need for clearer procedures and guidelines for special education services at the local and national level. Some Japanese children with disabilities missed opportunities for receiving special education services until they externalized their problems—for example, through aggressive behaviors or refusing to go to school. Uniformity in the quality of services also may be affected because the majority of educators currently teaching in special education classrooms and resource rooms in general public elementary schools do not have formal training in special education. They may have inadequate skills and understanding of the qualitatively different approaches to providing instruction that children with disabilities such as dyslexia and autism spectrum disorders may require to reach their potential. This inadequate understanding was perhaps reflected in some teachers' struggles and frustrations, including with Dai and his mother.

The credibility of our interpretation of Japanese practices and policies as reflecting strong cultural preferences for relationship-based, non-coercive services is supported by similar preferences and practices within the Japanese child welfare system (Bamba & Haight, 2011). Japanese parents are guided and provided with opportunities to use child welfare services but rarely forced or required to participate. Even in cases of families with suspected child maltreatment, professionals prefer to nurture supportive relationships with struggling parents that are sustainable over time and also allow children to retain connections to their families. Services are flexible and individualized for children and families. In cases of child maltreatment, the court system is rarely involved—parents rarely lose their parental rights. Japanese ways provide a model to the United States of family engagement and relationship building, a perennial problem for U.S. child welfare professionals.

On the other hand, some Japanese child welfare professionals, like Japanese educators, struggle with social policies that are relatively less structured. For example, when Japanese children are in out-of-home care, their guardians may not have the same legal tools to protect them from some kinds of parental maltreatment as are provided in the United States. Bamba and Haight (2011) report on the case of a child in out-of-home care who was battered during a home visit. The child loved his mother, and his guardian did not insist that he no longer visit her; rather, he provided her with opportunities to visit the child at his placement. When the mother declined the invitation and again battered her child during a home visit, the guardian expressed frustration that he did not have the legal tools to discontinue these visits. Eventually, the *child* decided to discontinue the home visits, and his mother then visited him at his placement. Nevertheless, the respect the guardian showed for this child's autonomous decision is similar to that shown to Dai and Yusuke by their educators as these children eventually decided to study in the Challenge and Rainbow Rooms.

The Evolution of a Japanese Model of Disability

Our research was conducted during the transition period into formal special education for children with "developmental disabilities." It illustrates the transformation of a Western "medical model" of disabilities and special education, which uses disability labels as a guide to provide services, into a blended bio-psycho-sociocultural Japanese model of developmental disabilities. In this model of disability, the biological variations underlying children's challenges with particular school tasks are recognized, but the focus is primarily on the psychosocial and cultural consequences of such human variation.

Before the special education reform, Japanese special education was characterized by two extremes. Children with severe disabilities received full support in a segregated setting. In contrast, children with milder disabilities were fully included in general education classrooms but without individualized support by specialists. After the reform, increasing numbers of children who are identified as having developmental disabilities receive support within or outside of their general education classrooms. Examination of this transition is significant, in part, because it widens our understanding of the extent and ways in which cultures vary in beliefs and responses to disability, as well as the impact of such differences on the developing child. Japanese educators have responded to the dilemma posed by children's less visible disabilities by recognizing the neurological basis of developmental disabilities. For educational purposes, however, they relocated problems from within individual children to those social contexts and relationships within which their differences arise.

In many respects Japan has been an international leader in progressive early and elementary school education (e.g., Lewis, 1995; Stevenson & Stigler, 1992). Yet Japan did not begin providing formal services to children with "developmental disabilities" until nearly four decades after the United States had begun providing such services. Following World War II, available resources were limited. Providing services to children with more severe disabilities such as global intellectual disabilities, and physical and sensory disabilities was, understandably, prioritized. In addition, the "uneven" abilities of children with developmental disabilities can make their needs for extra help less visible. Pulling apparently well-functioning (but struggling) children with mild developmental disabilities out from their peer groups to provide additional support deprives them of participation in a developmental context central to supporting those values, morals, and personality characteristics valued in successful Japanese adults. It also may disrupt education for *kokoro* (heart/mind) both for children with disabilities and their peers. Further, removing children from their peer groups exposes them to the risk of stigmatization, a particularly devastating experience in Japan where joy and belonging typically are found in group membership. On the other hand, peer group membership can be a burden for some children including those with disabilities like Yusuke and Dai. For these children, general education classrooms may not be the best place for them to learn. Accordingly, Japanese educators are currently challenged to meet the needs of individual children with developmental disabilities while maintaining the benefit of educating children within peer groups and avoiding stigmatization.

Given the Japanese emphasis on relationships, we considered the issue of stigma and disability through the everyday experiences of children, their parents, and educators. For Bakhtin, everyday experience is a source of responsibility, meaning, and creativity (Morson & Emerson, 1990). Bourdieu also stressed children's experiences as one element that contributes to the formation of "habitus" (Bourdieu, 1991; Jenkins, 2002). In short, children's everyday experiences shape their beliefs and values and have a long-lasting effect on their lives. Children's experiences of disability emerge within interactions with others, including their parents, teachers, and peers. The three children, Dai, Yusuke, and Kakeru, had some similar challenges, but they responded to and dealt with them differently, in part because they had varied experiences and relationships with peers, their parents, and teachers.

Many Japanese educators and parents recognized the neurobiological bases of difficulties some children face within the classroom in learning to read, calculate, and control their behavior and attention. Educators at Greenleaf Elementary School also used disability labels when describing individual children. Further, Dai's and Yusuke's parents noted that "labels" might help us to understand their children's disabilities and receive the necessary services. Nevertheless, in practice, they did not embrace children's medical diagnoses as useful in educating these children. Rather, their focus was transactional. Japanese educators formed the new category of "developmental disability," in part to avoid stigma attached to particular medical diagnoses (Tsuge, 2004). These educators avoided singling children out from their peers as much as possible. In addition to paying attention to children's individual needs and preferences, they located and responded to children's difficulties within sociocultural contexts focusing on interpersonal interactions—for example, by involving peers in supporting one another, creating supportive and home-like classrooms, and guiding children's voluntary cooperation and learning. In addition, Japanese educators extended their focus on the contexts of children's relationships to practices supporting parents' acceptance of their children's need for services and voluntary collaboration with educators in providing such services. As previously noted, an unintended consequence of these practices was that some children did not receive the support they needed in a timely fashion.

Some U.S. scholars (e.g., Hood et al., 1980; McDermott et al., 2006; Minow, 1990) have embraced a sociocultural model of disability with similarities to the Japanese model. They argue that examining the characteristics of individual children with learning disabilities is not enough to help them succeed at school. In addition, we need to pay attention to the contexts in which children with learning disabilities interact with various people, including their peers and educators, to define problems they are facing at school. The basic idea is that disabilities can be exacerbated or ameliorated through children's interactions with others in everyday contexts. The Japanese case illustrates how children's educational experiences may be supported through collaborative relationships formed with parents, educators, and peers.

What U.S. Educators and Policy Makers can Learn from Japanese Educators About Stigma-Sensitive, Inclusive, Non-Coercive Educational Practices

The cultural preferences of Japanese educators and policy makers focus our attention on complex issues of inclusion and stigmatization. In instances where the practices employed by elementary school teachers from Japan and the United States are similar (e.g., in their attention to children's holistic development), the Japanese case can serve to sensitize U.S. professionals to their significance for supporting inclusion and reducing stigma. In instances where the practices of Japanese educators seem unfamiliar (e.g., the practice of *mimamori*), the Japanese case may help U.S. professionals to think differently about complex issues related to disability. Below are a few of the lessons that we found important. Readers surely will identify others.

Create Supportive and Accepting Peer Groups

Peers are an increasingly important context for development during middle childhood in many cultural groups (e.g., Chen, French, & Schneider, 2006). Educators at Greenleaf Elementary School worked to create supportive peer groups into which children with developmental disabilities were included. In general, children's classrooms are intended to be places where they can create their *Ibasho*, where they feel safe, comfortable, and accepted. Children's classrooms were not only places to learn academic skills, but their homes at school. Teachers intentionally created environments and opportunities for children to interact with others. For example, through collaboration within peer groups comprised of children with diverse abilities, interests, and personalities, children learned not only academic skills but to respect each other's strengths and establish friendships. Teachers also served as "interpreters" of children who were struggling so that these children could find their *Ibasho* in the classroom and all children could learn to help each other. In other words, Japanese educators used contextual factors, such as peer group membership, not only to understand the experiences of children with disabilities but also as a tool to intervene and facilitate their development.

Similarly, cooperative learning groups in which children with diverse abilities work and play together is a recognized strategy used in inclusive classrooms in the United States. Such environments facilitate social interactions between children with disabilities and their typically developing peers (Taylor, Peterson, McMurray-Schwartz, & Guillou, 2002). By involving individuals with whom they have daily interactions at home, school, and other places, educators can modify or even create a social ecology for development in which children with disabilities are motivated to participate and adults can guide them in positive directions.

Further, peer awareness of the capabilities and struggles of children with disabilities can facilitate their voluntary involvement of these peers in collaborative activities. In their ethnographic study on U.S. children with high-functioning autism, Ochs and colleagues observed that class-mates were most supportive and voluntarily helped children with autism when their conditions and struggles were explained to their classmates. Such positive interactions were further enhanced through educators' direct interventions, for example, in cases of conflict (Ochs et al, 2001; Ochs and Solomon, 2010).

Facilitate Children's Voluntary Cooperation in Learning

Japanese non-coercive socialization practices also underscore the value of chil-dren's voluntary cooperation in learning and building interpersonal relation-ships. Azuma (1994) explained that in Japanese classrooms, when a teacher presents a lesson to the whole classroom, the instruction may be designed to facilitate interactions among children, in which children are motivated and learn spontaneously. At Greenleaf Elementary School, for example, in the third grade classroom, children learned the concept of weight through group activities and through writing and reflecting on what they learned each time a new term was introduced. To make this type of instruction effective, rela-tionships between teachers and children as well as between children become critical.

Unlike U.S. public schools, Japanese schools traditionally do not have specialists, such as school social workers, psychologists[3], and speech and language pathologists, to teach specific skills. Accordingly, classroom teach-ers have broader roles in and outside of their classrooms including teach-ing emotional and social skills. Given the broad, holistic goals of Japanese elementary school education, children's learning is designed to occur not only through classroom instruction and direct interventions but also through everyday interactions with peers and educators. Through participation in everyday activities, adults helped children to "naturally," or spontaneously and voluntarily, acquire socially desirable attitudes and values expected in fully integrated members of Japanese society.

These socialization practices occur during mundane, everyday activities, such as serving and eating lunch, cleaning, recess, and other activities in small groups in which children with diverse abilities and personalities work collaboratively. In these activities, adults generally guide children in setting their own goals and monitoring their own behaviors and progress—a com-mon strategy in Japanese schools intended to help children to take respon-sibilities for their own actions (e.g., Cave, 2007; Lewis, 1995). For example, at Greenleaf Elementary School, during a school wide reading program, "Book walk," children kept a record of books they read on their "Book walk card" for

2 weeks. On the first day, they filled out their goals, including the number of books they would like to read. Children received a certificate if they exceeded their goals. There were children who read 5 books and received a certificate, but children who read 20 books did not receive a certificate if their goals were higher than 20. During this period, children were excited when teachers told them they could go to the library after they completed the assigned tasks. They finished their tasks as early as possible and went to the library. Some children in the Rainbow Room also received the certificate.

Facilitate Children's "Natural" Learning of Culturally Desired Behaviors Through mimamori

The National Curriculum Standard for Elementary Schools includes many opportunities for children to "naturally" be socialized into Japanese society. For example, Japanese children have longer recesses and breaks than U.S. children, which provide Japanese children with more opportunities to interact and play with their peers (Stevenson & Stigler, 1992). Educators understand these unsupervised periods as a "natural" learning context in which children voluntarily learn interpersonal and problem-solving skills. Adults also create opportunities for children to learn by using children's real interpersonal problems in their daily lives and by guiding them to handle these problems and reflect on the outcomes. At Greenleaf Elementary School, educators did not necessarily provide immediate discipline for misbehaviors but allowed children to experience the natural and sometimes unpleasant consequences of their behaviors. There are times, of course, when adults must actively intervene and teach basic social skills, but Japanese educators created as many opportunities as possible, and appropriate, for children to learn through their everyday interactions with others.

Aspects of Japanese discipline are similar to the practices of master teachers in U.S. classrooms (Paley, 2004). For example, Vivian Paley, a veteran teacher at the John Dewey Laboratory School at the University of Chicago, described how she eliminated a time-out chair in her preschool classroom and revised her approach to a child who had frequent interpersonal problems. After carefully observing this child, who often engaged in arguments with other children in the block area, Paley gave him the opportunity to explain his behaviors. She found that the boy was trying to "help" other children to build, but the way he helped was neither appropriate nor appreciated. She invited the boy and his peers to role play, so he was able to observe his behaviors objectively and learn appropriate ways to help. Her approach was more structured than what was observed in Japanese classrooms, but they share similar underlying goals, creating a social context in which children are motivated to behave responsibly.

Similarly, Kramer and colleagues' research with U.S. families (e.g., Kramer, Perozynski, & Chung, 1999; Perozynski & Kramer, 1999) also indicates the importance of child-centered strategies including "active nonintervention" to prompt children to use skills they already have to resolve conflicts with siblings. This approach may take more time initially to deal with problems than giving children immediate directions or using tangible rewards and punishments, but once children learn the lessons, they may more easily retain and apply them to similar situations in the future.

Provide "Supportive" not "Special" Education

At Greenleaf Elementary School, some of the supportive strategies educators provided for children with disabilities were available to all children. The practice of providing support for children regardless of the type of "difficulties" at Greenleaf Elementary School may be similar to other Japanese schools. For example, "Sugar Creek Elementary School", located in another city, has implemented "support education" to meet the needs of every child who needs extra help. There is no "special" in this system, and any child with additional needs regardless of disability is able to receive the necessary support.[4] As the assistant principal at Greenleaf Elementary School stated, special education and support for children who are struggling for any reason are similar in that they take care of children's individual educational needs. Regardless of the reasons for their struggles (their family environment, language, disability, etc.), some approaches and practices utilized to help them may be quite similar.

Ideally, if the support for children who are struggling is integrated into activities and instruction "naturally," then all children who need the support can benefit from it without being singled out. In addition, other children without disabilities may benefit from these supports. Teachers can design such activities, for example, by using visual aids in addition to verbal instructions. Indeed, in the United States, "universal design for learning" has been found to be effective for teaching all children, not only those with disabilities. In this approach, as we observed in Greenleaf Elementary School, instruction may be delivered using a combination of verbal explanations and directions, visual cues such as drawings and pictures, and hands-on activities. Class materials may be provided in multiple formats, such as printed page, computers, and audio recordings. The content of materials is also adjustable to the level of understanding of individual students to motivate students with diverse backgrounds to learn while maintaining high expectations for all children. For example, if students are allowed to verbally respond, draw, or write answers to teachers' questions, they can participate in the instruction at the level of their ability and understanding (e.g., Blamires, 1999; Kohn, 2012; Smith, 2007).

Stay Close to Children's kokoro (Hearts/Minds)

By staying close to children's *kokoro*, educators were able to notice children's emotional and intellectual readiness for change and provide sensitive, developmentally appropriate support for each child. At Greenleaf Elementary School, educators and parents demonstrated flexibility and creativity in their support for individual children. They listened to each child and thoughtfully observed their progress and ongoing peer interactions. Rather than forcing Dai and Yusuke to interact with peers, for example, educators helped them become ready to return to their peer groups by creating a context where they were able to formulate their own strategies to cope with hardships. Socialization into a group of children in the Rainbow and Challenge rooms who were experiencing similar difficulties provided them with emotional support to handle hardships within peer groups in their general education classrooms. In this context, Dai and Yusuke were able to find their *Ibasho* (places where they felt comfortable and accepted) at school. Similarly, Kakeru's parents and teachers carefully observed him to determine his readiness to understand his "difficulties" and provided timely support for his transition into special education.

Support Children's Autonomous Participation in Decision Making

The Japanese case at Greenleaf Elementary School also raises the issue of how adults might support children's understanding and acceptance of support for disabilities. The three children were given opportunities to behave autonomously and to express their preferences—for example, when and where to receive additional support. This allowed children to find their *Ibasho* in which they were motivated to handle difficulties. In the United States, elementary school-aged children with disabilities are not always allowed this degree of autonomy. Their IEPs typically are created by teams of adults. The IDEA and its regulations describe that children also participate in these meetings when "appropriate." Children's participation, however, is only required when a purpose of the meeting is to discuss their postsecondary goals or transition services to reach these goals (Department of Education, 2013). Using a national representative sample, Barnard-Brak and Lechtenberger (2010) found a positive association between children's participation in IEP meetings and their academic achievement at the elementary school level. Yet involvement of children in the decision-making process (e.g., through participation in the meetings and incorporation of their preferences and interests in intervention programs), although encouraged, is not yet widely practiced.

Support Parents

Although children might benefit from specialized services, their parents' permission is necessary and their active collaboration desirable. At Greenleaf Elementary School, parents were concerned with the risk of stigmatizing otherwise well-functioning children by singling them out from their peers for formal intervention. Of course, sensitivity to stigma is not unique to Japanese parents; it is felt by U.S. parents as well. At Greenleaf Elementary School, supporting parents in resolving this dilemma posed by their children's differences was one of the priorities for educators.

Findings from Greenleaf Elementary School illustrate ways of supporting the parents of children with developmental disabilities and establishing trusting partnerships with them that may provide new perspectives for Western educators as we reflect on our own practices. For example, in the United States, litigation aimed at finding and punishing school districts and states for technical violations of the IDEA[5] also has bred attitudes of distrust between parents and educators, which hinders their capacities to cooperate in supporting children (IDEA Reauthorization, 2005). The IDEA requires parents' participation in creating and implementing children's IEPs. Yet at the practice level, parents and professionals express concerns regarding their partnerships, partly because of system requirements for special education. Parents' perspectives frequently are not given equal weight or respect with those of educators and other professionals. Some parents experience frustration, and many express the need for more empowerment, so that they can fully participate in the decision-making processes (e.g., Blue-Banning et al., 2004). In addition, first-generation Asian-American mothers of children with disabilities were critical of professionals who looked at their children from a medical perspective of finding something negative to correct. In responding to their children's challenges, they emphasized the importance of respectful and trusting relationships with professionals and holistic assessments that also recognized children's strengths (Jegatheesan, 2009).

Japanese educators recognized the challenges parents were facing, including emotional reactions to their children's disabilities and associated stigma toward them and their children. After they had identified children who were struggling, they did not necessarily communicate explicitly or immediately to parents that their children needed additional support. They anticipated how parents might feel and respond to direct discussions of their children's struggles and need for additional support. They spent time developing relationships with parents in which parents would be comfortable in expressing their concerns and needs to them. Educators also guided parents toward any support they might need to manage their own feelings of stress and were available when parents needed to be listened to. These practices reflect teachers' *omoiyari*—finely tuned empathy and sensitivity to what other people think and feel. Although subtle and implicit, significant communication occurred between Japanese parents and teachers as their thoughts, emotions, and desires were exchanged prior to the implementation of special education services for children.[6]

What Japanese Educators can Learn from U.S. Special Education Policies

The new special education system has created more opportunities for Japanese children who are struggling within general education classrooms to receive the necessary services, but educators identified significant challenges to insuring that all children with developmental disabilities receive timely and appropriate services, in part because of relatively flexible guidelines in special education policies. United States policies and practices may provide some models for Japanese educators in addressing the ongoing challenges they have identified. Indeed, educators at Greenleaf Elementary School were interested in hearing about special education in the United States and other countries but anticipated shaping these practices within their own systems.

Classroom Size

The classroom size in Japanese public elementary schools is generally larger than those of U.S schools. Currently in Japan, one general education classroom teacher is assigned for every 40 children[7] (Ministry of Internal Affairs and Communications, 2011a). Because Japanese classroom teachers now have to provide special education in their classrooms, both children and classroom teachers could benefit from smaller classroom sizes. At Greenleaf Elementary School, one grade level had classrooms of 20 children. Children with additional needs were able to receive necessary support and were stabilized within their general education classroom. However, when these classrooms were combined the next school year and children were in large groups, several children who had been stabilized began exhibiting problems.

At the governmental level, benefits and risks associated with smaller classroom sizes have been discussed (Ministry of Education, 2010c). A council within the Ministry officially announced its opinions regarding classroom sizes and stressed that the individual needs of children must be balanced with the functioning of groups. The goal was to attend to the needs of individual children while maintaining the traditional Japanese holistic approach, which seeks to create an educational environment in which children learn academic and social skills by establishing trusting relationships with their peers and classroom teachers. Therefore, the classroom size must be small enough for classroom teachers to attend to the individual needs of children but large enough for children to benefit from learning in groups.

The Ministry of Education has suggested that in small classrooms of 20 or fewer children, activities and instruction involving children from multiple classrooms should be actively utilized, so that children have more time to interact with others (Ministry of Education, 2010c). Greenleaf Elementary School has adopted this practice. Children in two small classrooms frequently studied as a large group and they came to know each other well. Greenleaf Elementary School also utilizes groups consisting of children from all grade levels, who interact and work together. By utilizing group activities outside of their classrooms, children with disabilities may be able to benefit from both individualized instruction in small classrooms and larger group learning experiences in general education classrooms.

Professional Education

In the United States, special education is an established program of study at colleges of education. To teach children with disabilities, educators are required to complete education programs, meet licensure requirements, and hold a special education certificate (Department of Education, 2013). The principal at Greenleaf Elementary School identified gaps in educators' knowledge and skills in special education as a challenge to supporting the school functioning of children with developmental disabilities. In addition to a general teaching certificate, Japanese teachers in special education schools are required to hold a special education certificate in their specialization—for example, hearing and visual impairments, intellectual disabilities, and physical disabilities. However, the same law that determines teacher certification also allows schools to postpone implementing this requirement for an unspecified period of time (Ministry of Internal Affairs and Communication, 2008b). During the 2011–2012 school year, 70% of teachers at special education schools held the special education certificate for their students' disabilities (Ministry of Education, 2012a).

Further, the law does not require special education certification for teaching in special education classrooms in general public schools. It is typical for children in special education classrooms and resource rooms to be taught by teachers who only have a general teaching certificate. In 2011, approximately one-third of special education classroom teachers at general public elementary schools held a special education certificate (Ministry of Education, 2012a). Consequently, in 2010, the Central Council for Education discussed the necessity of expanding the "certification for special education schools" to "certification for special education" involving educational services at general public schools (Ministry of Education, 2010d).

Ideally, teachers should learn skills for teaching children with disabilities at university before they begin teaching. Considering the shortage of teachers who hold special education certificates at special education schools, it is not currently realistic to assign special education teachers with certification to all general public schools to work with children with developmental disabilities. In addition to expanding teacher education at the college and university level, educating teachers currently working in schools—for example, through regular continuing education workshops on special education—is critical.

Systematic Procedures for Identifying Children and Providing Services

In U.S. public schools, general education screening coupled with formal assessment procedures for determining eligibility and implementing special education services are intended to identify children in need of support early and provide them with appropriate services. Our Japanese participants indicated a need for a clearer framework and set of guidelines that describe procedures for early identification of children in need of support and prompt provision of additional supports. When children with developmental disabilities are not identified early and provided with services, they may develop secondary disabilities (e.g., Saito, 2009); for example, they may lose motivation and confidence, refuse to come to school, struggle with peer relationships, and exhibit problem behaviors. Once secondary disabilities are established, children require even more intensive support. Currently, children's secondary disabilities are sometimes used as one of the indicators that services need to be *initiated*, as in the cases of Dai and Yusuke.

Educators also noted a need for additional resources for providing special education services. The School Education Law states that schools "can" create special education classrooms but does not say that schools "have to." This allows flexibility in the implementation of special education but also under resourcing. In addition, for children who do not need intensive support at special education classrooms, currently, not all schools have resource rooms and/or special support rooms and access may be limited. Educators described cases in which teachers had identified children's need for more intensive support, but staff or rooms for individual or small group instruction were not available. There is also the need for more specific procedures and clearer guidelines on the use of special support rooms, such as the Challenge Room. Because Japanese laws do not determine how to utilize special support rooms, their implementation and functioning depend on decisions made by local boards of education and schools.

Educational Funding

The principal at Greenleaf Elementary School indicated that schools may not receive enough money to implement the new educational support for children with developmental disabilities. In the United States, the IDEA determines reporting requirements for states and schools, including the number of children receiving the services, to receive federal grants for special education (Department of Education, 2013). In contrast, the Japanese government distributes special education budgets to local governments based on the number of educators teaching children with disabilities, rather than the number of children in special education. A modest increase in the number of children in special education may not be reflected in the educational budget local governments receive from the national government but can substantially increase the demands on classroom teachers. On the other hand, the principal also observed that the limited financial support available to implement the new special education system has encouraged teachers to work together as a team and to utilize resources in the community. This response may reflect the Japanese cultural preference for collaboration based on personal relationships of empathy and emotional connection.

Full-Time Special Education Coordinators

Under the current special education system in Japan, special education coordinators are educators who retain their regular responsibilities in addition to their roles as coordinators. Sano *sensei,* who as a school nurse had a more flexible schedule than classroom teachers, stated that she frequently found it difficult to complete her work. When classroom teachers serve as special education coordinators, it is even more difficult to balance their responsibilities as classroom teachers and coordinators. There is a definite need for a full-time special education coordinator in each school. Local boards of education are beginning to consider hiring full-time coordinators. For example, in 2008, eight local governments sent a request to the Ministry of Education to place full-time special education coordinators in all special education schools and as many general public elementary and junior high schools as possible (Kanagawa Prefecture, 2008).

If schools are able to hire full-time special education coordinators, then school social workers could be ideal candidates. Special education coordinators' roles include many characteristics of those of school social workers in the United States. For example, Sano *sensei* worked as a liaison with parents to initiate communications regarding their children's additional needs, and coordinated the support children received at general education classrooms and the resource room. She also provided direct services to children[8]. Currently, some Japanese school social workers are assigned to particular schools on a regular basis, but others are sent from local boards of education as needed. In the latter case, school social workers may not be able to stay at one school long enough to establish relationships with children and their parents. Further, school social workers in Japan primarily focus on children with problems caused by extended periods of absence, bullying, and child abuse and neglect. Some school social workers in several prefectures have begun to work with children with disabilities in general public schools (Kadota, 2009).

A Lesson for Both U.S. and Japanese Professionals: Interpret "Best Practices" With Caution

Our strategy of engaging multiple cultural perspectives contrasts with a tradition of research and practice that elevates one way of doing things, typically Western, as "best practice." Some researchers and professionals have treated "best practice" as if it were a culture-neutral matter that can be applied regardless of the sociocultural context in question. The Japanese case clearly illustrates the limitations of such an approach. To be effective, we must consider how the practices from other cultures intersect within particular cultural contexts. Practices from other cultural contexts, and even subcultural contexts, are interpreted within local communities by professionals and their clients (e.g., Lightfoot, 2004). Individuals from various cultural and subcultural contexts, for example, can interpret "disabilities" and appropriate responses, including services available for them, very differently. In addition, complex ethical issues can be interpreted and weighted very differently—for example, the balance between providing children with individualized disability services to facilitate their school learning versus exposing them to the risk of stigmatization. These ethical issues can be especially complex in cases on the border, such as children with mild cognitive and behavioral disabilities.

Strengths and Limitations

Our research program benefited from a variety of strengths and also suffered from a number of weaknesses. Misa's native fluency in Japanese was essential to keeping up with and sorting through a barrage of government documents during the design and implementation of the new, formal special education program. On the other hand, systematic information regarding the fidelity of the implementation of new laws in various locales, or the educational outcomes of children with developmental disabilities experiencing the new special education system, were not yet available.

Throughout the field study, our standpoint was to learn from participants. Therefore, developing relationships with them was critical. For this purpose, Misa's wheelchair was a useful tool in initiating relationships with participants, especially with children. A classroom teacher of one of the children Misa worked with noted that the child was able to ask her for help without feeling negatively because he knew he could help her as well. This reciprocal relationship also was important for Misa in learning children's honest thoughts.

Misa also was both an insider and an outsider at Greenleaf Elementary School. She was treated more as a staff member than as a researcher from the United States, an unfamiliar role. Although Misa's dual roles as a teaching assistant and a researcher helped her establish relationships with participants and allowed her to follow up with the same children across two school years, they also brought her several difficulties. First, although she was able to observe children and their interactions with peers and educators in natural settings, her role as a teaching assistant sometimes influenced their interactions and behaviors; for example, she occasionally had to give children directions and talk to parents as a "teacher." On the other hand, without this opportunity to be a teacher, she would not have been able to establish relationships with staff members, children, and their parents.

Although most teachers welcomed Misa when she went to their classrooms, there were a few teachers who were competitive with her or did not know how to utilize teaching assistants in their classrooms. For example, during the first wave of data collection, Misa spent time with two children almost continuously while they were at school. She developed relationships with them. When she went back to the school for the second wave of data collection several months later, one of these children was struggling with establishing a relationship with his classroom teacher. The teacher asked the special education coordinator not to involve Misa in the support for this child. On such occasions, Misa consulted with the special education coordinator who supervised teaching assistants.

As a researcher, Misa knew that she should not be involved in conflicts with teachers and children but, rather, observe participants' interactions and how they solved problems. Yet as long as she was at school as a teaching assistant, she had to take some responsibility and work as the special education coordinator suggested. Balancing her roles as researcher and "teacher" became more challenging as she was accepted and viewed by educators, children, and their parents as a teaching assistant.

To minimize the negative impact of study participation, participant children were limited to those who already received support within or outside of their classrooms and whose parents had accepted their child's disabilities or "difficulties." During participant observation in general education classrooms, several children were identified as at risk of failure and their possible developmental disabilities were discussed with educators. They and their parents, however, were not invited to individual interviews. Educators were concerned that participation in the study would have a negative effect on parents who were not yet ready to talk about their children's "disabilities."

Finally, this research presents an in-depth examination of children's experiences within a Japanese public elementary school contextualized by examination of national educational policies. This thick description allows us to develop an understanding of how these national educational policies are implemented and experienced by adults and children at the local level. At the same time, the scope of this field research is limited to Greenleaf Elementary School. Additional research is needed to further explore children's experiences of, and creative responses to, special education services, examine the broad range of parent and educator perceptions of "developmental disabilities," consider the transferability of findings from this study to other Japanese elementary schools, and examine the outcomes of the new policies and practices over time for children with developmental disabilities, their parents, their peers, and educators.

Conclusion

It seems appropriate to conclude our book with a brief update on the three children who served as case studies. Eight months after the large earthquake hit northeastern Japan in 2011, Misa returned to Greenleaf Elementary as a 1-day teaching assistant. Kakeru was a fourth grader studying in the Rainbow Room. In addition to his interest in bugs, he had developed a keen interest in the daily earthquake reports, which he reported to Misa. He still exhibited inappropriate behaviors occasionally, and his new classroom teacher struggled to respond to these behaviors. Dai was now a fifth grader. He was having some difficulties adjusting to his new classroom teachers in the Rainbow Room, and his attendance had become an issue again. His mother had a new job and could no longer escort him to school as she had previously. Sano *sensei* was concerned about how they could help him and his mother get back on track before he graduated from sixth grade next year. Yusuke graduated from Greenleaf Elementary School in March, 2011. In his graduation ceremony, rather than "hiding" that he was in the Rainbow Room, he and another six grade student chose to graduate as members of the Rainbow Room, not as members of their general education classroom. Educators accepted and respected their decision. In seventh grade, Yusuke studied primarily in a special education classroom. He still had interpersonal struggles but enjoyed school with a classroom teacher who understood his needs.

Notes

1. The implementation of the national achievement tests is, in part, out of a concern for the declining academic functioning of children. For example, results of the Programme for International Student Assessment in 2003 indicated that 10th grade students scored lower on reading comprehension tests than in the past (Ministry of Education, 2007c).
2. Teachers are also pressured by parents who send their children to cram schools after school. More parents are interested in sending their children to private junior high schools, which require children to pass entrance exams.
3. Since the late 1990s, public schools began to utilize school counselors/psychologists to provide support for children and their parents who were experiencing difficulties, including attendance issues and bullying. Since the government implemented a school social work project in 2008, school social workers' roles have gradually become known to the public.
4. This information is from a guideline developed by Sugar Creek Elementary School.
5. Schools' and states' failure to follow detailed IDEA requirements can lead to the withdrawal of federal funds.
6. Of course, there was individual variation among parents concerning their readiness to accept, and understanding of, their children's difficulties. Some parents in our study even initiated conversations with educators advocating for services for their children who were struggling. In addition, there was variation among teachers in their sensitivity to parents' emotional reactions and concerns.
7. As of 2012, the maximum classroom size is 35 in first and second grade classrooms.
8. Providing direct services is not described as a role of special education coordinators. Not all special education coordinators provide direct intervention.

GUIDELINE FOR THE REORGANIZATION OF SPECIAL EDUCATION SYSTEM

(from 2007 Ministry of Education notice to local boards of education)

1. In-school committee on special education

Under the leadership of the principal, each school must have a committee to establish a school-wide system to assess and discuss the needs of children, including children with disabilities. The committee includes administrators, a special education coordinator, a teacher who is in charge of academic affairs, a student guidance director, resource room teachers, special education classroom teachers, a school nurse, classroom teachers of a particular child, a teacher in charge of each grade level, and other staff members who can contribute to the committee... [The notice continues describing roles of the committee at special education schools.]

2. Understanding children's needs

Each school must try to understand and keep updated information on every child, identify any children who need special support, and assess their needs. For those who need special support, staff members must work collaboratively with a special education coordinator within the school, give careful explanation to parents in ways parents can understand, and discuss with parents support [for their children] at school as well as at home. Communications with parents are critical, as children may need medical attention depending on their conditions. At preschools[1] and elementary schools, [educators should] keep in mind that early identification and interventions are important, and make certain to assess and provide necessary support.

3. Designation of a special education coordinator

The principal of each school must select and assign one educator to serve as a special education coordinator, which is considered part of his/her administrative duties.[2] To promote special education in each school, a special education coordinator's role includes organizing and administrating a committee on special education and in-school training/workshops; communicating and collaborating with other related agencies, facilities, and schools; and being a contact person for parents. The principal oversees [the whole process] so that a special education coordinator functions as part of the system at school.

4. Develop and utilize individualized educational support programs in collaboration with related agencies and facilities.

Special education schools must provide special education services efficiently by utilizing individualized educational support programs incorporating support from multiple viewpoints, including medicine, social welfare, and employment, to provide long-term educational support consistently from infancy throughout public education and after leaving school. [General public] elementary and junior high schools also can develop individualized educational support programs as needed to provide support efficiently in collaboration with other related agencies and facilities.

5. Develop individualized education programs.

Special education schools must promote the establishment of education for children whose disabilities are multiple, severe, and diverse and strengthen instruction by utilizing individualized education programs. [General public] elementary and junior high schools must promote education that meets the needs of individual children—for example, by developing and utilizing individualized education programs.

6. Continuing education and specialization of educators

To promote special education, it is critical that educators acquire more professional knowledge about special education. Accordingly, each school has to make an effort to provide education—for example, by holding in-school workshops and sending educators to out-of-school workshops. Educators who have completed certain programs also have to continue their education—for example, by participating in more specialized workshops, collecting the most recent information, and utilizing training workshops for instructors offered by the National Institute of Special Needs Education. Further, workshops organized by local boards of education and other organizations [targeting educators and staff members at public schools] should be open to national and private schools and preschools (Ministry of Education, 2007a).

Notes

1. Japanese preschools correspond to Preschool and Kindergarten in the United States.
2. At public schools, the School Education Law describes that administrators can assign educators to perform some administrative duties. The duties may include collaboration with the community, curriculum development, and human rights education. Roles special education coordinators are supposed to play are considered one of the duties educators have to perform in addition to their regular teaching responsibilities.

   Typically, an educator who serves as a special education coordinator also has full responsibility in teaching.

REFERENCES

Abe, Y. (1998). Special education reform in Japan. *European Journal of Special Needs Education, 13*, 86–97.

Abell, J., Locke, A., Condor, S., Gibson, S., & Stevenson, C. (2006). Trying similarity, doing difference: The role of interviewer self-disclosure in interview talk with young people. *Qualitative Research, 6*(2), 221–244.

APA (2013). *Diagnostic and statistical manual of mental disorders* (5th ed. text revision). Arlington, VA: Author.

Artiles, A. J., Kozleski, E. B., Trent, S. C., Osher, D., & Ortiz, A. (2010). Justifying and explaining disproportionality, 1968-2008: A critique of underlying views of culture. *Exceptional Children, 76*(3), 279–299.

Artiles, A. J., Thourius, K. K., Bal, A., Neal, R., Waitoller, F. R., & Hernandez-Saca, D. (2011). Beyond culture as group traits: Future learning disabilities ontology, epistemology, and inquiry on research knowledge use. *Learning Disabilities Quarterly, 34*(3), 167–179.

Assouline, S. G, & Whiteman, C. S. (2011). Twice-exceptionality: Implications for school psychologists in the Post-IDEA 2004 era. *Journal of Applied School Psychology, 27*, 380–402.

Azuma, H. (1994). *Nihon jin no shitsuke to kyo-iku: Hattatsu no nichi bei hikaku ni motozuite [Discipline and education for Japanese people: Comparison of child development between the U.S. and Japan]*. Tokyo, Japan: Tokyo Daigaku Shuppan-kai.

Bakhtin, M. M. (1981). *The dialogic imagination: Four essays*. Austin, TX: University of Texas Press.

Bamba, S. & Haight, W. (2007). Helping maltreated children to find their Ibasho: Japanese perspectives on supporting the well-being of children in state care. *Children and Youth Services Review, 29*, 405–427.

Bamba, S., & Haight, W. (2009a). The developmental-ecological approach of Japanese child welfare professionals to supporting children's social and emotional well-being: The practice of mimamori. *Children and Youth Service Review, 31*, 429–439.

Bamba, S., & Haight, W. (2009b). Maltreated children's emerging well-being in Japanese state care. *Children and Youth Service Review, 31,* 797–806.

Bamba, S. & Haight, W. (2011). *Child welfare and development: A Japanese case study.* New York: Cambridge University Press.

Barnard-Brak, L., & Lechtenberger, D. (2010). Student IEP participation and academic achievement across time. *Remedial and Special Education, 31,* 343–349.

Benjamin, G. R. (1997). *Japanese lessons: A year in a Japanese school through the eyes of an American anthropologist and her children.* New York: New York University Press.

Blamires, M. (1999). Universal design for learning: Re-establishing differentiation as part of the inclusion agenda? *Support for Learning, 14*(4), 158–163.

Blue-Banning, M., Summers, J. A., Frankland, H. C., Nelson, L. L., & Beegle, G. (2004). Dimensions of family and professional partnerships: Constructive guidelines for collaboration. *Exceptional Children, 70*(2), 167–184.

Bourdieu, P. (1991). *Language and symbolic power.* Cambridge, MA: Harvard University Press.

Briggs, C. L. (1986). *Learning how to ask: A sociolinguistic appraisal of the role of the interview in social science research.* New York: Cambridge University Press.

Briggs, J. L. (1998). *Inuit morality play: The emotional education of a three-year-old.* New Haven, CT: Yale University Press.

Cabinet Office, the Government of Japan (2002a). Basic Programme for Persons with Disabilities. Retrieved October 5, 2010, from http://www8.cao.go.jp/shougai/english/basicprogram/3.html#3-4

Cabinet Office, the Government of Japan (2002b). Five-Year Plan for Implementation of Priority Measures. Retrieved October 5, 2010, from http://www8.cao.go.jp/shougai/english/5yearplan/5yearplan.html

Cabinet Office, the Government of Japan (2010). Kokusai teki na torikumi [What happens in the world: The Asian and Pacific Decade of Disabled Persons]. Retrieved October 11, 2010 from http://www8.cao.go.jp/shougai/asianpacific/index-ap.html

Cabinet Office, the Government of Japan (2011). Sho-gai sha kihon-ho no kaisei ni tsuite (Heisei 23 nen 8 gatsu) [The amendment of the basic law for persons with disabilities, August, 2011]. Retrieved August 17, 2011 from http://www8.cao.go.jp/shougai/suishin/kihonhou/kaisei2.html

Cave, P. (2007). *Primary school in Japan: Self, individuality and learning in elementary education.* New York: Routledge.

Chan, S. (1998). Families with Asian roots. In E. W. Lynch & M. J. Hanson, (Eds.), *A guide for working with children and their families: Developing cross-cultural competence* (pp. 251–354). Baltimore, MD: Paul H. Books Publishing Co.

Charmaz, K. (2002). Stories and silences: Disclosure and self in chronic illness. *Qualitative Inquiry, 8*(3), 302–328.

Chen X., French, D. C., & Schneider, B. H. (2006). Culture and peer relationships. In X. Chen, D. C. French, & B. H. Schneider (Eds.). *Peer relationships in cultural context* (pp. 3–20). New York: Cambridge University Press.

Clandinin, D. J., & Connelly, F. M. (2000). *Narrative inquiry: Experience and story in qualitative research.* San Francisco, CA: Jossey-Bass.

Clark, C. D. (2003). *In sickness and in play: Children coping with chronic illness.* New Brunswick, NJ: Rutgers University Press.

Clark, C. D. (2010). *In a younger voice: Doing child-centered qualitative research.* New York: Oxford University Press.

Cohen, C. B., & Napolitano, D. (2007). Adjustment to disability. *Journal of Social Work in Disability & Rehabilitation, 6*(1/2), 135–155.

Corsaro, W. A. (1997). *The sociology of childhood.* Thousand Oaks, CA: Pine Forge Press.

Corsaro, W. A. (2003). *We're friends, right? Inside Kids' culture.* Washington, D.C.: Joseph Henry Press.

Corsaro, W. A., & Rosier, K. B. (1992). Documenting productive-reproductive processes in children's lives: Transition narratives of a black family living in poverty. In W. A. Corsaro, & P. J. Miller (Eds.), *Interpretive approaches to children's socialization: New directions for child development* (pp. 5–23). New York: Jossey-Bass.

Crystal, D. S., Watanabe, H., & Chen, R. (1999). Children's reaction to physical disability: A cross-national and developmental study. *International Journal of Behavioral Development, 23*(1), 91–111.

Data Accountability Center (2012). Individuals with Disabilities Education Act Data, Retrieved December 7, 2012 from https://www.ideadata.org/PartBData.asp

Davis, J. M., & Watson, N. (2001). Where are the children's experiences? Analyzing social and cultural exclusion in 'Special" and "Mainstream" schools. *Disability & Society, 16,* 671–687.

Deford, F. (1997). *Alex: The life of a child.* Nashville, TN: Rutledge Hill Press.

Dekovic, M., Engels, R. C. M., Shirai, T., DeKort, G., & Anker, A. L. (2002). The role of peer relations in adolescent development in two cultures: The Netherlands and Japan. *Journal of Cross-Cultural Psychology, 33*(6), 577–595.

Department of Education (2013). Building the legacy: IDEA 2004. Retrieved April 21, 2013 from http://idea.ed.gov/explore/home

Department of Health and Human Services (2000). The developmental disabilities assistance and bill of rights act of 2000. Retrieved December 27, 2010 from http://www.acf.hhs.gov/programs/aidd/resource/dd-act

Dickson-Swift, V., James, E. L., Kippen, S., & Liamputtong, P. (2007). Doing sensitive research: What challenges do qualitative researchers face? *Qualitative Research, 7*(3), 323–353.

Doi, T. (2001). *The anatomy of dependence* (J. Bester, Trans.). Tokyo, Japan: Kodansha International. (Original work published 1971 under the title Amae no kozo)

Duncan, G. J., Huston, A. C., & Weisner, T. S. (2007). *Higher ground: New Hope for the working poor and their children.* New York: Russell Sage Foundation.

Dyson, A. H. (2003). *The brothers and sisters learn to write: Popular literacies in childhood and school cultures.* New York: Teachers College Press.

Fadiman, A. (1997). *The spirit catches you and you fall down: A Hmong child, her American doctors, and the collision of two cultures*. New York: Farrar, Straus, and Giroux.

Fine, G. A., & Sandstorm, K. L. (1998). *Knowing children: Participant observation with minors*. Newbury Park, CA: Sage Publications, Inc.

Ford, D. Y., Moore, J. L., III, & Scott, M. T. (2011). Key theories and frameworks for improving the recruitment and retention of African American students in gifted education. *The Journal of Negro Education, 80*(3), 239–253.

Garcia Coll, C., & Marks, A. K. (2008). *Immigrant stories: Ethnicity and academics in middle childhood*. New York: Oxford University Press.

Gaskins, S., Miller, P. J., & Corsaro, W. A. (1992). Theoretical and methodological perspectives in the interpretive study of children. In W. A. Corsaro, & P. J. Miller (Eds.), *Interpretive approaches to children's socialization: New directions for child development* (pp. 5–23). New York: Jossey-Bass.

Genishi, C., & Dyson, A. H. (2009). *Children, language, and literacy: Diverse learners in diverse times*. New York: Teachers College Press.

Goets, J. P., & LeCompte, M. D. (1981). Ethnographic research and the problem of data reduction. *Anthropology and Education Quarterly, 12*(1), 51–70.

Goffman, E. (1963). *Stigma: Notes on the management of spoiled identity*. Englewood Cliffs, NJ: Prentice-Hall, Inc.

Goldberg, M. P. (1989). Recent trends in special education in Tokyo. In J. J. Shields, Jr. (Ed). *Japanese schooling: Patterns of socialization, equality, and political control (pp. 176–184)*. University Park, PA: The Pennsylvania State University Press.

Green, S., Davis, C., Karshmer, E., Marsh, P., & Strauggtm B. (2005). Living stigma: The impact of labeling, stereotyping, separation, status loss, and discrimination in the lives of individuals with disabilities and their families. *Sociological Inquiry, 75*, 197–215.

Hagiwara, K. (2001). Kodomo wakamono no Ibasho no Jouken. [Conditions needed for children's and youth's Ibasho]. In H. Tanaka (Ed.), *Kodmo wakamono no Ibasho no kousou: "kyoiku" kara "kakawarinoba" he [Children's and Youth's ideas about Ibasho: From "Education" to "a Place for Interaction"]* (pp. 51–65). Japan: Gakuyoushobou.

Haight, W. L. (2002). *African-American children at church: A sociocultural perspective*. New York: Cambridge University Press.

Hall, J. P. (2002). Narrowing the breach: Can disability culture and full educational inclusion be reconciled? *Journal of Disability Policy Studies, 13*, 144–152.

Haynes, C., Hook, P., Macaruso, P., Muta, E., Hayashi, Y., Kato, J., & Sasaki, T. (2000). Teachers' skill ratings of children with learning disabilities: A comparison of the United States and Japan. *Annals of Dyslexia, 50*, 215–238.

Helton, J. J., & Cross, T. P. (2011). The relationship of child functioning to parental physical assault: Linear and curvilinear models. *Child Maltreatment, 16*(2), 126–136.

Heyer, K. (2008). No one's perfect: Disability and differences in Japan. In T. Berberi, E. C. Hamilton, & I. M. Sutherland (Eds.). *Worlds apart? Disability and foreign language learning* (pp. 232–251). London: Yale University Press.

Ho, A. (2004). To be labeled, or not to be labeled: That is the question. *British Journal of Learning Disabilities, 32,* 86–92.

Holland, D., Lachictte, W., Skinner, D., & Cain, C. (1998). *Identity and agency in cultural worlds.* Cambridge, MA: Harvard University Press.

Hood, L., McDermott, R. & Cole, M. (1980). "Let's *try* to make it a good day"—Some not so simple ways. *Discourse Processes, 3,* 155–168.

Hosaka, T. (2005). School absenteeism, bullying, and loss of peer relationships in Japanese children. In D. W. Shwalb, J. Nakazawa, and B. J. Shwalb (Eds.). *Applied developmental psychology: Theory, practice, and research from Japan.* Greenwich, CT: Information Age Publishing.

Hudley, E. V. P., Haight, W., & Miller, P. J. (2003/2009). *Raise up a child: Human development in an African-American family.* Chicago: Lyceum Books, Inc.

Hunt, P. F. (2011). Salamanca Statement and IDEA 2004: Possibilities of practice for inclusive education. *International Journal of Inclusive Education, 15,* 461–476.

Hymes, D. (1982). What is ethnography? In P. Gilmore & A. A. Glatthorn (Eds.), *Children in and out of school: Ethnography and education* (pp. 21–32). Washington, D.C.: Center for Applied Linguistics.

Ichiki, R. (2010). Sho-gai sha no kenri ni kansuru jyo-yaku no rinen wo fumaeta tokubetu shien kyo-iku no arikata ni kansuru ikennsho [Opinions for special education based on the philosophy of the Convention on the Rights of Persons with Disabilities] Retrieved April 21, 2013 from http://www.mext.go.jp/b_menu/shingi/chukyo/chukyo3/044/attach/1298937.htm

IDEA Reauthorization. (2005). *Congressional Digest, 84*(1), 10–12, 32.

Illinois State Board of Education (2009). *Parent guide – Educational rights and responsibilities: Understanding special education in Illinois.* Retrieved May 20, 2013 from http://www.isbe.net/spec-ed/html/parent_rights.htm

Itagaki, Y. & Toki, K. (1993). Current developments and the problems of culture and special education in Japan. In S. J. Peters (Ed.). *Education and disability in cross-cultural perspective* (pp. 127–166). New York: Garland Publishing, Inc.

Jegatheesan, B. (2009). Cross-cultural issues in parent-professional interactions: A qualitative study of perceptions of Asian American mothers of children with developmental disabilities. *Research & Practices for Persons with Severe Disabilities, 34,* 123–136.

Jegatheesan, B., Fowler, S., & Miller, P. J. (2010). From symptoms recognition to services: How South Asian Muslim immigrant families navigate autism. *Disability & Society, 27*(7), 797–811.

Jegatheesan, B., Miller, J. P., & Fowler, S. A. (2010). Autism from a religious perspective: A study of parental beliefs in South Asian Muslim immigrant families. *Focus on Autism and Other Developmental Disabilities, 25*, 98–109.

Jenkins, R. (2002). *Pierre Bourdieu* (2nd ed.). New York: Routledge.

Jessor, R., Colby, A. & Shweder, R. A. (Eds.) (1996). *Ethnography and Human Development: Context and Meaning in Social Inquiry.* Chicago: University of Chicago Press.

Kadomoto, J. (1990). Gakushu sho-gai oyobi sono shu-hen gun no gainen no kento [Review on the concepts of learning disabilities and other related disabilities]. *Japanese Journal of the Problems of the Handicapped, 61*, 2–8.

Kadota, K. (2009, June). Tokushu-go: 2008 nen-do suku-ru so-sharu wa-ku katsuyo jigyo: Genjyo to kadai [Special issue: Current status and problems from the school social work utilization project: Fiscal year 2008]. *Japanese Journal of School Social Work.*

Kanagawa Prefecture (2008). Hachi to-ken-shi shuno kaigi: tokubetsu shien kyo-iku suishin no tame no seido no kaizen ni kansuru youbou no jisshi nit suite [Eight prefectures-cities summit meeting: Regarding the request for changes in the current system to promote special education]. Retrieved December 21, 2010 from http://www.pref.kanagawa.jp/press/0805/001/index.html

Kasahara, M., & Turnbull, A. P. (2005). Meaning of family-professional partnerships: Japanese mothers' perspectives. *Exceptional Children, 71*(3), 249–265.

Kataoka, M., van Kraayenoord, C. E., & Elkins, J. (2004). Principals' and teachers' perceptions of learning disabilities: A study from Nara prefecture, Japan. *Learning Disability Quarterly, 27*(3), 161–175.

Kawabata, Y., Nicki, R. C., & Hamaguchi, Y. (2010). The role of culture in relational aggression: Associations with social-psychological adjustment problems in Japanese and US school-aged children. *International Journal of Behavioral Development, 34*(4), 354–362.

Kayama, M. (2010). Parental experiences of children's disabilities and special education in the United States and Japan: Implications for school social work. *Social Work, 55*, 117–125.

Kelly, B. (2005). 'Chocolate…makes you autism': Impairment, disability and childhood identities. *Disability & Society, 20*, 261–275.

Kendall, R. M., & DeMoulin, D. F. (1993). Mainstreaming students with disabilities using self-efficacy. *Education, 114*(2), 201–205.

Kennedy, R., & Yaginuma, M. (1991) Up and down etiquette. In B. Finkelstein, A. E. Imamura, J. J. Tobin (Eds.). *Transcending stereotypes: Discovering Japanese culture and education.* Yarmouth, ME: Intercultural Press, Inc.

Kimura, B. (1972). *Hito to hito no aida [Between one person and another].* Tokyo, Japan: Kobundo.

Kirk, S. A. (1977). Specific learning disabilities. *Journal of Clinical Child Psychology, 60*(3), 23–26.

Kirk, S. A. & Kirk, W. D. (1983). On defining learning disabilities. *Journal of Learning Disabilities, 16*(1), 20–21.

Kock, E., Molteno, C., Mfili, N., Kidd, M., Ali, A., King, M., et al., (2012). Cross-cultural validation of a measure of felt stigma in people with intellectual disabilities. *Journal of Applied Research in Intellectual Disabilities, 25*, 11–19.

Kohn, P. (2012). QUWAR: A collaborative professional development model to meet the needs of diverse learners in K-6 science. *Psychology in the Schools, 49*(5), 429–443.

Koro-Ljungberg, M., & Bussing, R. (2009). The management of courtesy stigma in the lives of families with teenagers with ADHD. *Journal of Family Issues, 30*, 1175–1200.

Kramer, L., Perozynski, L. A., & Chung, T. (1999). Parental responses to sibling conflict: The effects of development and parent gender. *Child Development, 70*(6), 1401–1414.

Lalvani, P. (2008). Mothers of children with Down syndrome: Constructing the sociocultural meaning of disability. *Intellectual and Developmental Disabilities, 46*, 436–445.

Lebra, T. S. (1976). *Japanese patterns of behavior.* Honolulu, HI: University of Hawaii Press.

Lewis, C. C. (1995). *Educating hearts and minds: Reflections on Japanese preschool and elementary education.* New York: Cambridge University Press.

Lightfoot, E. (2004). Community based rehabilitation: A rapidly growing method of supporting people with disabilities. *International Social Work, 47*(4), 455–468.

Lincoln, Y. S., & Guba, E. G. (1985). *Naturalistic inquiry,* Newbury Park, CA: Sage Publications.

Linde, C. (1993). *Life stories: The creation of coherence.* New York: Oxford University Press.

Link, B. & Phelan, J. (2001). Conceptualizing stigma. *Annual Review of Sociology, 27*(1), 363–385.

Llewellyn, A. & Hogan, K. (2000). The use and abuse of models of disability. *Disability & Society, 15*(1), 157–165.

Lutz, B. J., & Bowers, B. J. (2005) Disability in everyday life. *Qualitative Health Research, 15*(8), 1037–1054.

Mackelprang, R. W. & Salsgiver, R. O. (2009). *Disability: A diversity model approach in human service practice* (2nd ed.). Chicago: Lyceum Books, Inc.

Mansfield, C. (2000). Ritualizing socialization: The non-academic agenda of Japanese schools. *Education and Society, 18*(3), 7–19.

Maret, J. D. (2008). An ethnography of invisibility: Education and special needs children in Japan. Unpublished doctoral dissertation, University of Hawaii at Manoa. (UMI No. 3311885)

Markus, H. R., & Kitayama, S. (1991). Culture and the self: Implications for cognition, emotion, and motivation. *Psychological Review, 98* (2), 224–253.

McDermott, R., Goldman, S., & Varenne, H. (2006). The cultural work of learning disabilities. *Educational Researcher, 35*(6), 12–17.

McDermott, R., & Varenne, H. (1995). Culture as disability. *Anthropology & Education Quarterly, 26*(3), 324–348.

McMaugh, A. (2011). En/countering disablement in school life in Australia: Children talk about peer relations and living with illness and disability. *Disability & Society, 26*, 853–866.

McNulty, M. A. (2003). Dyslexia and the life course. *Journal of Learning Disabilities, 36*, 363–381.

Meadan, H., & Halle, J. W. (2004). Social perceptions of students with learning disabilities who differ in social status. *Learning Disabilities Research & Practice, 19*(2), 71–82.

Mehan, H. (1998). The study of social interaction in educational settings: Accomplishments and unresolved issues. *Human Development, 41*, 245–269.

Miller, P. J., Fung, H., & Koven, M. (2007). Narrative reverberations: How participation in narrative practices co-creates persons and cultures. In S. Kitayama & D. Cohen (Eds.), *Handbook of cultural psychology* (pp. 595–614). New York: Guilford Press.

Miller, P. J., Fung, H., Lin, S., Chen, E. C-H, & Boldt, B. R. (2012). How socialization happens on the ground: Narrative practices as alternate socializing pathways in Taiwanese and European-American families. *Monographs of the Society for Research in Child Development, 77*(1), 1–140.

Miller, P. J., Hengst, J. A., & Wang, S-H. (2003). Ethnographic methods: Application from developmental cultural psychology. In P.M. Camic, J. E. Rhodes, & L. Yardley (Eds.), *Qualitative research in psychology: Expanding perspectives in methodology and design* (pp. 219–241). Washington, D. C.: American Psychological Association.

Ministry of Education (1953). Waga kuni no kyo-iku no genjyo: Showa 28 nen-do [Current status of education in Japan: Fiscal year 1953]. Retrieved October 3, 2010 from http://www.mext.go.jp/b_menu/hakusho/html/hpad195301/hpad195301_2_201.html

Ministry of Education (1981). Gaku-sei hyaku-nen shi [History of education: One hundred years]. Retrieved October 2, 2010 from http://www.mext.go.jp/b_menu/hakusho/html/others/detail/1317552.htm

Ministry of Education (1992). Gaku-sei hyaku-nijyu-nen shi [History of education: One hundred and twenty years]. Retrieved October 2, 2010 from http://www.mext.go.jp/b_menu/hakusho/html/hpbz199201/

Ministry of Education (1993a). Waga kuni-no bun-kyo sesaku: Heisei 5 nen-do [Educational policies in Japan: Fiscal year 1993]. Retrieved October 3, from http://www.mext.go.jp/b_menu/hakusho/html/hpad199301/hpad199301_2_118.html

Ministry of Education (1993b). Heisei 5 nen Monbu kagaku sho kokuji dai 7 go: Gakko kyo-iku ho shiko kisoku dai 73 jyo no 21 no kitei ni yoru tokubetsu no kyo-iku katei [The 7th notice from the Ministry of Education, Science, and Culture, 1993: Special educational curriculum based on the article 73-21 of the School Education Law]. Retrieved May 6, from http://www.mext.go.jp/b_menu/hakusho/nc/k19930128001/k19930128001

Ministry of Education (1995). Gakushu sho-gai ji ni taisuru shido ni tsuite: Chu-kan houkoku [Instructions for children with learning disabilities: Interim report]. Retrieved October 3, 2010 from http://www.mext.go.jp/b_menu/hakusho/nc/t19950329001/t19950329001

Ministry of Education (1999). Gakushu sho-gai ji ni taisuru shido nit suite: Houkoku [Instructions for children with learning disabilities: Report]. Retrieved October 3, 2010 from http://www.mext.go.jp/a_menu/shotou/tokubetu/material/002.htm

Ministry of Education (2001a). 21 seiki no tokushu kyo-iku no arikata ni tsuite: Saishu houkoku [Future direction of special education in the 21st century: Final report]. Retrieved October 3, 2010 from http://www.mext.go.jp/b_menu/shingi/chousa/shotou/006/toushin/010102.htm

Ministry of Education (2001b). Heisei 13 nen-do monbu kagaku hakusho [An educational white paper: Fiscal year 2001]. Retrieved October 6, 2010 from http://www.mext.go.jp/b_menu/hakusho/html/hpab200101/hpab200101_2_005.html

Ministry of Education (2002a). Tsujyo no gakkyu ni zaiseki suru tokubetu-na kyo-iku teki shien wo hitsuyo to suru jido seito ni kansuru zenkoku jittai chousa [National research on children who needed special educational support in regular classrooms]. Retrieved October 3, 2010, from http://www.mext.go.jp/b_menu/shingi/chousa/shotou/018/toushin/030301i.htm

Ministry of Education (2002b). Sho-gai no aru jido seito no shu-gaku ni tsuite [Notice regarding school attendance of pupils and students with disabilities]. Retrieved October 3, 2010, from http://www.mext.go.jp/b_menu/hakusho/nc/t20020527001/t20020527001.html

Ministry of Education (2002c). Ko-ritsu gimu kyo-iku sho gakko no gakkyu hensei oyobi kyo-shokuin teisu no hyojyun ni kansuru ho-ritsu shiko-rei no ichibu kai-sei ni okeru kyo-iku jyo tokubetsu no hairyo wo hitsuyo tosuru jido mataha seito ni taisuru tokubetsu no shido tou ni taisuru kyo-shokuin teisu no tokurei kasan ni tsuite [Notice regarding amendment of the regulation of the Law determining standards for classroom sizes and the number of staff members at public schools providing compulsory education in order to assign additional staff members to provide educational support to pupils and students with additional educational needs]. Retrieved October 3, 2010, from http://www.mext.go.jp/b_menu/hakusho/nc/t20020401002/t20020401002.html

Ministry of Education (2002d). Sho-gakko secchi kijun [Standards necessary to establish an elementary school]. Retrieved December 26, 2011 from http://www.mext.go.jp/a_menu/shotou/koukijyun/1290242.htm

Ministry of Education (2002e). Tashika-na gakuryoku ko-jyo no tame no 2002 api-ru: Manabi no susume [2002 Appeal to improve children's academic standards and ability: Encouragement of learning]. Retrieved April 21, 2013 from http://www.mext.go.jp/a_menu/shotou/actionplan/03071101/008.pdf

Ministry of Education (2003). Kongo no tokubetsu shien kyo-iku no arikata ni tsuite [The future direction of special education in Japan: Final report]. Retrieved April 26, 2005, from http://www.mext.go.jp/b_menu/shingi/chousa/shotou/018/toushin/030301.htm

Ministry of Education (2004). Sho chu gakko ni okeru LD (gakushu sho-gai), ADHD (chu-i kekkann/tadou sei sho-gai), ko-kinou jihei-sho no jidou seito he no kyo-iku shien taisei no seibi no tame no gaidorain (shi-an) no kouhyo ni tsuite [Publication of the tentative guideline to establish the system to provide educational support for children with LD (learning disabilities), ADHD (attention deficit/ hyperactivity disorder), high functioning autism at elementary and junior high schools]. Retrieved November 12, 2010, from http://www.mext.go.jp/a_menu/shotou/tokubetu/material/1298152.htm

Ministry of Education (2005a). Hattatsu sho-gai sha shien ho no shiko ni tsuite [Enforcement of the Support for Persons with Developmental Disabilities Act]. Retrieved October 4, 2010, from http://www.mext.go.jp/b_menu/hakusho/nc/06050816.htm

Ministry of Education (2005b). Hattatsu sho-gai no aru jidou seito he no shien ni tsuite (Tsu-chi) [Notice: Support for pupils and students with developmental disabilities]. Retrieved October 3, 2010 from http://www.mext.go.jp/b_menu/hakusho/nc/06050815.htm

Ministry of Education (2005c). Tokubetsu shien kyo-iku wo suishin suru tame no seido no arikata ni tsuite (Toshin) [Report: A system promoting special needs education]. Retrieved October 5, 2010 from http://www.mext.go.jp/b_menu/shingi/chukyo/chukyo0/toushin/05120801.htm

Ministry of Education (2006a). Tsu-kyu ni yoru sidou no taisho to suru koto-ga tekitou na jihei-sho sha, jyo-cho sho-gai sha, gakushu sho-gai sha mataha chu-i kekkann tadou sei sho-gai sha ni gaitou suru jidou seito ni tsuite: Tsu-chi [Notice: Pupils and students with autism, emotional disorders, learning disabilities, or attention deficit hyperactivity disorders who are eligible to receive special education part-time at resource rooms]. Retrieved October 3, 2010 from http://www.mext.go.jp/b_menu/hakusho/nc/06050817.htm

Ministry of Education (2006b). Gakko kyo-iku ho shiko kisoku no ichibu kaisei ni tsuite: Tsu-chi [Notice: the amendment of the enforcement regulation of the School Education Law]. Retrieved October 5, 2010 from http://www.mext.go.jp/b_menu/hakusho/nc/06050814.htm

Ministry of Education (2006c). Kyo-iku kihon-ho no sikou ni tsuite: Tsu-chi [Notice regarding the enforcement of the Fundamental Law of Education]. Retrieved May 17, 2010 from http://www.mext.go.jp/b_menu/kihon/about/06122123.htm

Ministry of Education (2006d). Tokubetsu shien kyo-iku no suishin no tame no gakko kyo-iku ho tou no ichibu kaisei ni tsuite: Tsu-chi [Notice: Amendment of the School Education Law and other related laws in order to promote special education]. Retrieved October 6, 2010 from http://www.mext.go.jp/b_menu/hakusho/nc/06072108.htm

Ministry of Education (2006e). Gakko kyo-iku ho tou no ichibu wo kaisei suru ho-ritsu an ni kansuru futai ketsugi [A supplementary resolution for a draft of the law amending the School Education Law and other related laws]. Retrieved October 5, 2010 from http://www.mext.go.jp/b_menu/hakusho/nc/06072108/002.htm

Ministry of Education (2006f). Heisei 18 nen-do monbu kagaku hakusho [An educational white paper: Fiscal year 2006]. Retrieved August 22, 2011 from http://www.mext.go.jp/b_menu/hakusho/html/hpab200601/002/002/017.htm

Ministry of Education (2006g). Tokubetsu shien kyo-iku shiryo: Heisei 17 nen-do [Special education statistics: 2005]. Retrieved December 1, 2012 from http://www.mext.go.jp/a_menu/shotou/tokubetu/material/003.htm

Ministry of Education (2007a). Tsu-chi: Tokubetsu shien kyo-iku no suishin ni tsuite [Notice: Implementing special needs education]. Retrieved October, 6, 2010 from http://www.mext.go.jp/b_menu/hakusho/nc/07050101.htm

Ministry of Education (2007b). "Hattatsu sho-gai" no yo-go no shiyou ni tsuite [Regarding the use of the term, "developmental disabilities"]. Retrieved October, 3, 2010 from http://www.mext.go.jp/a_menu/shotou/tokubetu/main/002.htm

Ministry of Education (2007c). Dokkai-ryoku koujyo ni kansuru shidou shiryou [Instructional materials to improve reading comprehension]. Retrieved February 4, 2013 from http://www.mext.go.jp/a_menu/shotou/gakuryoku/siryo/05122201.htm

Ministry of Education (2008). Sho-gakko gakushu shido yo-ryo [National Curriculum Standard for elementary schools]. Tokyo, Japan: Author.

Ministry of Education (2009a). Jyocho sho-gai sha wo taisho to suru tokubetsu shien gakkyu no meisho ni tsuite: Tsu-chi [Notice regarding the name of special education classrooms for children with emotional disorders]. Retrieved May 6, 2010 from http://www.mext.go.jp/b_menu/hakusho/nc/1246163.htm

Ministry of Education (2009b). Tokubetsu shien kyo-iku no saranaru jyu-jitsu ni mukete (Shingi no chu-kan tori matome): Souki kara no kyo-iku shien no arikata ni tsuite [Further enhancement of special education (Interim report of the council): Educational support since early childhood]. Retrieved March 29, 2010 from http://www.mext.go.jp/b_menu/shingi/chousa/shotou/054/gaiyou/1236337.htm

Ministry of Education (2009c). Tokubetsu shien gakko no gakushu shido yo-ryo tou no ko-ji oyobi iko sochi ni tsuite [The national curriculum standard for special education schools and steps to implement the new curriculum]. Retrieved October 13, 2010 from http://www.mext.go.jp/a_menu/shotou/new-cs/youryou/tsuuchi2/__icsFiles/afieldfile/2009/04/06/003_1.pdf

Ministry of Education (2009d). *Tokubetsu shien gakko kyo-iku yo-ryo, gakushu shido yo-ryo [National Curriculum Standard for special education schools].* Tokyo, Japan: Author.

Ministry of Education (2010a). Showa 22 nen kyo-iku kihon ho seitei ji no jyo-bun [The Fundamental Law of Education of 1947]. Retrieved October 6, 2010 from http://www.mext.go.jp/b_menu/kihon/about/a001.htm

Ministry of Education (2010b). Sho-gai sha seido kaikaku no shuishin no tame no kihon teki na houkou: Dai 1-ji iken [A reform of support systems for people with disabilities: The first suggestions]. Retrieved October 15, 2010 from http://www.mext.go.jp/b_menu/shingi/chukyo/chukyo3/siryo/attach/1295927.htm

Ministry of Education (2010c). Kongo no gakkyu hensei oyobi kyo-shokuin teisu no kaizen ni tsuite (Teigen) [Opinions offered by the Council: Future direction of classroom size and numbers of staff members]. Retrieved October 28, 2010 from http://www.mext.go.jp/a_menu/shotou/hensei/005/1296296.htm

Ministry of Education (2010d). Tokubetsu shien kyo-iku no arikata ni kansuru toku-betsu iin-kai (Dai 4 kai) gijiroku [The minutes of the fourth meeting: The ad hoc committee on the future direction of special education]. Retrieved December 21, 2010 from http://www.mext.go.jp/b_menu/shingi/chukyo/chukyo3/044/siryo/1298919.htm

Ministry of Education (2011a). Tokubetsu shien kyo-iku shiryo: Heisei 22 nen-do [Special education statistics: Fiscal year 2011]. Retrieved December 1, 2012 from http://www.mext.go.jp/a_menu/shotou/tokubetu/material/1309805.htm

Ministry of Education (2011b). Ko-ritsu gimu kyo-iku sho gakko no gakkyu hensei oyobi kyo-shokuin teisu no hyojyun ni kansuru ho-ritsu no ichibu wo kaisei suru ho-ritsu [The amendment of the Law determining standards for classroom sizes and the number of staff members at public schools providing compulsory educa-tion]. Retrieved December 2, 2012 from http://www.mext.go.jp/b_menu/houan/kakutei/detail/1305316.htm

Ministry of Education (2012a). Tokubetsu shien kyo-iku shiryo: Heisei 23 nen-do [Special education statistics: 2011]. Retrieved February 28, 2013 from http://www.mext.go.jp/a_menu/shotou/tokubetu/material/1322973.htm

Ministry of Education (2012b). Gakko kihon chousa: Heisei 23 nen-do [School sta-tistics: 2011]. Retrieved February 28, 2013 from http://www.mext.go.jp/b_menu/toukei/chousa01/kihon/kekka/k_detail/1315581.htm

Ministry of Education (2012c) Zenkoku gakuryoku gakushu jyoukyo chousa no gaiyou [Overview of the National research on academic achievement and learn-ing]. Retrieved February 28, 2013 from http://www.mext.go.jp/a_menu/shotou/gakuryoku-chousa/zenkoku/07032809.htm

Ministry of Health, Labour and Welfare (2004a). Hattatsu sho-gai sha shien ho [Support for Persons with Developmental Disabilities Act]. Retrieved October 4, 2010 from http://www.mhlw.go.jp/topics/2005/04/tp0412-1b.html

Ministry of Health, Labour and Welfare (2004b). Hattatsu sho-gai sha shien ho shiko rei [Support for Persons with Developmental Disabilities Act, enforcement ordinance]. Retrieved October 14, 2010 from http://www.mhlw.go.jp/topics/2005/04/tp0412-1c.html

Ministry of Health, Labour and Welfare (2004c). Hattatsu sho-gai sha shien ho shiko kisoku [Support for Persons with Developmental Disabilities Act, enforcement regulation]. Retrieved October 14, 2010 from http://www.mhlw.go.jp/topics/2005/04/tp0412-1d.html

Ministry of Internal Affairs and Communication (2006) Kyo-iku kihon ho [The Fundamental Law of Education]. Retrieved May 15, 2010 from http://law.e-gov.go.jp/htmldata/H18/H18HO120.html

Ministry of Internal Affairs and Communication (2007). Gakko kyo-iku ho [The School Education Law]. Retrieved October 6, 2010 from http://law.e-gov.go.jp/htmldata/S22/S22HO026.html

Ministry of Internal Affairs Communication (2008a). Jido fukushi ho [The Child Welfare Act]. Retrieved October 12, 2010 from http://law.e-gov.go.jp/htmldata/S33/S33HO116.html

Ministry of Internal Affairs and Communication (2008b). Kyo-in menkyo ho [Teacher certification law]. Retrieved March 5, 2011 from http://law.e-gov.go.jp/htmldata/S24/S24HO147.html

Ministry of Internal Affairs and Communication (2011a). Ko-ritsu gimu kyo-iku sho gakko no gakkyu hensei oyobi kyo-shoku in teisu no hyojyun ni kansuru ho-ritsu [Law determining standards for classroom sizes and the number of staff members at public schools providing compulsory education]. Retrieved October 5, 2010 from http://law.e-gov.go.jp/htmldata/S33/S33HO116.html

Ministry of Internal Affairs and Communication (2011b). Gakko kyo-iku ho shiko kisoku [The School Education Law enforcement regulation]. Retrieved September 11, 2011 http://law.e-gov.go.jp/htmldata/S22/S22F03501000011.html?sess=88d57b4cfb4f5741a47f

Ministry of Internal Affairs and Communication (2011c). Gakko kyo-iku ho shiko-rei [The School Education Law enforcement ordinance]. Retrieved September 11, 2011 http://law.e-gov.go.jp/htmldata/S28/S28SE340.html

Minow, M. (1990). *Making all the difference: Inclusion, exclusion, and American law.* Ithaca, NY: Cornell University Press.

Mogi, T. (1992). The disabled in society. *Japan Quarterly, 39* (4), 440–448.

Morson, G. S., & Emerson, C. (1990). *Mikhail Bakhtin: Creation of a prosaics.* Stanford, CA: Stanford University Press.

Murakami, Y., & Meyer, H. D. (2010). Culture, institutions, and disability policy in Japan: The translation of culture into policy. *Comparative Sociology, 9,* 202–221.

Nakamura, M. & Arakawa, S. (2003). *Sho-gai ji kyo-iku no rekishi [History of special education].* Tokyo, Japan: Akashi Shoten.

National Archives of Japan (1947) Gakko kyo-iku ho: Go-shomei genpon [The School Education Law, Signed original]. Retrieved October 13, 2010 from http://www.archives.go.jp/ayumi/kobetsu/s22_1947_01.html

National Association of Parents of Children with Learning Disabilities (2013). Zenkoku LD oya no kai no ayumi [History of the National Association for Parents of Children with Learning Disabilities]. Retrieved February 27, 2013 from http://www.jpald.net/ayumi.html

National Institute of Special Needs Education (1975) Jyu-do, jyu-fuku sho-gai ji ni tai-suru gakko kyo-iku no arikata ni tsuite (Houkoku) [School education for children with severe and multiple disabilities: Report]. Retrieved July 13, 2011 from http://www.nise.go.jp/blog/2000/05/b2_s500331_01.html

National Institute of Special Needs Education (1978). Kei-do shin-shin sho-gai ji ni taisuru gakko kyo-iku no ari-kata: Houkoku [School education for children with minor disabilities: Report]. Retrieved July 13, 2011 from http://www.nise.go.jp/blog/2000/05/b2_s530812_01.html

National Institute of Special Needs Education (1992). Tsu-kyu ni yoru shido ni kan-suru jyu-jitsu housaku ni tsuite: Shin-gi no matome [Strategies to establish and implement pull out instructions: A summary of the council]. Retrieved August 14, 2010 from https://www.nise.go.jp/blog/2000/05/b2_h040330_01.html

Nishimaki, K. (2005). Byo-jyaku kyo-iku no rekishi to seido 1 [History and policies pertaining to education of children with chronic illness]. Retrieved December 2, 2012 from http://www.nise.go.jp/portal/elearn/rekishi1.html

Nugent, M. (2008). Services for children with dyslexia—The child's experience. *Educational Psychology in Practice. 24,* 189–206.

Ochs, E., Kremer-Sadlik, T., Solomon, O., & Sirota, K. G. (2010). Inclusion as social practice: Views of children with autism. *Social Development, 10*(3), 399–419.

Ochs, E., & Solomon, O. (2010). Autistic Sociality. *Ethos, 38*(1), 69–92.

Okamoto, K (2006). *Education of the rising sun 21: An introduction to education in Japan* (2nd ed.). Tokyo, Japan: National Federation of Social Education.

Olney, M. F., Kenedy, J. Brockelman, K. F., & Newsom, M. A. (2004). Do you have a disability? A population-based test of acceptance, denial, and adjustment among adults with disabilities in the U.S. *Journal of Rehabilitation, 70,* 4–9.

Ototake, H. (1998). *Gotai Fumanzoku.* Tokyo, Japan: Kodansha. (Also published in English in 2000 as *No One's Perfect*)

Paley, V. (1990). *The boy who would be a helicopter.* Cambridge, MA: Harvard University Press.

Paley, V. (1993). *You can't say you can't play.* Cambridge, MA: Harvard University Press.

Paley, V. (2004). *A child's work: The importance of fantasy play.* Chicago: University of Chicago Press.

Peak, L. (1991). *Learning to go to school in Japan: The transition from home to preschool life.* Berkeley, CA: University of California Press.

Perozynski, L., & Kramer, L. (1999). Parental beliefs about managing sibling conflict. *Developmental Psychology, 35*(2), 489–499.

Peters, S. J. (Ed.). (1993). *Education and disability in cross-cultural perspective.* New York: Garland Publishing, Inc.

Peters, S. J. (2010). The heterodoxy of student voice: Challenges to identity in the sociology of disability and education. *British Journal of Sociology of Education, 31,* 591–602.

Phillips, M. J. (1990). Damaged goods: Oral narratives of the experience of disability in American culture. *Social Science and Medicine, 30*(8), 349–857.

Poindexter, C. C. (2003). The ubiquity of ambiguity in research interviewing: An exemplar. *Qualitative Social Work, 2*(4), 383–409.

Portelli, A. (2003). *The order has been carried out: History, memory, and meaning of a Nazi massacre in Rome.* New York: Palgrave MacMillan.

Portway, S. M., & Johnson, B. (2005). Do you know I have Asperger's syndrome? Risks of a non-obvious disability. *Health, Risk & Society, 7,* 73–83.

Quinn, N., & Strauss, C. (1997). *A cognitive theory of cultural meaning.* New York: Cambridge University Press.

Rogoff, B. (2003). *The cultural nature of human development.* New York: Oxford University Press.

Rogoff, B. (2011). *Developing destinies: A Mayan midwife and town.* New York: Oxford University Press.

Rogoff, B., Mistry, J., Göncü, A., & Mosier, C. (1993). Guided participation in cultural activity by toddlers and caregivers. *Monographs of the Society for Research in Child Development, 58*(8, Serial No. 236).

Saito, K. (2009). *Hattatsu sho-gai ga hiki-okosu niji sho-gai he no kea to sapo-to. [Care and support of secondary disabilities caused by developmental disabilities.].* Tokyo, Japan: Gakken Kyoiku Shuppan.

Sato, N. E. (2004). *Inside Japanese classrooms: The heart of education.* New York: Routledge Falmer.

Shimizu, H. (2001a). Japanese cultural psychology and empathic understanding: Implications for academic and cultural psychology. In H. Shimizu & R. A. LeVine (Eds.), *Japanese frame of mind: Cultural perspectives on human development* (pp. 1–26). New York: Cambridge University Press.

Shimizu, H. (2001b). Japanese adolescent boys' sense of empathy (omoiyari) and Carol Gilligan's perspectives on the morality of care: A phenomenological approach. *Culture & Psychology, 7*(4), 453–475.

Shimizu, K. (1999). *Nozoite miyou! imano sho-gakko: Henbo suru kyo-shitsu no esu-nogurafi [Look into current elementary schools: Ethnography of evolving classrooms]*. Tokyo, Japan: Yushin-do Koubunsha.

Shweder, R. (2009) Introduction: An invitation to the many worlds of childhood. In R. Shweder (Ed. In Chief) *The Child: An encyclopedic companion* (pp. xxvii–xxxvii). Chicago: University of Chicago Press.

Shweder, R. A., Goodnow, J. G., Hatano, G., LeVine, R. A., Markus, H. R., & Miller, P. J. (2006). The cultural psychology of development: One mind, many mentalities. In W. Damon & R. Lerner (Eds.), *Handbook of child development: Vol. 1 Theoretical models of human development* (6th ed., pp. 716–792). Hoboken, NJ: John Wiley & Sons, Inc.

Smith, D. D. (2007). *Introduction to special education: Making a difference* (6th ed.). Boston: Allyn and Bacon.

Stake, R. E. (2010). *Qualitative Research: Studying how things work*. New York: The Guilford Press.

Steedman, C. K. (1986). *Landscape for a good woman: A story of two lives*. New Brunswick, NJ: Rutgers University Press.

Stevenson, H. W., & Stigler, J. W. (1992). *The learning gap: Why our schools are failing and what we can learn from Japanese and Chinese education*. New York: Simon & Schuster Inc.

Sugawara, N. (2011). *Tokubetsu shien kyoiku wo manabu hito-he [For those who are learning special needs education]*. Kyoto, Japan: Minerva Shobo.

Summers, J. A., Marquis, J., Mannan, H., Turnbull, A. P., Fleming, K., Poston, D. J.,…Kupzyk, K. (2007). Relationship of perceived adequacy of services, family-professional partnerships, and family quality of life in early childhood service programmes. *International Journal of Disability, Development and Education, 54*(3), 319–338.

Tachibana, T., & Watanabe, K. (2004). Attitudes of Japanese adults toward persons with intellectual disability: Comparisons over time and across countries. *Education and Training in Developmental Disabilities. 39*(3), 227–239.

Takahashi, N. (2003). Learning of disabled children in Japan: Simultaneous participation in different activity systems. *Mind, Culture, and Activity, 10*(4), 311–331.

Taylor, A. Peterson, C., McMurray-Schwartz, P., & Guillou, T. (2002). Social skills interventions: Not just for children with special needs. *Young Exceptional Children, 5*, 19–26.

Tobin, J., Hsueh, Y., & Karasawa, M. (2009). *Preschool in three cultures revisited: China, Japan, and the United States*. Chicago: The University of Chicago Press.

Tobin, J. J., Wu, D. Y. H., & Davison, D. H. (1989). *Preschool in three cultures: Japan, China, and the United States*. New Haven, CT: Yale University Press.

Tregaskis, C., & Goodley, D. (2005). Disability research by disabled and non-disabled people: Towards a relational methodology of research production. *International Journal of Social Research Methodology, 8*(5), 363–374.

Tsuge, M. (2004). *Gakushu-sha no tayo na ni-zu to kyo-iku sesaku [Diverse needs of learners and educational policies]*. Tokyo, Japan: Keiso Shobo.

Tsuneyoshi, R. (1994). Small groups in Japanese elementary school classrooms: Comparisons with the United States. *Comparative Education, 30*(2), 115–129

Tsuneyoshi, R. (2001). *The Japanese model of schooling: Comparisons with the United States*. New York: RoutledgeFalmer.

Ueno, K., & Hanakuma, S. (2006). *Kei-do hattatsu sho-gai no kyo-iku: LD, ADHD, and ko-kinou PDD tou he-no tokubetsu shien [Education for mild developmental disabilities: Special education for LD, ADHD, and high functioning PDD]*. Tokyo, Japan: Nihon Bunka Kagaku-sha.

UNESCO (1994). The Salamanca statement and framework for action on special needs education. Retrieved May 21, 2013 from http://www.unesco.org/education/pdf/SALAMA_E.PDF

United Nations (1989). Convention on the Rights of the Child. Retrieved May 21, 2013 from http://www.ohchr.org/en/professionalinterest/pages/crc.aspx

United Nations (1993). Standard Rules on the Equalization of Opportunities for Persons with Disabilities. Retrieved August 16, 2011 from http://www.un.org/disabilities/default.asp?id=26

United Nations (2004). The international decade of disabled persons 1983-1992. Retrieved October 10, 2010 from http://www.un.org/esa/socdev/enable/disunddp.htm

United Nations (2006). Convention on the rights of persons with disabilities and optional protocol. Retrieved October 8, 2010 from http://www.un.org/disabilities/documents/convention/convoptprot-e.pdf

United Nations (2010) Convention on the Rights of Persons with Disabilities. Retrieved October 8, 2010 from http://www.un.org/disabilities/default.asp?navid=13&pid=150

United Nations (2013) Convention and Optional Protocol Signatures and Ratifications. Retrieved August 26, 2011 from http://www.un.org/disabilities/countries.asp?id=166

Varenne, H., & McDermott, R. (1998). *Successful failure: The school America builds. Boulder*, CO: Westview Press.

Vygotsky, L. S. (1978). The role of play in development. In M. Cole, V. John-Steiner, S. Scribner, & E. Souberman (Eds.), *Mind in society* (pp. 92–104). Cambridge, MA: Harvard University Press.

Walsh, D. J. (2004). Frog boy and American monkey: The body in Japanese early schooling. In L. Bresler (Ed.), *Knowing bodies, feeling minds* (pp. 97–109). Amsterdam: Kluwer Academic Publishers.

Ware, L. P. (2002). A moral conversation on disability: Risking the personal in educational contexts. *Hypatia, 17*, 143–171.

Weisner, T. S. (Ed.). (2005). *Discovering successful pathways in children's development*. Chicago: University of Chicago Press.

Wertsch, J. V. (1991). *Voices of the mind*. Cambridge, MA: Harvard University Press.

Wertsch, J. V. (2008). From social interaction to high psychological processes: A clarification and application of Vygotsky's theory. *Human Development, 51*, 66–79.

White, M. (1987). *The Japanese educational challenge: A commitment to children.* New York: The Free Press.

WHO (2007). International statistical classification of diseases and related health problems 10th revision version for 2007. Retrieved October 5, 2010 from http://apps.who.int/classifications/apps/icd/icd10online/

Zambo, D. (2004). Using qualitative methods to understand the educational experiences of students with Dyslexia. *The Qualitative Report, 9*, 80–94.

INDEX

IDEA Reauthorization, 190, 191, 200
IEPs (Individualized Education
    Programs), 73–74, 190, 199
inclusive education, 57, 59
individual beliefs and responses to
    disabilities, fluidity of, 6–7
individual informal interactions,
    39–40
individual interviews (research
    methodology), 35–36
individualized education, 63–65,
    73, 210
Individualized Education Programs
    (IEPs), 73–74, 190, 199
individuals with disabilities
    marginalization of, 7–8
    self-understanding, fluidity of, 6–7
    stories of, 20–23
    See also children with disabilities
Individuals with Disabilities Education
    Act (IDEA, PL.94–142), 4–5,
    190–191, 204
inexperienced teachers, 146
in-school committees on special
    education, 209
intercultural learning, 4
intergenerational interactions,
    86–87
inter-grade groups, 90, 124, 174
internalized stigma, 8
interpersonal relationships
    as context for disabilities, 14–15
    Dai's struggles with, 161
    group learning and, 99
    as locus for disabilities, 190
    problems with, in peer groups,
        135–137
    responding to problems with, 133
interpersonal skills, 93–94, 94–95
interviews, self-disclosure in, 45
isolation from peers, 100
Itagaki, Y., 56, 57

James, E. L., 39
Japan
    child welfare policies, 55, 191–192
    concepts of self in, 12–13
    developmental disabilities as new
        category, 9–12
    disabilities, response to, 2
    education, holistic approach to, 202
    elementary school education, 15–17
    formal special education,
        implementation of, 50, 55
    model of disabilities, evolution of,
        192–194
    socialization practices, 13–15
    social policies, 55
    special education, cautious approach
        to, 72
    special education policies and
        practices, 189–190, 191
Japanese Language classes, 101n8
Jegatheesan, B., 3, 8, 21, 200
Jenkins, R., 193
Jessor, R., 46
jibun (interpersonal-self), xvii, 12
John Dewey Laboratory School,
    University of Chicago, 197
Johnson, B., 3, 8, 9
Jun (Dai's classmate), 134

Kadomoto, J., 11, 50, 72
Kadota, K., 205
Kakeru (case study subject)
    about, 32, 175–176
    bugs, knowledge of, 138, 177
    Challenge Room, transition to,
        179–181
    in general education classroom,
        178–179
    Ibasho, struggles to maintain,
        181–182
    interview with, 36
    parents' support for, 107

special education classrooms
  eligibility for, 98–99
  emergence of, 52–54
  extent of, 27, 56, 104
  group dynamics in, 94
  lack of, 57
  School Education Law on, 56, 69
  teacher certification, 203
  types of, 97–98
  See also Rainbow Room; resource
    rooms
special education coordinators, 11, 66,
    204–205, 210
special education reform
  challenges of, 51–52
  challenges to implementation, 73–75
  description of, 11–12
  in Japanese elementary schools, 1–2
  need for, 62
  report on, 65
special education schools, 55–57, 68,
    69, 202
special needs education, implementa-
    tion of, 1
special support rooms, 47n6, 70–71, 204
  See also Challenge Room; resource
    rooms
specific learning disabilities. *See*
    developmental disabilities
Stake, R. E., 23
standardized achievement tests, 188
Standard Rules on the Equalization of
    Opportunities for Persons with
    Disabilities, 59
Steedman, C. K., 22
Stevenson, C., 1, 43, 193, 197
Stigler, J. W., 1, 193, 197
stigma and stigmatization
  avoidance of, 17
  as challenge to parents' support of
    children, 109–112
  courtesy stigmatization, 8–9, 120

definition, 8
difference as source of, 103, 120–121
invisible nature of developmental
    disabilities and, 113–114
other parents as source of, 112–113
overview, 7–9
parents' rejection of, 6
sensitivity to, 190
from special education, 2, 74
special education services usage and,
    105
stories, 20–23, 38–42, 42–45
Straight, B., 23
Strauss, C., 149
Sugar Creek Elementary School, 198
Sugawara, N., 53
summer camp, 142–143
Summers, J. A., 190
Support for Persons With
    Developmental Disabilities Act,
    66–71, 73
supportive education, 198–199

Tachibana, T., 21
Takahashi, N., 7
Tanaka (teacher), 137, 142–143, 163–164,
    173
Taylor, A., 195
teachers
  children, bonds with, 79–80, 99–100
  disabilities, responses to, 2
  home visits by, 85–86
  inexperienced, 146
  moral education, role in, 91
  parents, collaboration with, 88–89
  role in Japan vs. U.S., 196
  skill variations, 144–146
  values and attitudes, 111–112
  working hours, 150n5
  See also Akiyama; Aoki; Hashimoto;
    Kawai; Maekawa; Nagai; Ono;
    Sano; Sekine; Tanaka